SAINTS AND OURSELVES

Saints and Ourselves

Edited by
Philip Caraman, S.J.

SERVANT BOOKS
Ann Arbor, Michigan

Cover Photo: Lawrence Zink, Inc.
Book Design: John B. Leidy

Published by
Servant Books
P.O. Box 8617
Ann Arbor, Michigan 48107

Printed in the United States of America
ISBN 0-89283-123-5

CONTENTS

Contributors

Donald Attwater • Author of the *Penguin Dictionary of the Saints* and the *Catholic Dictionary*.

James Brodrick, S.J. • A noted biographer, whose works include *St. Francis Xavier, St. Ignatius: The Pilgrim Years,* and the *Procession of Saints*.

Katharine Chorley • Author of *Armies and the Art of Revolution* and *Arthur Hugh Clough, the Uncommitted Mind: A Study of His Life and Poetry*.

Alice Curtayne • Author and translator, whose works include *A Recall to Dante* and *St. Catherine of Siena*.

Christopher Dawson • A noted historian, whose works include *The Making of Christendom, The Dividing of Christendom,* and *The Making of Europe*.

Anne Fremantle • A well-known biographer, she is the author of *Saints Alive* and *George Eliot* and the editor of *The Age of Belief: The Medieval Philosophers*.

Nicolete Gray • Author of *Rossetti, Dante, and Ourselves*.

Renée Haynes • Novelist and historian, she is the author of *Hillaire Belloc* and *Philosopher King: The Humanist Pope Benedict XIV*.

Douglas Hyde • Former editor of the London *Daily Worker,* he resigned in 1948 and later joined the Roman Catholic Church. He is the author of *Dedication and Leadership: Learning from the Communists, Communism Today,* and *A Literary History of Ireland*.

Sheila Kaye-Smith • Her works include *Quartet in Heaven, John Galsworthy,* and *Joanna Godden Married and Other Stories.*

Sir John McEwen • Scottish statesman, poet, and playwright.

Leslie Macfarlane • Author of *Violence and the State* and *Modern Political Theory.*

J.B. Morton • Journalist and author, whose works include *Brumaire: The Rise of Bonaparte* and *Hillaire Belloc: A Memoir.*

Muriel Spark • Author of numerous novels, including *The Prime of Miss Jean Brodie, The Mandelbaum Gate,* and *Loitering with Intent.*

Robert W. Speaight • Actor, lecturer, and author of at least twenty books, including *The Christian Theatre, The Life of Teilhard de Chardin,* and *Shakespeare: The Man and His Achievement.*

Evelyn Waugh • A satirical novelist, whose major works include *Brideshead Revisited* and *Scoop.*

Hugh Ross Williamson • Actor, playwright, historian, and novelist. His works include *The Poetry of T.S. Elliot, Jeremy Taylor,* and *Historical Enigmas.*

Preface

THIS BOOK PRESENTS a selection from three volumes entitled *Saints and Ourselves,* each containing sketches of twelve saints, that first appeared in the English periodical *The Month,* of which I was then editor. The idea behind the series was to get the leading Catholic writers of the day to contribute an essay on the saint that particularly appealed to them. Curiously, two writers chose St. Joan of Arc, but otherwise there was no competition for any single saint. Today, more than twenty-four of the original thirty-six contributors have joined the company of the men or women about whom they wrote: they, along with those still at work, are now in retrospect acknowledged among the finest authors of a silver decade of Catholic writing.

The choice made by the contributors told a great deal about themselves. Evelyn Waugh, for instance, wrote on St. Helena, who had already been the subject of his only historical novel. Giving the reason for his choice he wrote: "The Cross is very plain for us today; plainer perhaps than for many centuries. What we learn from Helena is something about the workings of God; that he wants a different thing from each of us, laborious or easy, conspicuous or quite private, but something that only we can do and for which we were each created."

As I read each essay, I recalled the lines of Gerard Manley Hopkins, who wrote of the diversity of sanctity in one of his sonnets. Christ, he said, "plays in ten thousand places, lovely in limbs and lovely in eyes not his, to the Father through the features of men's faces." And, one could add, not only in limbs but in mind and heart, for no saint is like any other and none is wholly imitable, though all offer some light to guide us in the twilight of this life. The reading of their lives gives us glimpses of what God is really like and also brings us into touch with the kind of world loved by Christ and ever full of promise waiting to be renewed.

Great men and women have always an appeal; some are admirable and some not—few are imitable. It is the mark of a saint that he fulfills the highest ideal given to man and is at the same time a friend and inspiration. They tell us what is possible for us, whether we have one talent or ten, whether we live in sorrow or joy, in days of menace or in times of hope. They combine the almost impossible—weakness with strength, darkness with joy, self-denial with profound humanity and affection. Unlike so many other distinguished men in science, literature and statesmanship, they remain ever contemporary in that they reveal the everlasting source of happiness, the secret of how to turn the common into what is perfect and unique. Each, as Evelyn Waugh shows in his essay, manages to find the true Cross, the emblem of life and hope.

PHILIP CARAMAN
December 8, 1981

The Early Martyrs

Donald Attwater

IT IS FITTING that a series such as is contained in this book should begin with a consideration of some martyrs, for it is from veneration of the early martyrs that the whole great business of the *cultus* of the saints in the Christian Church derives. Whatever the dignity and importance and interest of the saints whose festivals figure in the various calendars of the Church, those feasts must all, without exception, give place to the anniversaries of the martyrs in point of antiquity. Already in the second century the annual commemoration of St. Polycarp (referred to below) was celebrated in Smyrna from the time of his passion; from the beginning of the third century such commemorations were becoming general.

There is nothing surprising about this. For the first three hundred years of their history Christians lived in an atmosphere of martyrdom, of witness by blood. Persecution was not continuous, and it varied in intensity from time to time and from place to place, but the possibility of being called on to die for the name of the Lord Christ was never far away; and that state of affairs, again at times and in places, has recurred ever since. Mankind was redeemed by the willing death of the incarnate Son of God, who on the third day rose again from the dead: redeemed man is never so Christlike as when he willingly goes to death for his Saviour, to await the resurrection that is to come. In those early days such a death might be the lot of any Christian; it was, and is the ultimate indefeasible Christian right—if the call comes, to die for the Lord. And those to whom

1

the call came and who accepted it (for not all did so) created a tradition that was to endure, the classic tradition of the supreme witness to Christ and of how that holy witness by violent death should be met. In reading the authentic accounts of early martyrdoms one cannot but notice an, as it were, liturgical quality about them. And that, too, is not surprising: for Christian martyrdom is essentially a *leitourgia*, a sacred action publicly done for the common good.

That good has several aspects. Part of it is the creation of the tradition itself; but also the edifying, the building-together, of that body within which the tradition energizes: that the martyrs' blood is the Church's seed is one of the most oft-quoted of truths. It has been acutely remarked that the martyrs made subsequent saints possible by making subsequent Christianity possible. And the debt to the martyrs, as well as the public nature of holiness, is recognized when we call all other saints "confessors" (in its non-technical sense the word applies equally to women), for "confessor" too means "a witness."

Saints are as heterogeneous a human category as can be imagined, and those considered in this book are a very varied company, widely separated, too, in time and place. They came timelessly together in the waters of baptism, they were held together in and by the Body of Christ, His mystical body and His eucharistic body, and they are presented here in virtue of their common sanctity. In the first place stands a brief record of some of those martyrs who were their forerunners, whose lives and deaths spoke more effectively than any words to those who came after: "This is the Way. Walk ye in it."

This group of early martyrs must be defined. "Early" I take in the conventional historical sense of those who suffered in the classical Ten Persecutions before the Peace of the Church in the year 313. This is a very large body indeed, and again not homogeneous: they differ endlessly in character, condition, circumstances. Crucial for my purpose, they differ seriously in how much we know about them. Early martyrs, as defined, must bring first to most minds such names as Lawrence, Cecilia, Agnes, George, Catherine, Christopher, Barbara, Lucy,

Alban in England. Yet with those, and others hardly less well known, I am not here concerned. Who then?

Our knowledge of the early martyrs mainly depends on documents—letters, chronicles, "acts" or "passions"—which vary greatly in authenticity, scope and historical value. The learned have classified these documents into six categories, according to their worth. The first two of these categories comprise the official reports of the trials of martyrs and the accounts of eyewitnesses and of other trustworthy, well-informed contemporaries. Of these precious testimonies there are very few: less than a score have so far been generally recognized. The very circumstances of the composition of these few unquestionably genuine and almost unadulterated narratives give to the martyrs concerned an interest, an appeal, an actuality, a movingness that is irresistible to the reader sixteen hundred or more years afterwards.

"It is a refreshing experience for any religious-minded person of today to shut his eyes for once to the many complex, and in some degree unpleasant, aspects of religious life and look into the soul of a great man who succeeded in reducing this complexity to one or two engrossing facts or ideas and putting them in the center of his everyday life." Those are the words of Dr. James Kleist, S.J., written with reference to St. Ignatius of Antioch who, however little is known about his life, has left an intimate picture of his mind and spirit in his letters, six addressed to Christian communities and one to an individual. And what Dr. Kleist says about Ignatius can be applied equally well, in their degree and circumstances, to what we are told in the narratives referred to above of the lives, and more particularly of the deaths, of other Christians in the early days, ranging from bishops and a learned apologist in great centers of the Roman empire to slave girls and a Gothic convert near the lower Danube. The "engrossing facts and ideas" to which Dr. Kleist refers are, quite simply, God and Jesus Christ. That indeed is what would be expected of Christians; what is striking is the simplicity, the firmness, the sobriety with which those facts were clung to, those ideas lived. And should martyrdom be called for, the supreme witness to those facts and ideas, that too was met as being, as it were, "all in the day's work."

If we except St. Stephen, the protomartyr, the account of whose passion in the Acts of the Apostles is the prototype of straightforward, unadorned martyr narratives, the first in order of time about whom we have this sort of evidence is that same St. Ignatius of Antioch, called "the God-bearer." About the year 107 the old man was dispatched for execution from what was to be "the god-beloved city" of Antioch to Rome; he was in charge of a file of soldiers who, he tells us, were like "ten leopards": he was "fighting these wild beasts on land and sea, by day and night," and "the more courteously they are treated the worse they get." During that journey he wrote his letters, and it is from them, and particularly from the incomparable letter to the Roman Christians written from Smyrna, that Ignatius can be known.

The form of those letters, written from the heart in view of death, have no attraction for the grammarian and the rhetor; but for the Christian they are among the most precious testimonies of antiquity. Ignatius was worried lest the brethren at Rome should seek to save his life. "Do not show me unseasonable kindness, I beseech you," he writes. "Let wild animals devour me, for so shall I reach God." And he adds the words that are sung as the communion verse of the Mass of his feast: "I am Christ's wheat, and I am to be ground by the teeth of beasts that I may become good bread."—I do not give orders to you, as Peter and Paul did. They were apostles, I am a convict. They were free, I am even yet a slave. But once I have suffered I shall become a freedman of Jesus Christ, made one with him I shall arise free. Just now I learn in my bonds to desire nothing." Nothing but martyrdom. And that martyrdom came soon, when he was cast to the lions, perhaps in the Colosseum.

The last of the letters of St. Ignatius was addressed to Polycarp, the young bishop of Smyrna whom Ignatius had met when his ship touched at that port. Fifty or so years later Polycarp himself gave his life for Christ, and an account thereof was sent by the Smyrniot Christians to their brethren at

Philomelium in Pisidia. When the police came to arrest him at a farm outside the city, St. Polycarp gave them supper, while he stood a long while praying aloud, "remembering all who had ever come his way, great and small, high and low, and the whole Catholic Church throughout the world." He was taken straight to the stadium where, amid a tremendous uproar, the proconsul urged him to "Swear by the *genius* of Caesar; repent; say 'Away with the atheists!'" And Polycarp, "looking on all the crowd of lawless heathen," indicated them with a gesture of his hand and said, "Away with the atheists!"

He would neither swear by the imperial *genius* nor curse his Master: "Eighty and six years have I served Christ and he has done me no wrong. How can I blaspheme my King, who saved me?" He was ready to expound his religion to the proconsul but not to the people, whom "I do not deem worthy to hear any defence from me." The mob howled that a lion be loosed on him; but this could not be legally done as the games were officially over, so they clamoured that he be burned, running forward with fuel from workshops and baths. Bound to a stake, St. Polycarp prayed in a loud voice, a prayer of praise and thanksgiving, and when he had said Amen the fire was lighted. "And the fire made a sort of space, like a ship's sail bellying in the wind, surrounding the martyr's body as with a wall, and he in the midst, not like burning flesh but as bread in the baking or gold and silver refined in a furnace. And we caught a sweet fragrance, as it were the breath of incense or other precious spice."

During the persecution under Marcus Aurelius, and therefore not far removed from the death of St. Polycarp, there took place the martyrdom of St. Justin, the apologist who after his conversion "preached the word of God in the guise of a philosopher." He appears to have been denounced by a Cynic whom he had worsted in public debate, and was brought before the prefect Rusticus with several others.

Justin, who gave his address as "Martin's house, near Timothy's baths," declared his belief in one eternal God, the Creator, and in God's Son, the Lord Jesus Christ; he said that he, Justin, was a man of little worth, but he recognized the testimony of the prophets; and he explained in reply to a question that his fellow-believers met where they would and could: "for our God is not confined by place, but unseen fills heaven and earth, and is worshipped and glorified by the faithful everywhere."

"To come to the point, then," said the prefect, "you are a Christian?" "Yes, I am a Christian," replied Justin. And so said the others, one of whom was a woman, another a slave in the imperial household, another one of the bystanders, seven in all—"a motley crew," remarks Msgr. Duchesne. Asked if he, "said to be a learned man," thought that were he executed he would go up into Heaven, Justin replied, "I hope if I endure such things to have God's gifts. I do not think, I know and know certainly." And with one voice they refused to sacrifice: "Do what you will. We are Christians, and we offer no sacrifice to idols." So Rusticus gave sentence that they be scourged and then beheaded in accordance with the law: which was done, "and some of the faithful took their bodies by stealth and laid them in a fitting place."

The year 177 was marked by the passion of numerous martyrs of Lyons and Vienne in Gaul; this fact was unfolded in a letter to the churches of Asia and Phrygia which has been called "the pearl of the Christian literature of the second century." The persecution began with social pressure—exclusion from houses, public baths, markets; then there were casual mobbings and stoning; then the authorities took it up, the public being whipped up to hysteria by charges of cannibalism and incest made against the Christians.

The bishop of Lyons, St. Pothinus, was over ninety years old, and sick; after being manhandled before the governor he was thrown into prison, where he died two days later. But the individual of whom we are told most is St. Blandina, a slave girl, "in whom Christ made manifest that things which appear insignificant and uncomely and contemptible are accounted most honorable with God, for their love of him, which is manifested not in outward show but in power." She was tortured bitterly, but would only say, "I am a Christian; nothing vile is done amongst us." When she was brought into the arena with three others and suspended from a pole with arms outstretched, the wild beasts would not touch her; so she was put aside for another day, when she appeared "as though she were called to a wedding feast," with the fifteen-year-old boy Ponticus. "After the whips, after the beasts, after the fire, she was put at last into a net and thrown to a bull. When she had been tossed about for a long time, no longer knowing what was happening, being upheld by her hope and faith and communing with Christ, she too was offered up, the very heathen declaring that they had never known a woman show such endurance. But even so their rage and savagery against the saints were not appeased."

St. Cyprian, bishop of Carthage, is an important figure in the history of the Western Church and the development of Christian thought in his age; he stands out no less among the martyrs of Africa in the middle of the third century. His first interrogation took place in the private hall of the proconsul Paternus, who treated him with some deference: the account gives a strong impression of an interview between two gentlemen, the one carrying out a painful duty, the other quietly and courteously firm in his refusal to betray his clergy, without any hint of defiance. Cyprian was banished to Curubis. On his return all the faithful gathered outside the house where the bishop was detained, and Cyprian gave special orders for the care of the young women among them. His second examination was very short. The proconsul, Galerius Maximus, asked whether Cyprian had taken it on himself to be the father of these sacrilegious men, and he said he had. "The most sacred emperors have ordered you to sacrifice."—"I refuse."—"Think about it."—"Do your duty. In so clear a matter there is nothing to think about." So Galerius Maximus, after consultation with his colleagues, "most reluctantly" gave sentence: Thascius Cyprianus was to be put to death by the sword. To which Cyprian replied, "Thanks be to God."

A crowd accompanied him to the field of Sextus; there,

having bowed himself in prayer, Cyprian took off his outer
clothes and stood in his linen undergarment to await the
executioner (to whom he left twenty-five gold pieces). Linen
cloths were strewn around him by the brethren, while Julian the
priest and Julian the subdeacon helped him to blindfold his
eyes. "So suffered the blessed Cyprian; and his body was laid
out near by to satisfy the curiosity of the heathen."

Three among these martyrs were soldiers. St. Marinus,
stationed at Caesarea in Palestine, was due for promotion, when
it was discovered he was a Christian. The local bishop,
Theotecnus, led him to the church, and they stood together
before the altar. "Drawing back the soldier's cloak a little,
Theotecnus pointed to the sword at his side; at the same time he
showed him the book of the gospels, bidding him choose
between the two. Without hesitation, Marinus stretched out his
right hand and touched the sacred writings." Taken back to
court, "after showing wonderful zeal, he was led away to
death." St. Marcellus, a centurion, suffered at Tangier in 298.
At a regimental dinner to honor the emperor's birthday he had
refused to take part: he threw his belt down before the
standards, exclaiming, "I serve Jesus Christ, the eternal king. I
will serve your emperors no longer. I scorn to worship your
gods of wood and stone." St. Maximilian, on the other hand, the
son of a veteran in Numidia, refused to serve at all. Like St.
Martin of Tours and St. Victricius of Rouen later, he was what
is nowadays called a conscientious objector; unlike them, he
paid for it with his life.

The narratives abound in lively touches and enlightening
details. Polycarp, getting down from the police captain's
chariot, scraped his shin but concealed his pain. . . . When
soldiers came to arrest St. Fructuosus, bishop of Tarragona in
Spain, he was going to bed; he asked if he might be allowed to
put on his shoes. At his interrogation the governor Aemilian
asked, "Are you a bishop?" "I am," replied Fructuosus. "You
were," retorted the governor, and sentenced him to be burned.
Members of Aemilian's household saw a vision of Fructuosus
and his deacons going up in glory to Heaven; but when the

governor was sent for, "he was not worthy to behold them." . . .
St. Papylas was asked if he had children. "Yes, many, thank
God." And a man in the crowd shouted, "He means that some
of the Christians are his children according to his faith." His
companion, St. Carpus, smiled while being bound to the stake.
"I saw the glory of the Lord and was glad," he explained.
"Moreover, I am rid of you and have no part in your evil
deeds." . . . There were attempts by main force to make St.
Pionius sacrifice in a temple (he was seized at Smyrna while
celebrating the anniversary of St. Polycarp's martyrdom); he
resisted so violently that it took six men to overpower him. . . .
In their speech we can hear the patrician dignity of St. Cyprian,
the preciseness of St. Justin, the soldierly terseness of St.
Marcellus; above all, perhaps, the three voices in the *Passion of
St. Perpetua and St. Felicity.*

This last holds a position all of its own among the records of
the martyrs, nor is that simply due to the interest of later times:
for during the fourth century it was publicly read in the
churches of North Africa, and was so popular that St.
Augustine protested that it must not be put on a level with the
books of the Bible. There were six martyrs in this group at
Carthage on the nones (7th) of March in the year 203. They
were Vibia Perpetua, twenty-two years old, a married woman of
noble birth with a baby son; Felicity, a slave girl, who was with
child; Revocatus, also a slave; Saturninus, Secundulus, and
Saturus. They were all catechumens except Saturus, who
seemingly had been the means of their conversion. Over a third
of the narrative was written by St. Perpetua herself, a little of it
by St. Saturus, and the remainder by an unknown editor, whom
several scholars have identified as Tertullian.

During a period of open arrest the five catechumens received
baptism, and a few days later were taken to prison. Perpetua was
much troubled for the welfare of her baby, who was with her,
and by the entreaties of her aged father; he, poor man, was a
pagan and could not at all understand his favorite child's
resolution. "And I grieved for my father's sake, for he alone of
all my kin would find no comfort in my suffering"; she felt

relieved when he left her and ceased his importunities for a time. Just before her interrogation Perpetua had the first of several dreams or visions: of the dragon-guarded ladder up which she followed Saturus into a garden, where there was a white-haired Shepherd milking sheep, around whom stood thousands clad in white; "And he said to me, 'Welcome, child,' and from the curd he had from the milk he gave me a morsel. I received it in my joined hands, and ate; and all that stood by said, 'Amen.' "

At the trial the procurator appealed to Perpetua in the name of her father and her child, but in vain. Her father was given blows for interrupting ("I grieved for his unhappy old age"), and all were condemned to the beasts. Perpetua's baby was taken from her, and he, "as God willed, wanted no more to be suckled, nor did I take fever, that I might not be troubled by anxiety for the baby or by pain in my breasts."

A few days later she dreamed of her seven-year-old brother Dinocrates, who had died of a horrible disease. He looked feverish, thirsty, and miserable, and was trying to drink from a fountain that was too high for him to reach. So she set herself to pray for him; and she again saw Dinocrates, now drinking the waters of the fountain and playing happily. On the day before her passion Perpetua had another vision. She seemed to be in the arena, confronted by an ugly Egyptian; and a Man of huge stature, gloriously clothed, told her she must fight with the Egyptian, and if she triumphed she would receive the branch that he carried, on which were golden apples. Perpetua was stripped and rubbed down with oil by attendants, and "I became a man." And she fought with the Egyptian and overcame him (the description of the contest is most vivid). She received the branch, and the bearer of it kissed her, saying, "Peace be with you, daughter." "And I awoke, understanding that I should not fight with beasts but with the Devil. But I knew that victory was mine."

Saturus too had a vision. With Perpetua he was carried by angels to Heaven, a garden full of trees "whose leaves sang without ceasing," and they were invited to "go in and greet the

Lord." As they entered, voices as one voice were singing *Agios, agios, agios* ("Holy, holy, holy,"); and in the midst sat One like unto a man, with snow-white hair but youthful countenance, surrounded by elders. "The four angels lifted us up; and we kissed him and he stroked our faces with his hand [cf. Apoc. 7:17]. And the elders said, 'Stand up.' And we stood up, and gave one another the kiss of peace. Then said the elders to us, 'Go and play.' And I said to Perpetua, 'You have what you desired.' She said to me, 'God be thanked that I who was merry in the flesh am still merrier now.' " Those are the very accents of Thomas More thirteen hundred years later.

Felicity meanwhile was troubled lest her pregnancy should delay her martyrdom till after the others (for it was unlawful to execute a woman who was with child). She was eight months gone, and her fellows prayed together in her behalf. Two days before the games she gave birth to a girl, who was straightway adopted by one of the faithful. The labor was difficult, and a warder said to her, "You are suffering now: what about when you are thrown to the beasts?" "Now I suffer what I suffer," Felicity replied, "but then Another will be in me who will suffer for me, because I am to suffer for Him." On their last night the condemned celebrated a love feast, and many came out of curiosity to watch them. Saturus told these sightseers to be about their business: "Won't you see enough of us tomorrow?" They went away astonished; and some believed.

The contest of these martyrs took place at the games held in honor of the festival of Geta Caesar. As they entered the amphitheater, "with gay and gallant looks," the three men (Secundulus had died in prison) threatened the onlookers with God's judgment, even the president where he sat in state. Felicity came rejoicing, "from blood to blood, from the midwife to the gladiator, to be washed after childbirth in a second baptism." Last of all Perpetua, "true bride of Christ and darling of God, her piercing look abashing all eyes, . . . singing victoriously."

Saturninus and Revocatus were exposed to a leopard and then to a bear. Saturus was twice put back unhurt, and then was mauled by the bite of a leopard. Dipping a ring in his blood he gave it to a soldier, Pudens, saying, "Farewell! Remember the faith and me. And let not these things disturb but strengthen you" (Pudens was afterwards himself a martyr). And so Saturus died. But the two women, against all custom, were thrown to a savage cow, which tossed them both. Perpetua sat up, drew her torn tunic about her, and pinned up her hair, "for it was not seemly that a martyr should suffer with hair dishevelled, lest she should seem to mourn in her glory." Then she helped Felicity to her feet, and they were put back. Perpetua—"so lost was she in the Spirit and in ecstasy"—asked when they were to be thrown to the cow, and would hardly believe it had already happened. She turned to her brother and another catechumen: "Stand fast in faith," she said, "and love one another. And do not let our sufferings be a stumbling-block to you."

They kissed one another, "that they might fulfill their martyrdom with the rite of peace," and moved to a place where all might see the final swordstroke. Saturninus and Revocatus and Felicity died without sound or stir. But Perpetua's executioner was a novice and failed to kill her at the first blow, so that she shrieked with pain: then she herself guided the gladiator's wavering hand to her throat. "Perhaps so great a woman, feared by the unclean spirit, could not have been slain unless she so willed it."

These few notes do but scant justice to the theme; but they are enough to show these martyrs as men and women, not as puppets; that their records are of what happened, uncontaminated by folklore and fairy tales. There is none of the accumulation of monstrous statements, of pointless and often fantastic marvels, with which the appeal of simple stories was afterwards heightened or lack of information supplied. The writers were not yet didactic, composing manifestos for, as an instance, the dignity of virginity; or expanding proconsular interrogations into theological arguments and apologies. (In an elaboration of the sober account of St. Procopius given by the historian Eusebius, the martyr is made to refer to Hermes Trismegistus, Homer, Plato, Aristotle, Galen, and Scamandrus in support of the oneness of God; what Eusebius says he did was to accommodate one line from the Iliad.) Here are plain men and women, from all states of life, reminding us, *mutatis mutandis*, of none so much as the English martyrs of the sixteenth and seventeenth centuries.

And for what did they suffer? Christopher Dawson rightly says, "The Roman empire was antichristian not so much because of an official worship of Jupiter and Mars and the rest, but because it made its own power and greatness the supreme law and the only measure of its social action." The record is plain. "Have you heard what the emperors have ordered?"— "Swear by Caesar's *genius*."—"Obey the gods, and submit to the princes."—"Sacrifice to the gods." Christians were sacrilegious, impious atheists, because they would not thus sacrifice or swear. They were haters of the human race because, in what touched religion—and there only—they dissociated themselves from the solidarity of the Roman empire. It was, in modern terms, an attempt by the state, the civil power, to coerce the conscience of its citizens. So it has been, many times and in many places, throughout the ages, from that day to this. And the Christian answer has likewise been the same: from the Apostles' "We ought to obey God rather than men," through Thomas More's "The king's good servant, but God's first," down to our times. "Give honor to Caesar as unto Caesar, but fear to God," said St. Donata before the proconsul at Scillium. "I am a Christian; I worship Christ," declared St. Carpus at Pergamos, "So be assured, O proconsul, that I do not sacrifice to these counterfeits." By such words they convicted themselves. As Tertullian says, "The only thing needed to satisfy the general hatred is, not the investigation of a charge, but the confession of the Name."

Near the beginning of these pages I quoted Dr. Kleist's observation about the freedom from religious complexity shown in the letters of St. Ignatius of Antioch. That concentration runs through all these martyr narratives: on God, Jesus Christ, the gathering of the brethren in the Church, indwelt, corporately and individually, by the Holy Spirit. The thought and life of these Christians is permeated by the Sacred Scriptures: in thirteen of these narratives there are over 250 separate quotations from or allusions to the text of the Bible, mostly of course the New Testament. There is no "multiplicity," no complication, no hint of dissipation of spiritual energy: as Dr. Kleist says of St. Ignatius, they are concentrated on that "upholding of your traditions just as I have handed them on to you" for which St. Paul praised the Corinthians. Even for those who might desire it, the recovery of such primitive simplicity is doubtless impossible.

But, connected with this "unsophisticated" atmosphere, there is something that is perhaps a practical and insistent message for Christians today, who also feel that upon them "the ends of the world are come." Again Dr. Klesit refers to it. It is the note of triumph, of victory, among these early Christians; they were fully conscious of being "a chosen race, a royal priesthood, a consecrated nation," a society of which, in the words of St. Augustine, "the king is Truth, the law is Love and the duration is Eternity." Their Christianity is "indubitably confident and absolutely certain. . . . Consciousness of victory animated them all. . . . Blandina no less than Tertullian or Lactantius." Was there, on the human level, any more ground for triumph among the Christians of the two and a half centuries from Nero to Diocletian than there is today? Or less? The victorious aspect of martyrdom is decisive: but they saw in it simply a special participation in the victory of Christ. It was in that they triumphed, martyrs or not. Fallen mankind was redeemed on Calvary; and on the third day redeemed mankind triumphed with the Saviour. It is that which the Church relives on every Lord's Day, on every day. "Christ conquers, Christ reigns, Christ rules"; every Christian shares his triumph, and "neither death nor life, nor angels or principalities or powers, neither what is present nor what is to come, no force whatever" can take it away from us.

I have written, with affection and enthusiasm, about some early martyrs. But love and reverence for them must not withdraw attention from those of the ages that followed, and those of our own age. The opening passage of the *Passion of St. Perpetua and St Felicity* would seem to be relevant: "If ancient examples of faith, which both witness to the grace of God and strengthen man, were therefore set out in writing that by their reading and recalling of the past God might be glorified and man strengthened, should not new examples which serve these ends also be set forth? For these too will some day be old and needful for those who come after us. . . ." *In pace illi, nos in spe.*

St. Helena Empress

c.250 – c.330

Evelyn Waugh

WE ARE ADVISED to meditate on the lives of the saints, but this
precept originated in the ages when meditation was a more
precise and arduous activity than we are tempted to think it
today. Heavy apparatus has been at work in the last hundred
years to enervate and stultify the imaginative faculties. First,
realistic novels and plays, then the cinema have made the urban
mentality increasingly subject to suggestion so that it now
lapses effortlessly into a trance-like escape from its condition. It
is said that great popularity in fiction and film is only attained
by works into which readers and audience can transpose
themselves and be vicariously endangered, loved and ap-
plauded. This kind of reverie is not meditation, even when its
objects are worthy of high devotion. It may do little harm,
perhaps even some little good, to fall day-dreaming and play the
parts of Sir Thomas More, King Lewis IX or Father Damien.
There are evident dangers in identifying ourselves with Saint
Francis or Saint John of the Cross. We can invoke the help of
the saints and study the workings of God in them, but if we
delude ourselves that we are walking in their shoes, seeing
through their eyes and thinking with their minds, we lose sight
of the one certain course of our salvation. There is only one saint
that Bridget Hogan can actually become, Saint Bridget Hogan,
and that saint she *must* become, here or in the fires of purgatory,

17

if she is to enter heaven. She cannot slip through in fancy-dress, made up as Joan of Arc.

For this reason it is well to pay particular attention to the saints about whom our information is incomplete. There are names in the calendar about which we know nothing at all except those names, and then sometimes in a form that would puzzle their contemporaries. There are others about whom, humanly speaking, we know almost everything, who have left us a conspectus of their minds in their own writings, who were accompanied through life by pious biographers recording every movement and saying, who were conspicuous in the history of their times so that we can see them from all sides as they impressed friends and opponents. And mid-way between these two groups are the saints who are remembered for a single act. To this class Helena eminently belongs. In extreme old age, as Empress Dowager, she made a journey into one part of her son's immense dominions, to Jerusalem. From that journey spring the relics of the True Cross that are venerated everywhere in Christendom. That is what we know; most else is surmise.

Helena was at a time, literally, the most important woman in the world, yet we know next to nothing about her. Two places claim to be her birthplace: Colchester in England and Drepanum, a seaside resort, now quite vanished, in Turkey. The evidence for neither is so strong that Englishman or Turk need abandon his pretension. She was probably of modest rank, not servile, not illustrious. Constantius married her early in his rise to power and abandoned her later for a royal match. She may have been brought up at one of the post-stables on an Imperial trunk road and have there attracted Constantius's attention on one of his offical journeys. Or she may, conceivably, have been what legend makes her, the daughter of a British chief. She bore one son, Constantine the Great, probably at Nish in Serbia. After her divorce she settled at Trier (Trèves) where the Cathedral probably stands on the foundations of her palace. Almost certainly it was there that she became Christian. Lactantius, who was tutor to her grandson Crispus, may have helped instruct her. At the very end of her life she suddenly emerged for her great adventure. She died at Constantinople and her body was thereupon or later moved to Rome. Her tomb never became a great centre of pilgrimage. She, herself, seems never to have attracted great personal devotion; but she was a popular saint. Numberless churches are dedicated to her; numberless girls baptized with her name; she appears everywhere in painting, sculpture and mosaic. She has fitted, in a homely and substantial way, into the family life of Christendom.

There is little of heroism or genius in any of this. We can assume that she was devout, chaste, munificent; a thoroughly good woman in an age when palaces were mostly occupied by the wicked; but she lived grandly and comfortably whereas most of the saints in every age have accepted poverty as the condition of their calling. We know of no suffering of hers, physical, spiritual or mental, beyond the normal bereavements, disappointments and infirmities which we all expect to bear. Yet she lived in an age when Christians had often to choose between flight, apotasy or brutal punishment. Where, one may ask, lies her sanctity? Where the particular lesson for us who live in such very different circumstances?

For the world of Constantine, as we catch glimpses of it, is utterly remote from ours. There are certain superficial similarities. Poetry was dead and prose dying. Architecture had lapsed into the horny hands of engineers. Sculpture had fallen so low that in all his empire Constantine could not find a mason capable of decorating his triumphal arch and preferred instead to rob the two-hundred-year-old arch of Trajan. An enormous bureaucracy was virtually sovereign, controlling taxation on the sources of wealth, for the pleasure of city mobs and for the defence of frontiers more and more dangerously pressed by barbarians from the East. The civilized world was obliged to find a new capital. All this seems familiar but for the event of supreme importance, the victory of Christianity, we can find no counterpart in contemporary history. We cannot by any effort of the imagination share the emotions of Lactantius or Macarius. Helena, more than anyone, stands in the heart of that mystery.

She might claim, like that other, less prudent queen: "In my end is my beginning." But for her final, triumphant journey she would have no fame. We should think of her, if at all, as we think of Constantine: someone who neatly made the best of both worlds. The strong purpose of her pilgrimage shed a new and happier light on the long years of uneventful retirement showing us that it was by an act of will, grounded in patience and humility, that she accepted her position. Or rather, her positions. We do not know in exactly what state Constantius found her. She certainly did not choose him for his hopes of power. Those hopes, indeed, proved her undoing and dismissed her, divorced, into exile. In a court full of intrigue and murder she formed no party, took no steps against her rival, but quietly accepted her disgrace. Constantine rose to power, proclaimed her empress, struck coins in her honour, opened the whole imperial treasury for her use. And she accepted that too. Only in her religious practices did she maintain her private station, slipping in to mass at Rome among the crowd, helping with the housework at the convent on Mount Sion. She accepted the fact that God had His own use for her. Others faced the lions in the circus; others lived in caves in the desert. She was to be St. Helena Empress, not St. Helena Martyr or St. Helena Anchorite. She accepted a state of life full of dangers to the soul in which many foundered, and she remained fixed in her purpose until at last it seemed God had no other need of her except to continue to the end, a kind, old lady. Then came her call to a single peculiar act of service, something unattempted before and unrepeatable—the finding of the True Cross.

We have no absolute certainty that she found it. The old sneer, that there was enough "wood of the cross" to build a ship, though still repeated, has long been nullified. All the splinters and shavings venerated everywhere have been patiently measured and found to comprise a volume far short of a cross. We know that most of these fragments have a plain pedigree back to the early fourth century. But there is no guarantee which would satisfy an antiquary, of the authenticity of Helena's discovery. If she found the True Cross, it was by direct supernatural aid, not by archaeological reasoning. That, from the first, was its patent of title. There are certain elements about the surviving relics which are so odd that they seem to preclude the possibility of imposture. The "Label," for example—the inscription *Jesus of Nazareth, King of the Jews*—now preserved in Santa Croce seems the most unlikely product of a forger's art. And who would have tried to cheat her? Not St. Macarius certainly. But it *is* nevertheless possible that Helena was tricked, or that she and her companions mistook casual baulks of timber, builders' waste long buried, for the wood they sought; that the Label, somehow, got added to her treasure later. Even so her enterprise was something life-bringing.

It is not fantastic to claim that her discovery entitles her to a place in the Doctorate of the Church, for she was not merely adding one more stupendous trophy to the hoard of relics which were everywhere being unearthed and enshrined. She was asserting in sensational form a dogma that was in danger of neglect. Power was shifting. In the academies of the Eastern and South-Eastern Mediterranean sharp, sly minds were everywhere looking for phrases and analogies to reconcile the new, blunt creed for which men had died, with the ancient speculations which had beguiled their minds, and with the occult rites which had for generations spiced their logic.

Another phase of existence which select souls enjoyed when the body was shed; a priesthood; a sacramental system, even in certain details of eating, anointing and washing—all these had already a shadowy place in fashionable thought. Everything about the new religion was capable of interpretation, could be refined and diminished; everything except the unreasonable assertion that God became man and died on the Cross; not a myth or an allegory; true God, truly incarnate, tortured to death at a particular moment in time, at a particular geographical place, as a matter of plain historical fact. This was the stumbling block in Carthage, Alexandria, Ephesus and Athens, and at this all the talents of the time went to work, to reduce, hide, and eliminate.

Constantine was no match for them. Schooled on battle fields and in diplomatic conferences, where retreat was often the highest strategy, where truth was a compromise between irreconcilable opposites: busy with all the affairs of state; unused to the technical terms of philosophy; Constantine not yet baptized, still fuddled perhaps by dreams of Alexander, not quite sure that he was not himself divine, not himself the incarnation of the Supreme Being of whom Jove and Jehovah were alike imperfect emanations; Constantine was quite out of his depth. The situation of the Church was more perilous, though few saw it, than in the days of persecution. And at that crisis suddenly emerged God-sent from luxurious retirement in the far north, a lonely, resolute old woman with a single concrete, practical task clear before her; to turn the eyes of the world back to the planks of wood on which their salvation hung.

That was Helena's achievement, and for us who, whatever our difficulties, are no longer troubled by those particular philosophic confusions that clouded the fourth century, it has the refreshing quality that we cannot hope to imitate it. The Cross is very plain for us today; plainer perhaps than for many centuries. What we can learn from Helena is something about the workings of God; that He wants a different thing from each of us, laborious or easy, conspicuous or quite private, but something which only we can do and for which we were each created.

St. Basil

c.329-379

Anne Fremantle

ST. BASIL is not only one of the "great ecumenical Doctors" of the Eastern Church, but one of the very few Fathers of the Church to be styled "Great." He was a founder—of a Rule for monks still followed today by Greek monastics both Catholic and Orthodox; he was the initiator of a liturgy still in current use; he was a legislator—three of his letters, known as "canonical," are the basis of certain rulings in Canon Law, and he was one of the saints who, in the fourth century, laid the foundations of the Christian social order and mapped the broad outlines of social justice. It is this last aspect of his life and work, perhaps, that brings him nearest to us today—indeed, many of his pronouncements against capital, against investments and inheritance, might have got him into trouble with American Senate committees. St. Basil was also a great stylist, and one of the best letter-writers among the saints, and he stands out as the first Christian champion of pagan literature: his *Treatise for Young Men* is a model of advice on the use of profane letters, still. St. Basil had, furthermore, a very warm and close family life: he had nine brothers and sisters, of whom two brothers— St. Gregory of Nyssa and St. Peter of Sebaste, and one sister, St. Macrina the Younger, also became saints. His grandmother, St. Macrina the Elder, and his mother, St. Emily, also were canonised, and his maternal grandfather was martyred during the Diocletian persecution. He had a genius, too, for friendship,

23

and such unlikely people as Antipater and Julian the Apostate were among his correspondents, whilst his friendship with St. Gregory Nazianzen, the third of the "Cappadocian triple constellation" (he and his brother Gregory of Nyssa being the other two) is one of the most famous in history: "more famous than Orestes and Pylades," St. Gregory Nazianzen wrote, in the funeral oration he made for St. Basil.

St. Basil was born into one of the great administrative families of Cappadocia—in what is now Turkey—about 329. His parents were rich, and profoundly Christian—they were none of your new bandwagon Christians following the Emperor Constantine's recent example. Basil's paternal grandfather and grandmother, with their children, had taken to the woods rather than renounce their faith under Diocletian. For seven years, winter and summer, they had lived the life of the *maquis* in the Pontine forests, sleeping out in shepherds' huts in winter, under the stars in summer, living on what they could catch, without benefit of dogs or horses, and on wild fruits. Their lands and wealth were confiscated. Later, Basil's father got back his family fortunes, and brought up Basil and his nine siblings to combine urbanity of manners and profound intellectual interests with deep and sincere piety.

When he was of an age seriously to study, his father sent Basil to Athens. His arrival there was eagerly awaited by a fellow-Cappadocian, Gregory of Nazianzen. "I had not been long in Athens," wrote the latter, "when Basil followed me. I was able to make the young men around me, who did not know what kind of a man Basil was, respect his serious character, the maturity of his demeanour . . . with the result that, almost alone among the new arrivals among us, he was able to escape the general fate," of being "hazed." Not long after his arrival, some Armenians ("I found Armenians an untruthful race, perfidious and overly dissimulating," comments Gregory) began questioning Basil. Gregory at first thought they merely were upholding the honour of Athens against Basil's birthplace, Caesarea, but soon saw they were out for blood. He quickly came to Basil's rescue, and the two worsted their rivals. This sealed their friendship, especially as Gregory then comforted Basil, who was sad: Athens was disappointing him. Thenceforward, for the five years they studied in Athens, they shared a room, ate at the same tables, "Our affection increased daily, for while carnal passions pass like spring flowers, chaste sentiments, because their object is stable, are more enduring, and the greater the beauty sought, the closer the unity between those dedicated to the same goal."[1]

"We two," Gregory goes on, after excusing himself for being moved to tears by his memories, "had virtue as our sole objective, and we lived with this future hope before us, that before leaving this world we would be from this world detached. Our eyes glued to this goal, we guided our life and all our actions by the commandments, and mutually egged each other on, being each for the other the measure by which we were able to discern the just from the unjust." Nor did they live apart from their fellow students: on the contrary, they made many friends, choosing, however, the best and the least quarrelsome. "They knew only two roads—one to church, the other to school." Some of their companions found them a bore, among these Julian the Apostate, who lost his faith while at Athens.

At last the time came to go home. The two friends had agreed to go together, but Gregory was persuaded to stay on. But he found Athens so empty without Basil that "I could not endure my unhappiness any longer, nor bear to be an object of pity any longer, nor to explain our separation to everyone . . . so I broke all the chains which bound me to Athens and went to join Basil." The two friends had decided, while at Athens, to seek the perfect life by answering the call to sell all they possessed, give it to the poor and follow Christ. But arrived home at Caesarea, Basil, covered with academic honours, was offered the top professorship in his native city, and accepted it. For several years he basked in the adulation of his fellow citizens, and, as W.K. Lowther Clarke puts it, "though Gregory, the friend, denies it, Gregory, the brother, declares expressly that Basil's head was completely turned by his success" (de Vita Macrinae).[2]

He became impossible, despising his colleagues, and lording

it even over the city fathers. Luckily Macrina, his eldest sister, gave Basil a terrific dressing down—what would be called, vulgarly, "a piece of her mind." In a letter (223) he describes the result:

> After I had wasted much time in vanity and had spent nearly all my youth in the vain labour in which I was engaged, occupying myself in acquiring a knowledge made foolish by God [his years of rhetoric], when at length as if aroused from a deep sleep, I looked upon the wondrous light of the truth of the Gospel and saw the futility of the wisdom of the rulers of this world who are passing away, having mourned deeply my piteous life, I prayed that guidance be given me for my introduction to the doctrines of religion. And before all things else, I was careful to amend my ways, which for a long time had been perverted by my companionship with the indifferent.

His sister, his brother Peter and his mother Emily, her family now grown, had given up their great wealth and retired to a little country place where they lived from the work of their hands. Basil, when he, too, gave away all he possessed, saw that thus to follow the family pattern was but a first step towards holiness. He decided to study the ascetic life, and set off on a voyage to the desert, to visit the monks there and learn from them.

> And in truth [he writes], I found many in Alexandria and throughout the rest of Egypt, and others in Palestine and Syria and Mesopotamia, the self-discipline of whose manner of living I admired. I marvelled, too, at their endurance in toil; I was amazed at their attention at prayers, their victory over sleep, being overcome by no physical necessity, always preserving lofty and unconquered the resolution of their soul, in hunger and thirst, in cold and nakedness, as if living in flesh not their own, they showed by their deeds what it is to dwell among those on this earth and what to have their citizenship in heaven.[3]

Basil's travels took two years. He had now only one tunic and one coat, and for the rest of his life he lived only on bread and water. He returned to his mother and sister, and wrote to Gregory to join him in a monastic life. Gregory replied he had to look after his old parents, but suggested they should divide their time, living together, now near the relatives of the one, now of the other. Evidently Basil did at some point visit Gregory at Tiberina, and tried to found a monastery there,[4] for Basil's jokes about the Tiberina mud, which evidently annoyed Gregory, seem taken from real incidents. Evidently, too, Tiberina didn't work, and Basil chose instead a lonely part of his family estate of Annesoi, but on the opposite bank of the Iris from where his mother and sisters had established themselves. Writing to Gregory, he described the place:

A landscape exactly as I wished it—as we used to imagine it in our dreams, so here it is in reality. A high mountain, covered with a thick wood, well watered with clear, cold streams. At its foot is a plain, whereinto flow these streams. This plain is almost an island, deep valleys bound it on two sides . . . there is only one entrance, of which we are in control. As to the dwelling, it is sheltered in another gorge, at one end of which is a high mountain. The plain unrolls itself before my eyes, and from the top, I can see the river flowing around . . . the fastest stream I know, which is thrown into a frenzy by a nearby rock. The sight is enchanting for me and for whomever sees it . . . not to speak of the advantage to us of the enormous crowd of fish it nourishes. And the best thing about this site is that together with the abundance of everything we need, it above all offers what is for me the greatest of goods: quiet. Not only is it free from city noises, but there are not even any visitors, except hunters.

Gregory's reply to this paean is to reproach his friend with his aversion to mud—the mud of Tiberina—"After all," says Gregory, "it's your own, native, Cappadocian mud, and squeamishness is not holiness."

What kind of a life does Basil lead in his Paradise, asks Gregory? Upon which Basil replies in a very different tone:

> I blush to tell you what I myself do night and day in my retreat. For I have renounced city occupations, as the occasions of innumerable misfortunes. But I have not been able to detach myself from myself. I am like those who, on the sea, because they are unaccustomed to sailing, are seasick: they grumble that it is the size of the boat makes them sick and seek refuge in the lifeboat or dinghy, but everywhere they are ill at ease and feel equally sick, for their own bile and their own nausea has followed them. That's about what has happened to us here: we brought our own domestic troubles with us, and are subject to the same troubles everywhere, to such an extent that we have not profited much from our isolation. But at least, the opportunities are here: here we have the calm necessary for contemplation; we are removed from the world by interior abandonment, we have prayer, interspersed with hymns; we read the Bible.[5]

This description brought Gregory to Annesoi—but he did not stay. Why he did not, is still a mystery—one of those "personality problems" that occur even between saints, even between saints who happen to have been the closest of friends for all their lives. Gregory's letters—two out of the three— referring to his stay, are written in an overbluffing, too hearty-hilarious, style.

> For me, I'll be glad to admire your Pontus, its pontic glooms and this place of true exile; the rocks suspended above your heads, the wild beasts that challenge your faith, and this mouse hole—let's give it its real name, in spite of its venerable designation of study, monastery and school . . . as for your peaceful river, full of fish—it's fuller still of stones than fish—as for the birds, they sing, but of starvation, and no one visits you except hunters—better add, who come to visit your corpses. . . .

In his second letter Gregory glooms over gardens without vegetables, "in spite of the manure we lugged out of the buildings to spread over the land. . . ." But in the third, he makes up for his kidding.

> What I wrote before was but in fun. What I write now, I write in all seriousness. Who will give me back the former months, where I found with you my delights in suffering? . . . Who will give me back those vigils and psalm-singings, those voyages to God by prayer, and that life in some way immaterial and incorporeal? Who will restore to me the unity, the fraternal sympathy you made sublime and divine? And the fight for virtue, the zeal enforced by laws and written rules? And our study of the divine maxims, and the discovery, with the help of the Holy Ghost—of the light they contain? Or, to speak of smaller things, who will restore to me the daily work we did with our own hands? Hewers of wood and haulers of stone, planters and waterers we were. . . . Help me, at least. . . . What we acquired that is useful, keep it for us by your prayers, so that we may not vanish like a shadow in the dawn. For I breathe you more than the air, and, present or absent . . . I live only the time I am with you.

In his funeral sermon Gregory explains: "I had to look after my old parents; a pack of misfortunes separated me from him. It was neither right nor reasonable, perhaps; yet these were the reasons that separated us." But if Gregory went, others came, and for these Basil wrote the *Moralia* and the *Great* and *Little Rules* which still serve many Eastern communities, and these early ascetical writings make of St. Basil the monastic legislator of the East, as later St. Benedict was of the West. He conceived monastic life as a community life, the hermit's life as the exception:

Question: Since your words have given us full assurance that the cenobitic life is dangerous for those who despise the commandments of the Lord, we wish to learn whether it is necessary that he who withdraws should remain alone, or live with brothers of like mind.

Answer: I think that the life of several in the same place is much more profitable. First, because for bodily wants no one of us is sufficient unto himself, but we need each other in providing what is necessary. In addition, the love of Christ does not permit each one to have regard only to his own affairs, for love, he says, seeks not her own. The solitary life has only one goal, the service of its own interests . . . further, no one in solitude recognises his own defects, since he has no one to correct him and in gentleness and mercy direct him on his way. . . . Also the commands may be better fulfilled by a larger community, but not by one alone, for while this thing is being done another will be neglected, for example, by attendance upon the sick the reception of strangers is neglected.

This, from St. Basil's Rule, shows his practical sense: he states quite simply that holiness comes *after* the ten commandments. And he is deeply a contemplative.

In tracking the footsteps of Him who is our guide [he says] we must strive after a quiet mind. He who is not yet married is harassed by frenzied cravings, and rebellious impulses, and hopeless attachments; he who has found his mate is encompassed with his own tumult of cares: if he is childless, there is desire of children; has he children, anxiety about their education, attention to his wife, care of his house, oversight of his servants, misfortunes in business, quarrels with his neighbours, . . . each day, as it comes darkens the soul in its own way, and night after night takes up the day's anxieties and cheats the mind with corresponding illusions.

How escape this repetition? By "separation from the whole world . . . not bodily separation, but the severance of the soul's sympathy with the body . . . and so to live that the heart may readily receive every impress of divine teaching. Preparation of heart is the unlearning of the prejudices of evil converse. It is the smoothing of the waxen tablet before attempting to write on it."

Basil welcomed all who came, even pagans, and "those who understood nothing of our way of life, and even mock it, for they will not return to bother us." Orphans and local children came to his monasteries to be educated. Basil made of all the monasteries he founded in the many towns of Pontus separate, independent institutions, although they all followed his constitutions. As an educator, Basil advised young men to study Greek as Moses had studied Egyptian and Daniel had studied Babylonian, wisdom: for he realised and preached that all good, everywhere, belongs to the Church. He wrote wonderfully of the "good things of the Greeks" and bade the young "load their ship with knowledge." His style is full of splendid phrases: "This game that the God inside is always playing with all of us," he writes, and again, "God's will is done on earth as it is in heaven, by incessant revolution." He cites Hesiod and Homer, Solon and Prodicos, as inciters to virtue, and Pericles, Euclid, Socrates, Alexander, and Clinias as practising it.

Basil's peaceful life in his beloved retreat lasted a scant five years—interrupted by a visit to the Council of Constantinople in 360. In 362 the pattern of his life, divided between prayer, study and the formation of his disciples, was changed by the Bishop of Caesarea, Eusebius, sending for him and ordaining him to the priesthood. In a few weeks, however, the bishop grew jealous of his brilliant new curate, and Basil withdrew into one of his monasteries until 365, when his friend Gregory insisted he must leave his solitude as the Emperor Valens, an Arian, was persecuting the Catholics and Caesarea needed all her strong men to defend the Faith. Eusebius now realised the true stature and quality of Basil, became entirely devoted to him, and died in his arms. Basil was chosen his successor, and became archbishop of Caesarea in 370, at the height of the Arian controversy. The Emperor was determined to stop at nothing to overcome Catholic resistance. He nominated as Archbishop of

Constantinople one of his Arian puppets. When eighty-four of the clergy bravely resisted the phoney election, the emperor deported and drowned them at sea. Then he sent his terrible praetorian prefect Modestus to summon Basil before him. The following account of their interview is by St. Gregory Nazianzen.

> "What is the meaning of this, you Basil," said the prefect, a bitter Arian, not deigning to style him bishop, "that you stand out against so great a prince, and are self-willed when others yield?"
>
> **Basil:** What do you want of me? And what is my extravagance? I have not yet learned it.
>
> **Modestus:** Your not worshipping after the Emperor's manner, when the rest of your party have given way.
>
> **Basil:** I have a Sovereign whose will is otherwise, nor can I bring myself to worship any creature—I am a creature of God, and commanded to be a god.
>
> **Modestus:** For whom do you take me?
>
> **Basil:** For a thing of nought, while such are your commands.

And so the dialogue goes on, Basil acknowledging the prefect to be "In a noble place: I own it. And it is much for me to have your fellowship, for we are both God's creatures." Presently Modestus lost his temper, and rose from his place, threatening Basil with "confiscation, exile, tortures, death." Basil is scornful:

> "Think of some other threat—these have no influence upon me. He runs no risk of confiscation who has nothing to lose, except these poor garments, and a few books. Exile is no threat to one who is at home wherever he is, or rather who dwells everywhere in God's home, whose pilgrim and wanderer he is. Tortures cannot harm a frame so frail as to break under the first blow. If you struck me once, I would be

dead. And that would but send me sooner to Him for whom I live and labour, for whom I am dead rather than alive, to whom I have long been journeying."

Modestus grumbled that no one had ever spoken before to Modestus with such freedom. "Perhaps," Basil said, "you have never met a bishop? Else under similar circumstances you would have heard identical language." Thereafter both Modestus and his master left Basil well alone.

During the worst famine Caesarea had ever known, which occurred shortly after Basil had become bishop, he took strong measures against the black marketeers and rent gougers.

What will you say to God when he asks you why you dressed the walls of your house, and not your brother, you who hoard your wheat and don't feed the hungry? Whom have I wronged, you ask, by keeping what is my own? From whom did you keep these goods and why do you think they were for your personal use? It's just as if someone in the theatre, having taken a seat, prevented others entering and making use of what belongs to all. Such is the attitude of those who possess: because they were the first to occupy common property, they think they can appropriate it.

And he goes on, using the same language Bernard Shaw was to use, "What is a thief? A thief is one who takes the good belonging to others. Are you not a thief, who turn to your sole profit that of which you received only the custodianship?" And he adds, as any Fabian might have: "the coat hanging in your closet belongs to the shivering; the shoes you are not wearing belong to the barefoot: the money you hid in your safe-deposit box belongs to your brother. You commit as many injustices as there are men to whom you might have given." But for Basil, the poor have just as many obligations as the rich: to be rich is not a fixed state, it is a state of mind. "You are poor," he cries, "but there's always someone poorer than you. You only have ten days to live? Here's a man who has but two."

Naturally, he showed what he meant by example. His mother, who had just died, had left him her tiny estate. "He sold it, and at once bought food with the proceeds and established a food kitchen. He gathered all those who were dying of hunger in one place, men, women, children, oldsters. He had managed to get hold of big saucepans full of vegetables. Like Christ, he himself fed the hungry," relates St. Gregory.

He could, like many, have limited his help to material assistance, or to the building of hospitals and schools. But he did not equate charity with alms: his first idea was to re-establish in every man his dignity, however miserable that man might be. There was at that time a hideous disproportion between the rich landowners and the landless people. Many wars had devastated the country, and the Barbarians, never far, pillaged the people during their raids. Basil regarded no person as too humble for his intervention: a runaway slave's master is exhorted to mercy; Basil disapproved the current use of torture and constantly inveighed against it; he wrote to Modestus about the iron-miners in the Taurus mountains, and begged him not to tax them "as it is to your interest not to make it impossible for them to work for the general good."

Meanwhile, a new war had broken out against the Goths, and on 9 August 378, the imperial army was terribly beaten: the Emperor Valens disappeared—some say he was burnt to death in a cabin where, wounded, he had taken refuge. A few months later Theodosius, a Catholic, became emperor, and under him peace was re-established in the Church. But Basil did not live to see the peace he so longed for. He died at forty-nine, worn out, on 1 January 379. "His life was the incessant movement which carried him continually towards God," wrote his friend St. Gregory. He would have wished no other epitaph. His feast is 14 June.

St. Monica

332-387

Muriel Spark

MONICA, THE MOTHER of St. Augustine, was born at Tagaste in North Africa in the year 332, and died at Ostia in the fifty-sixth year of her life.

Among saints, she is the most fortunate in her first biographer. St. Augustine does not give us a long history of his mother, but what he says of her is everywhere immediate and powerful. Her character pervades the first nine books of the *Confessions*. If that were merely a work of fiction Monica would still be one of the memorable women of literature, and the relationship between mother and son one of the most interesting.

Monica had intrigued her son's imagination. While his closest friends—those who exerted most influence on his mind—remain eloquent impressions, he renders Monica's personality in the round. His father, son and brother are portrayed in a glimpse but he gives to his mother totality and magnitude:

> Much I omit but I will not omit whatsoever my soul would bring forth concerning that Thy handmaid, who brought me forth, both in the flesh, that I might be born to this temporal light, and in heart, that I might be born to Light eternal.

Monica's character presents a number of curious contrasts. There is a difference between Monica up to the time of her widowhood and the type of woman she became after her husband's death; a difference between her attitude to the world in general and her dealings with Augustine. In the one aspect she is the exemplary type of woman saint, displaying the virtues of gentleness, patience, modesty and extreme tact; but in everything that touched her son she became a sort of holy terror, she was above tact, she pursued him recklessly over land and sea, badgered bishops on his behalf, parted him from a beloved mistress. In all her ordinary transactions she is that withdrawn, self-contained, "chaste and sober widow" whom Augustine extols:

> so frequent in almsdeeds, so full of duty and service to Thy saints, no day intermitting the oblation at Thine altar, twice a day, morning and evening, without any intermittance, coming to Thy church, not for idle tattlings and old wives' fables, but that she might hear Thee in Thy discourses, and Thou in her prayers.

While to other appearances, her behaviour was that of a tiresome possessive mother, one of those who wield over their children a tyranny of tears and long-suffering, who turn up at the least comfortable moments, who always know best and suffer from chronic rectitude. Monica, moreover, possessed the exasperating justification of the visionary. She was highly civilised, she was deeply primitive. If she had not been holy she would probably have been insufferable.

Tagaste, the birthplace of both Monica and Augustine, was situated in what is now Algeria, bordering on Tunisia; the region was at that time one of the most fruitful holdings of the Empire. They were of the great North African stock, the Berbers. Monica was born in the birth year of St. Jerome, of a Christian family and in an environment where schism was rife and paganism still bubbled below the surface.

She was brought up by a "certain decrepit maidservant" to whose diligence Monica claimed that she owed her religious disposition. This old woman must have been particularly grim, for she would not permit the children to drink between

meals—not even water, though they were parched with thirst—
in order to restrain their appetite for wine when it should later
come within their reach. An incident recorded of Monica's
childhood also has to do with wine-drinking.

When she, as though a sober maiden, was bidden by her
parents to draw wine out of the hogshead, holding the vessel
under the opening, before she poured the wine into the
flagon, she sipped a little with the tip of her lips . . . And
thus by adding to that little, daily littles, she had fallen into
such a habit as greedily to drink off her little cup brim-full
almost of wine. Where was then that discreet old woman,
and that her earnest countermanding? Would aught avail
against a secret disease, if Thy healing hand, O Lord,
watched not over us? . . . For a maid-servant with whom she
used to go to the cellar, falling to words with her little
mistress, when alone with her, taunted her with this fault,
with most bitter insult, calling her wine-bibber. With which
taunt she, stung to the quick, saw the foulness of her fault,
and instantly condemned and forsook it.

It is true that Monica retained a particular touchy reserve
about wine; she would taste it only for courtesy's sake, and
when, following a local custom, she distributed wine to the
faithful at the martyrs' tombs, she contrived to make it "not
only very watery, but unpleasantly heated with carrying
about."

She was married at about the age of twenty-two to a pagan
husband, Patricius, of noble origin and declining fortune, who
held some magisterial rank in Tagaste. He was notoriously
hot-tempered, and as a husband very generous, very unfaith-
ful. Monica handled him admirably:

She had learned not to resist an angry husband, not in
deed only, but not even in word. Only when he was smoothed
and tranquil, and in a temper to receive it, she would give an
account of her actions, if haply he had overhastily taken
offence.

Which piece of wisdom Monica was wont to dispense to the matrons of the town who suffered greatly from their husbands' beatings, such being the manners of Tagaste; and those who took her advice found it marvellously effective. By her tact and composure Monica also managed to quell and gain the affection of a troublesome mother-in-law and a houseful of murmuring servants. She gained a reputation as a peacemaker, receiving confidences which she never disclosed except to bring discordant parties to reconcilement. We are told that she was further endowed with pleasant conversational gifts and gracious ways, by which she endeared herself to her difficult husband.

Of course, many women, not particularly noted for sanctity, have done as much. The real test of Monica's quality in the early years of her marriage was her position as a Christian in a pagan household, for it was some seventeen years before Patricius became a Christian. Augustine declares, "it was her earnest desire that Thou my God, rather than he should be my father; and in this Thou didst aid her to prevail over her husband."

Monica had three children, Navigius who was mild and pious, marvellous Augustine and a daughter who it is thought was named Perpetua. Obtaining her husband's tolerance, she brought them up in Christian doctrine. Augustine was not baptised in his infancy, nor perhaps were his brother and sister. But he speaks of being dedicated by Monica in a special way to the Christian faith:

> As a boy I had already heard of an eternal life, promised us through the humility of the Lord our God stooping to our pride; and even from the womb of my mother, who greatly hoped in Thee, I was sealed with the mark of His cross and salted with His salt.

It is strange that Monica should have followed the dubious custom of late baptism, against which Augustine later inveighed in the same breath as he makes excuse for her, that she foresaw the great temptations of his youth, "and preferred to expose to them the clay whence I might afterwards be moulded, than the very cast, when made." When, as a child, Augustine was taken ill and thought to be dying, having himself asked to be baptised, Monica was in great anxiety to procure this sacrament for him, and would have done so had he not suddenly recovered. One of Monica's characteristics was her adherence to popular and local religious customs; this of the deferred baptism may have been an instance.

Towards the end of her husband's life Monica won him to the Christian faith, but she was not of one mind with him concerning Augustine who was then entering his sixteenth year. For when Patricius, "as already anticipating his descendants," observed with delight his son's growing into high-spirited manhood, Monica did not share this natural response; on the contrary, she was "startled with a holy fear and trembling" and took occasion privately to warn Augustine "not to commit fornication, but especially never to defile another man's wife." At this stage Monica's words seemed, as he says, womanish advices which he should blush to obey.

Augustine makes it a point that, for all his mother's fears for his chastity she was not for providing him with a wife:

> She feared lest a wife should prove a clog and hindrance to my hopes. Not those hopes of the world to come, which my mother reposed in Thee; but the hope of learning, which both my parents were too desirous I should attain; my father, because he had next to no thought of Thee, and of me but vain conceits; my mother, because she accounted that those usual courses of learning would not only be no hindrance, but even some furtherance towards attaining Thee.

Monica's ambitions for Augustine began to emerge at this time with some intensity, and as in later years, she combines, with a kind of economy, her intentions for his worldly success and those for his salvation. Already she has the end in view, and the means do not apparently trouble her. Consequently her actions are not directed towards simplifying any immediate situation that concerns Augustine. He is prevented from marriage or promised in marriage according as it seems expedient to Monica. One does not get the impression that she was greatly solicitous for his current well-being. In many ways she is like one of those inspired resolute women of the Old Testament, and a saint to be contemplated rather than copied.

It is not surprising that Monica acted as if her son was exceptional, since he was exceptional. Augustine, reviewing her life with his wonderful sense of Providence, saw the hand of God in all her actions. Her admonitions to chastity, he says, "were Thine, and I knew it not; and I thought that Thou wert silent and that it was she who spake." In such a case it is not surprising that Monica carried on as if the future shape of Christendom depended on her son's conversion, for it so largely did.

She became a widow about her fortieth year when Augustine entered his nineteenth. He was pursuing his studies with success at the new city of Carthage and had by this time embarked on his liaison with his faithful mistress who presently bore him a son. This irregularity did not apparently distress Monica nearly so much as his adherence to Manichean beliefs, on which account she mourned Augustine as one dead; "more than mothers weep the bodily deaths of their children. For she, by that faith and spirit which she had from Thee, discerned the death wherein I lay."

At first she closed her house to him, could hardly bear to eat at the same table; "abhorring and detesting" he says, "the blasphemies of my error." However, a dream to which she attached great authority persuaded her to receive him as before. In such matters she possessed the discrimination of the true visionary; "for she could, she said, through a certain feeling, which in words she could not express, discern between Thy revelations, and the dreams of her own soul." This dream which so changed Monica's attitude is recorded by Augustine:

She saw herself standing on a certain wooden rule, and a shining youth coming towards her, cheerful and smiling upon her, herself grieving, and overwhelmed with grief. But he having enquired of her the causes of her grief and daily tears, and she answering that she was bewailing my perdition, he bade her rest contented, and told her to look and observe, "That where she was, there was I also." And when she looked, she saw me standing by her in the same rule.

When she told Augustine this dream he interpreted it to mean, "that she should not despair of being one day what I was." But she, without hesitation, replied, "No, for it was not told me that Where he, there thou also; but Where thou, there he also."

This dream, in which she so closely identifies herself with the Catholic faith, she took as a promise of Augustine's conversion; it so thoroughly convinced her that she drew consolation and hope from it for years to come. Meanwhile the promptitude and correctness of her reply impressed Augustine. It appealed to the young logician in him:

> That she was not perplexed by the falsity of my interpretation, and so quickly saw what was to be seen, and which I certainly had not perceived before she spake, even then moved me more than the dream itself.

From his first interpretation of her dream, the possibility seems to have been in his mind that Monica might one day take to Manicheism; and it is, indeed, a wonder that she who always inclined to think of herself together with Augustine, and being of a visionary temperament, did not succumb to that poetic and imaginative heresy.

Augustine's Manicheism brought out the dramatic matriarch in Monica. He was outwardly more free of her control than in his boyhood when he had scorned her advice, but now a relationship less tangible yet closer appears between them. She holds him with her tears and by her visions, by refusing him her house and taking him back again, she arrests his attention by outwitting him in simple logic. At this period also, Monica went to a bishop for whom she had a particular regard, imploring him to discuss religion with Augustine. The bishop refused: Augustine was unteachable, and besides, very tricky to argue with. Monica would not be satisfied; "but urged him more, with entreaties and many tears, that he would see me and discourse with me; he, a little displeased with her importunity, saith, 'Go thy ways, and God bless thee, for it is not possible that the son of these tears should perish.' " Monica, who often discerned the voice of Heaven in the words of others, took this answer as a divine promise.

Augustine, surrounded by his friends, and under distinguished patronage, taught rhetoric in his native town for a time, and subsequently for some nine years at Carthage. During this period he cannot have been much in Monica's company. These were the critical years of his spiritual growth, and although throughout his writings Augustine speaks admiringly of his mother's perceptive mind—as that of a "natural philosopher"—she probably had no direct intellectual influence upon him. Her influence was rather personal and affective. And it is rather to the efficacy of her prayers and tears in obtaining his conversion that Augustine repeatedly draws attention: "Through her tears night and day poured out, with a sacrifice offered for me unto Thee." One does not know if Monica's thoughts were occupied on other matters throughout these years; the impression given by the *Confessions* is that she was wholly absorbed in Augustine, her attention fixed unremittingly on him. That this is probably true is indicated by the degree of Monica's alarm when he decided to leave Africa.

This was in 383. He made up his mind to go to Rome. Monica put up a strong opposition, but without success. Distracted, she then followed him as far as the coast. Here the scene was set for a battle of wills. Monica clung to him passionately; he should go no further, or if he did she would accompany him.

Augustine was thirty years of age; he was intent on going to Rome, and without his mother; and, understandably, with the least possible distress to himself. The story of his escape is a dramatic one, and in telling it Augustine seems to recapture the original exhilaration and pathos:

I feigned that I had a friend whom I could not leave, till he had a fair wind to sail. And I lied to my mother, and such a mother, and escaped. Refusing to return without me, I scarcely persuaded her to stay that night in a place hard by our ship, where was an Oratory in memory of the blessed Cyprian. That night I privily departed. The wind blew and swelled our sails, and withdrew the shore from our sight, and she on the morrow was there, frantic with sorrow. And with complaints and groans filled Thine ears, who didst then disregard them; while through my desires Thou wert hurrying me to end all desire, and the earthly part of her affection to me was chastened by the allotted scourge of sorrows. For she loved my being with her, as mothers do, but much more than many. . . . And yet, after accusing my treachery and hardheartedness, she betook herself again to intercede for me, went to her wonted place, and I to Rome.

Augustine probably got the escape idea from the *Aeneid,* but Monica was no wretched Dido. Less than two years later she embarked for Milan where Augustine was established. It was a stormy passage, but having received in a vision assurance of their safe arrival, "she comforted the very mariners by whom passengers unacquainted with the deep used rather to be comforted."

On her arrival she learned that Augustine had abandoned the Manichean heresy, "though not yet a Catholic Christian"; he was apparently surprised that she did not seem overjoyed at this news. She looked for a more positive decision, and told him calmly: "She believed in Christ, that before she departed this life, she should see me a Catholic believer." At the same time she intensified her efforts to intercede for him.

In Milan she conceived a great love for the saintly bishop Ambrose, for his having lately exerted a benign influence on her son: "That man she loved as an angel of God." So high was her reverence for St. Ambrose that on his account she was induced to give up certain religious customs to which she had been greatly attached all her life. In Africa it had been the custom to fast on Saturdays. Also, it had been her habit to commemorate the martyrs by distributing food and wine to Christians assembled at the shrines. She did not find the Saturday fast in Milan, and when she arrived at the church with her basket of food and wine she was turned away by the porter. Monica lost no time in enquiring about the reason, using Augustine as a messenger to Ambrose on these points. (Some say that she seized this opportunity to bring them together.) On the question of the Saturday fast Ambrose replied simply that it was not the custom in Milan because it had never been so. On the other point, he forbade the practice on the grounds that it might lead to excessive eating and drinking in the churches, and moreover, it resembled too closely some current pagan usages.

It went hard with Monica to give up her favourite obser-vances, but so she did. Augustine, knowing the strength of his mother's will, marvelled how readily she gave in to Ambrose, declaring it doubtful that she would have yielded to anyone else. Ambrose, in his turn, greatly admired Monica for her devout bearing, her eager spirit and the good things she did. So that, says Augustine, "when he saw me, he often burst forth into her praises; congratulating me that I had such a mother."

A few months after her arrival in Milan, Monica was involved in the exciting seige of the basilica where Ambrose usually officiated. There Ambrose and his people kept watch in the church while it was surrounded for some days by the soldiers of the Empress Justina, who wanted the building for her Arians. As might be expected, Monica was prominently present among the faithful, taking a leading part in their witness.

Augustine's mistress had joined him in Milan, together with their son Adeodatus. This union had become a hindrance both to Augustine's career and to his baptism which was now in prospect. "Continual effort," he writes, "was made to have me married. I wooed, I was promised, chiefly through my mother's pains."

At this time an amusing experiment was tried by Augustine on his mother, with her co-operation. Having a lively faith in her visionary powers he put her up to praying for a special vision which would reveal something concerning his future marriage. Monica heartily undertook this enterprise, but was unlucky in her visions so far as the marriage was concerned. What she "saw" she dismissed as vain and fantastic things.

Shrewd Monica eventually found a girl, two years under marriageable age, for whom Augustine agreed to wait. Procrastination probably seemed the wisest course to Monica. Meanwhile the woman with whom Augustine had lived so long was despatched to Africa, greatly to his misery, while the boy Adeodatus was left in Monica's charge.

When, in the summer of that year Augustine was resolved not only to receive baptism, but to follow a celibate life, Monica's ambitions were realised beyond her hopes. "She rejoiced, she triumphed."

At Cassiacum, a country villa had been placed at Augustine's disposal, and there he retired to prepare for his baptism with Monica and a small company of friends. The party included his son Adeodatus who was a catechumen like himself, and his untroublesome brother Navigius. Monica is seen at last tranquil and benevolent and satisfied. She took charge of the company "as though," writes Augustine, "she had been mother of us all; so served us, as though she had been child to us all."

In those dialogues of Augustine which refer to this idyllic interlude, Monica is given a revealing part. Allowing for the rhetoric of the occasion—for the speeches attributed to her are unlikely to be accurate reports—the role she occupies in the dialogues at least indicates Augustine's mental image of her at this time. He conceives her as a sort of Diotima figure in that country-house symposium. Hers is the role of untrammelled wisdom rather than a discursive one. It is stated that, listening to Monica, the company forgets her sex and believes it is listening to some divine doctor; and Augustine professes himself to be ravished with delight, contemplating the divine source whence flow Monica's thoughts. Although these and similar references, unlike those in the *Confessions,* have no claim to be considered historical, they certainly represent some aspects of the actual wise oracular Monica.

After Augustine's baptism he prepared to take Monica back to Africa with his brother and son. They travelled to Rome, staying nearby at Ostia on the Tiber. There the memorable scene occurred in which Monica and Augustine, standing by a window that overlooked a garden, shared a mystical experience or at least a kind of philosophical ecstasy:

> We were discoursing together, alone, very sweetly . . . enquiring between ourselves of what sort the eternal life of the saints was to be, which eye hath not seen, nor ear heard, nor hath it entered into the heart of man. And when our discourse was brought to that point, that the very highest delight of the earthly senses, in the very purest material light, was, in respect of the sweetness of that life, not only not worthy of comparison, but not even of mention; we raising ourselves with a more glowing affection towards the "self-same" did by degrees pass through all things bodily, even the very heaven whence sun and moon and stars shine upon the earth; yea, we were soaring higher yet, by inward musing, and discourse, and admiring of Thy works; and we came to our own minds, and went beyond them, that we might arrive at that region of never-failing plenty, where Thou feedest Israel for ever with the food of truth, and where life is the Wisdom by whom all these things are made. And while we were discoursing and panting after her, we slightly touched on her with the whole effort of our heart; and we sighed, and there we leave bound the first fruits of the Spirit; and returned to vocal expressions of our mouth, where the word spoken has beginning and end.

Towards the end of this sublime conversation Monica declared that, for her part, she had no further delight in this life, now that her hopes for Augustine were abundantly fulfilled. She had, in a sense, advanced ahead of herself into eternity. "What do I here?" she said.

About five days later Monica fell sick with fever. Unconscious for a while, she came round to see her two sons and grandson by her bed. "Where was I?" she enquired.

It was known to Monica's family that her heart had been set on being buried in her native town, in the ground prepared for her beside her husband. And apparently there had been in her mind some superstition that the place of burial affected the disposal of bodies at the Resurrection. But now on her death-bed, her family were amazed to hear her state calmly, "Here shall you bury your mother"; and Augustine especially rejoiced at her freedom from this last temporal anxiety. She died a few days later, leaving no instructions for her embalming or mode of burial, but "desired only to have her name commemorated at Thy altar, which she had served without intermission of one day."

On her death, says Augustine, his life was torn, since his life and hers had been as one life. This is probably more than a verbal conceit. Their spiritual affinity was more intense than their natural relationship, though it followed the same pattern. This is a recurrent theme with Augustine. He continually adapts the scriptural text, "I am in travail over you afresh, until I can see Christ's image formed in you," to illustrate Monica's spiritual motherhood. "The mother of my flesh," he writes, "even more lovingly travailed in birth of my salvation." And again, "With how much more vehement anguish she was now in labour of me in the spirit, than at her childbearing in the flesh."

Monica is often remembered for her persevering prayers and tears. In the office of St. Monica there is an emphasis on her weeping, curiously exultant and lyrical:

This mother wept and prayed assiduously to obtain Augustine's conversion.

She wept both day and night, did this afflicted mother, and interceded earnestly for her son.

Behold her, this widow, who knows how to weep; she who sheds such continuous and such bitter tears over her son.

Monica was not the lachrymose type of woman in the ordinary sense, on the contrary she strikes one as being good and tough. It is one more instance of her paradoxical nature, that her almost primitive capacity for weeping and bewailing her son combines with her restrained and happy bearing in other respects. Augustine was much taken up with the mystery of tears, when considering his own grief on the death of his young friend:

> May I learn from Thee why weeping is sweet to the miserable? Unless we mourned in Thine ears, we should have no hope left. Whence then is sweet fruit gathered from the bitterness of life, from groaning, tears, sighs, and complaints? Doth this sweeten it, that we hope Thou hearest?

The cultus of St. Monica emerged towards the thirteenth century, when her feast was observed in many places. About 1430, when devotion to Monica was widespread, a search was authorised for her remains which, though they had been moved from their original resting-place, still lay at Ostia. Her relics were discovered and translated to Rome on a Palm Sunday, and it is declared that in the course of the journey several sick children, brought by their mothers to the passing coffin, were healed.

St. Augustine

354-430

Robert Speaight

I HAVE SOMETIMES, to induce sleep or distract myself from worry, played a childish game. I have imagined that Charon has ferried me across the Styx and that there, on the other side, an emissary—of whom I am not quite sure—is waiting to receive me. He tells me that before proceeding to other and sterner business I may choose any single person from among the dead, as distinct from the damned, with whom to dine and spend the evening. Even when you have made the capital decision as to whether your companion shall be a man or a woman, the choice is still exasperating in its range. You may reject Dr. Johnson because he would talk too much, and St. Thomas Aquinas because he would talk too little; you may reject all the greatest beauties because they would so evidently be the greatest bores; but you still have to choose between Keats and Coleridge, Madame de Sévigné and Mozart. I must confess that in this particular game the saints do not offer much competition. One humbly hopes to have a glimpse of them later on. The very fact that they are so tremendous makes them somehow less companionable. What could one conceivably say to St. John of the Cross? In the still earthy and sullied condition in which one disembarks from Charon's ferry, one has the unworthy suspicion that a saint might spoil one's dinner.

There are, however, certain exceptions to this reluctance to face the best and wisest of mankind. One would give a great deal for an evening in the company of St. Thomas More—the questions and the answers and the slightly whimsy jokes. But of all the men who have ever lived I think that I would choose St. Augustine for the companion of a privileged evening. And since I cannot hope to add anything of the least importance to what has already been written about this prodigious man, I am simply going to ask myself why I should make this choice.

What follows here is neither criticism, nor informed comment; it is no more than the expression of a profound attachment.

You notice that although I do not hesitate to call St. Augustine a prodigy, I refer to him as a man, not as a soul or a mind. Some of the saints are so transparent that you hardly feel their bodily essences at all. The sorrowing eyes of St. Therese of Lisieux, as we see them in the untouched-up photographs, the stigmata of St. Francis, the mittened hands of Padre Pio—these have nothing in common with the life of the body, as we know it to our pleasure or our cost. Again, the massive countenance of Aquinas points to the *quinque viae* or the rout of the Albigensians. These appearances, to be frank, are an incitement to prayer and study; they are not an encouragement to conversation. But with St. Augustine it is different. Here the appearance is anybody's guess—and what a fascinating guess—but the physical man is with us, stirring us with his energy and singeing us with his flame. We see him in sandals and tunic, in cope and mitre, walking and talking in his habit as he lived. In one sense he is remote, radiant with wisdom and elevated by the exercise of heroic virtue; but in another sense he is there beside us speaking our language, knowing our difficulties, and acquainted with our crisis. It may sound presumptuous to say that one would like to have a conversation with St. Augustine; but how dearly one would love to hear him talk!

It is a truism to say that St. Augustine's time was in many respects analogous to our own. There were the same political earthquakes and morbid tyrannies, the same puerile superstitions, the same philosophic unrest. And it is the primary, important and saving fact about Augustine that he was born with a question mark in his mind. By that I mean not only that he went on asking the supreme question until he had found the answer to it, but that when he had found the answer, he went on trying to explain, and not merely to preach, his satisfaction. This set him apart from the dull mass of the indifferent—he would have understood no better than Pascal how anyone could fail to agonize over the answer to the question which haunted him; and it set him apart also from the complacent, from those who sat pretty in their possession of the Faith. There runs through all his writing a certain incredulous gratitude for the gift of grace. He is for ever interrupting his narrative to make room for some exclamation of contrition or praise. If he were a less gifted writer, this would be irritating; we often find it so in other works of spirituality. But Augustine was by far the greatest writer who has ever written in defence of Christianity. His style has the majesty of great music and the liveliness of good conversation. Father Martindale has compared it to César Franck, and Charles Du Bos used to say that it reminded him of Bach. It has the *sérieux* of the one and the structure, at once so durable and light, of the other.

For all the pleasure one would take in hearing Augustine talk, I fancy that at times I should prefer to play the part of a hidden witness; I should find it fascinating to overhear him discussing Plato with an Oxford don or psychology with a Harley Street specialist. I would gladly give my place at the table to a musician. But this is to play a different sort of game, and I only introduce these personalities to emphasize the several levels on which Augustine meets us. Unlike so many theologians and moralists, he meets us on the plane of the imagination. It is one thing to admit and to analyse the imagination; anyone with a little training in philosophy can do that. But only genius can exercise the imagination; just as sanctity alone can purify it. Many of the saints—humble, heroic, untutored people—have had what one may call the genius of sanctity. Those who knew the Carmelite Prioress Mother Mary of the Cross will know something about the common sense of sanctity; and in the spiritual life it may be that genius and common sense are one.

But Augustine had genius *and* sanctity; and this makes his use of the imagination so subtle and powerful an instrument for the discovery of truth.

To those who fear and condemn the imagination, who place it below the logical deductions of the schools, we are entitled to reply that it was by this method that Christ Himself had taught. For the imagination can reach those who are incapable of argument; those who, without being poets or children, have the mind of a poet or a child. It is true, of course, that the imagination often turns inward; it nourishes a sterile subjectivism. And it is perhaps because Augustine was himself so great a master of introspection that he appeals to an introspective century. His introspection fascinates us as much as at one time it fascinated him. But it was his mission to experience and to demonstrate the only possible issue of introspection. Many years ago W.B. Yeats remarked to me, "Man has for so long regarded himself in the mirror that he must now, from sheer boredom, either retreat into the anonymity of the herd, or go forward with wisdom." This observation is pertinent to Augustine. As Maritain has put it, "Mystical wisdom may be called in some sort the activating agent, the catalysing instrument of augustinian introspection, thanks to which it appears as the most marvellous instrument of spiritual observation." Even so loyal a scholastic as M. Maritain can admit that the mode of St. Augustine's teachings was nearer to the method of the Gospels than it was to the scientism of the Schools. In so far as it contained a philosophic doctrine, this was a metaphysic of conversion, a metaphysic of the inward life.

It would be fanciful, perhaps, to describe St. Augustine as a Christian Proust—he had greatnesses to which even a Christian Proust would never have attained—but it may be useful to invoke the name of Proust in order to measure the intelligibility of Augustine to the modern world, and to perceive the contrast between our disease and the cure that he proposes for it. I yield to no one in my admiration for Proust. He remains for me the most readable, the most seductive of writers. He had a genius, not only for expression but for organization, of a very rare kind.

But I do not see how one can deny that spiritually, as well as physically, he was an invalid. He was a man who did not, I think, really want to get well. His mind moved round and round in concentric circles, "mixing memory and desire." There was an alarming disparity between his gifts which were enormous and his moral sensibility which was impotent. He was a man who never felt for a moment that the world was too much with him. He did not find an issue to his introspection, because he never seriously looked for one.

Here he is very different from Henry James, with whom he has sometimes been compared. James, for all his introspection, his maddening minutiae of analysis, was, morally, a bracing writer. And the contrast with St. Augustine is naturally overwhelming. Augustine ran all the risks of introspection. He was, at first, more interested in himself than in other people; more interested in ideas than in men; more interested in truth than in charity. He was devoted to his mother, his mistress, and his son. He was very fond of his friends. He had an affectionate nature. But his mind was tuned vertically to his own misery and uncertainty, and to God. It did not embrace the variety and even the vulgarity of mankind, as the mind of Shakespeare or St. Francis embraced them. Whatever the dissipation or curiosity he may have been entertaining at the moment, he always lived in the presence of his problem. He had, in almost every respect, the character of a modern intellectual, who is trying to see things straight. He had the same ardours and reluctances, and the same embarrassing choice. Who shall it be—Ouspensky, Marx or Freud; Sartre or Rudolf Steiner; Santayana or Tagore? So, in Augustine's day, they crowded round him; the solemn physicians and the self-confident osteopaths of the soul.

For a time he seems to have believed that his greatest temptation was lust, and everything he says on this subject has a moving intensity. Only Shakespeare, with his "expense of spirit in a waste of shame," has expressed the same agony of desire and dissatisfaction. But many others, on the verge of conversion or contrition, have felt as he did the impossibility, the inhumanity, of giving up this person or this thing. Others, also, believing chastity to be possible and beneficial, have asked for it eventually, when the blood is cold; "but not yet." Augustine felt all this, and has described it to us; the sheer wall that the will must climb, forbidding in the terrible sun; the daunting difficulty of the last step. His fears are echoed in the stories of many contemporary conversions. Claudel's four years of waiting after the revelation in Notre Dame; the slow crisis in the convictions of Charles Du Bos, whom Augustine literally led by the hand; the painful stages, suggested in his *Journal*, of Julian Green's return. Augustine summed up the feelings of all who exclaim, "I believe—yes; but I simply have not the strength to behave."

There is in this final agony of the will, enfeebled by sexual habit, a hint of what we are told about the agony of death; the sense of loneliness, of a supreme effort to be made and no one near. In the eighth book of the *Confessions* Augustine expresses the truth, which heresy has sometimes deformed, of the helplessness of the soul until Grace has come to its rescue. No mountaineer describing his ascent of the Matterhorn has given us a greater sensation of vertigo than did Augustine in this passage. He is in the garden, sobbing on the bench, with Alypius close by; one feels the noonday heat and the normalities of social intercourse; a decanter of wine, perhaps, nearly empty on the table, with the Epistles of St. Paul beside it; a bird singing; and each detail of the story Ponticianus has just told hanging like motes in the air:

> For I kept saying within myself "Let it be now, let it be now," and by the mere words I had begun to move towards the resolution. I almost made it, yet I did not quite make it. But I did not fall back into my original state, but as it were stood near to get my breath. And I tried again and I was almost there, and now I could all but touch it and hold it: yet I was not quite there, I did not touch it or hold it. I still shrank from dying unto death and living unto life. The lower

condition which had grown habitual was more powerful than the better condition which I had not tried. The nearer the point of time came in which I was to become different, the more it struck me with horror; but it did not force me utterly back nor turn me utterly away, but held me there between the two. (Trans. F.J. Sheed.)

The unflinching realism of this speaks volumes to the modern mind; we are miles away from rhapsody. Augustine is here the perfect example of his own dictum, "etiam peccata serviunt." They do indeed, and I have no doubt that the main reason why I should like to spend an evening with him is because he was a sinner; and because his sins were so clearly not the peccadillos with which the saints seem so often unnecessarily to torment themselves.

Augustine, I have said, believed that his principal sin was lust. It was natural that he should have believed this, though there is no reason to think that his experiences were abnormal for a young man of his temperament and his time. It was natural because lust, unlike other sins, is always with us, only masking itself (as it did not, I think, mask itself for Augustine) under the cover of romanticism. Nevertheless, I am sure that Augustine's most insidious temptation was pride, and it had already been overcome when he stole away in the garden to weep. His crucifying consciousness of difficulty is proof of this. Pride, swaggering as courage, would have gone undaunted to the last assault—and fallen; or, if momentarily successful, would not have persevered. All the aquiline strength of Augustine came from his humility, just as humility came from the knowledge of his own weakness. Here also sin had served.

There had been perhaps a tincture of pride in his curiosity. A man may sincerely desire the truth; yet he may want it on his own terms. He is not prepared for unconditional surrender. If he is a natural philosopher and polemicist, he will enjoy the cut and thrust of discussion; and even when he has reached a provisional conclusion, he will like to feel that in the last resort he is *disponible*. Or even if his reason has surrendered to logic, he will rejoice that his will is uncommitted. These are subtle temptations and they stalk the salons and studios of twentieth-century London or Paris, as they stalked the *atria* of Carthage or Milan. Augustine, it is true, had never been blind to the vanity and snobbery, the petty jealousies, of the Schools. If one of his professors "had the worst of the argument with some fellow-master, he was more torn with angry vanity than I when I was beaten in a game of ball." It was more contemptible to talk with a vulgar accent than to hate one's fellow-men. These are recognizable traits in Oxford and Cambridge, as they are in Chelsea and Bloomsbury. The intellectual is almost by definition the most unforgiving of men.

The brilliant group to which Augustine belonged was also remarkable for its ignorance. Extraordinary things were happening in the world around them, of which they knew nothing. He learned of the great ascetic experience in the desert, of the vocation and the vigil of St. Antony, with the same astonishment (but with rather less incredulity) than an aesthete from King's might hear of Padre Pio, or a sceptic from the London School of Economics might listen to an eye-witness account of Lourdes. But where the pride of intellect menaced him most dangerously was in his dealings with Divinity itself. For a long time Augustine's God was essentially the God of the philosophers, and it is a curious thing that even with the example of Monica at his side and with the fact of a palpable organized Christianity around him, he could have gone so far without bringing himself face to face with Christ. He had sought to gain by intellectual effort alone the wisdom that must be brought by dispossession.

For I was not yet lowly enough to hold the lowly Jesus as my God, nor did I know what lesson His embracing of our weakness was to teach . . . I talked away as if I knew a great deal; but if I had not sought the way to you in Christ Our Saviour, I would have come not to instruction but to destruction.

Just as there are certain Christians who are tempted to bypass the Cross, to circumvent the necessity of suffering by an emphasis on more comfortable doctrines, so there have always been enquirers who think themselves too clever for Jesus Christ. The shattering second-rateness of their prescriptions is plain to read in the history of thought; they have not even the dignity of heresy; for they do not persist like the greater heresies, but fail for want of satisfying the human nature which they flatter. A false spirituality is the disease of carnal minds. Augustine had "thought of Our Saviour Himself . . . as brought forth for our salvation from the mass of Your most luminous substance: and I could believe nothing of Him unless I could picture it in my own vain imagination. I argued that such a nature could not possibly be born of the Virgin Mary, unless it were mingled with her flesh. And I could not see how that which I had thus figured to myself could be mingled and not defiled." Here there was perhaps a legacy of Platonic idealism— I have often detected a moutainous pride in people who call themselves Platonists; and in this sense the conversion of St. Augustine may be described as the consummation, the realization rather, of Plato's thought. So fine a structure, if men were safely to take refuge in it, needed the Cross and the Crib. It needed the charity of the one and the condescension of the other, although condescension and charity were in both.

One of the most striking passages in the *Confessions* is the story of Victorinus and Simplicianus, the master of St. Ambrose. Victorinus, a friend of Augustine, had become a kind of crypto-convert, not wanting the matter talked about and wishing, as so many people wish, to be a Christian in his own way. "I would have you know," he had said to Simplicianus, "that I am now a Christian." Simplicianus' reply was the voice of the Catholic Church, which has never shown the slightest disposition to indulge peculiar sensibilities. "I shall not believe it," he said, "nor count you among Christians unless I see you in the Church of Christ." Victorinus, we are told, retorted with some irony, "Then is it the walls that make Christians?" Each man persisted stubbornly in his position, for Victorinus was afraid to excite the ridicule of his important friends; and it was not until later that he suddenly remarked to Simplicianus, "Let us go to the Church. I wish to be made a Christian." He was subsequently instructed and baptized.

This story illustrates the cardinal vice of the intellectual, which is really the sin of the Pharisee; that he regards himself as a superior person. Hence the temptation of the *petite chapelle*. He does not realize that segregation stultifies his thought. Above all, of course, he fears the institution; Victorinus' retort about the "walls" has echoed all down the ages of individualism. "The Church," such a man will argue, "is all right for simple people who need guidance. It certainly had a good effect on Mrs. So-and-So. It is admirable as a custodian of morals and a cement of civilization. But for anybody like myself—" This reasoning is not always formulated, but it is often felt; and it was enormously to the credit of Augustine that he never seems to have entertained it for an instant. Being a Christian meant for him one thing only; it meant asking instruction, making confession, and receiving baptism like anybody else; it meant the use of the Sacraments and the pursuit of the good life; it meant membership of the Catholic Church. His superior intelligence was quite incapable of flirting with any such folly as a fancy religion of one's own.

And so it was that this great individualist found community by entering within the walls; and the wisdom he instils comes to us in large measure from the contacts he made there. He learned from the exercise of the espicopate, to reach men at all levels, no longer "redolent of the high cedars of the schools," but offering the "health-giving herbs" of Christian doctrine. Others have done this, to be sure, but no one was ever to occupy a position of high administrative authority and expound so ripe a wisdom with so sharp a psychological insight. Like Christ Himself, he knew what was in man; not with the knowledge of the Creator allied to the experience of the Creature, but with the purified knowledge of his own mistakes. Charles Du Bos recounts that as he was approaching the crisis of his conversion, a young priest of Saint-Pierre de Montrouge remarked to him: "For the

Christian discouragement is perhaps the only unforgivable fault. Remember that there was nothing that St. Augustine had not done, but that on the anniversary of his death we celebrate Mass with the white vestments, which are the symbol of purity." A nature so violent as Augustine's might easily have been twisted to fanaticism, and even today the temperaments which are inclined to stress the corruptibility of human nature are sometimes described as Augustinian. But it is not this aspect of his teaching that I wish to emphasize here; it is no lantern-jawed Jansenist whose image is reflected in the periods of Augustine's prose. It is a man possessed through and through by the sense of glory. It is the radiance rather than the exactitude of truth—though indeed the two are inseparable—that shines through all his commentary. We can easily discern how grace had softened as well as straightened his nature. The man who had know the ferocity of sexual passion could see in the meeting of Christ and the woman taken in adultery nothing more than "infinite misery face to face with infinite compassion." The intellectual who had jibbed at the Incarnation could now paint its paradox. "He lies in the manger, but contains the world; He sucks at the breast, but feeds the Angels; He is wrapped in swaddling clothes, but vests us with immortality; He is suckled, but adored; He found no place at the inn, but makes for Himself a temple in the hearts of believers. For in order that weakness might become strong, strength became weak."

Here we have precision of doctrine linked to an experienced spirituality and a luminous power of phrase. We catch the authentic accent of sanctity. But where Augustine is exceptional among the saints—where we think of him in company with St. Paul—is in the possibilities of error that were overcome in him. He was a great writer, and this he would always have been; but we might have turned against him his own reproach to Licentius, "You have received from God a mind of gold and you have placed it at the service of pleasure; you have made of it a vase in which you offer yourself to the devil." He might have been a great heresiarch, and he maintained that the great heresies were all the products of great minds. He might have refused the community of the "walls." Instead, it was by living inside the walls and looking at them, that he learnt to design the architecture of the City of God. Here he found the sense of proportion which saved him from fanaticism. He learnt that it needs all sorts to make a Church; that "humble wedlock is better than proud virginity"; that while the Church is an institution, she is "an institution of spiritual people" and only God knows who are really His own. "How many that are not ours are yet, as it were, within; how many that are ours are still, as it were, without. . . . And they that are not ours, who are within, when they find their opportunites go out; and they that are ours, who are without, when they find opportunities, return." He admitted the place of those "who . . . marry, who give in marriage, who till the fields, who build houses," He allowed the reasonable and disinterested rights of property. He saw not only the hierarchy but the wholeness of created things. "I realized that while certain higher things were better than lower things, yet all things together are better than the higher alone."

As always, it is the total man, spiritualized but not rarefied, who speaks to us—with eloquence but without exaggeration. His appeal is strong and his message significant for a generation in stress. He may fairly be described as crisis-minded, not because he suffered from the panic of the present moment, but because, basing himself on the Bible, he created a philosophy— or rather, as Maritain suggests, a wisdom of history. He enables you to feel the past, endure the present, and to some extent foresee the future. Through all the catastrophic changes he had witnessed, he saw the war of the Two Cities; here he corrects, though he does not always contradict, the historicism which can only see the material event. But his sense of crisis was fundamentally the Christian obligation of choice. This was all part of the question mark he was born with. "What shall I believe? What shall I do? How can I know Him without loving Him first?" These questions, we have seen, might have become the counters of a sophisticated game; a substitute for spiritual vigour. But we know that they were not, for the reason that Augustine, like all the greatest thinkers, was a man in whom intellect knew its place. He is the perfect illustration of Vauvenargues' maxim that "great thoughts spring from the heart."

St. Gregory the Great

c.540–604

Nicolete Gray

MY DEVOTION to St. Gregory is founded on the immense impression made upon me by his great work the *Moralia*. It seemed to me that my mind was laid open before me, all its thoughts read, the shifting, multifarious, discreditable ocean of its consciousness brought to light, described accurately, ordered. In form the book belongs to a tradition quite foreign to modern thought. It is a commentary on the book of *Job*, of which every sentence is taken and in principle interpreted three times; "historically," that is, concerned with the actual events and actors of the book, "allegorically," interpreting Job as a type of Our Lord, and "morally," in which the entire action of the book takes place in the mind of the believer. It is this last interpretation which is far the most original part of the book and has given it its name; though in modern terms it is rather concerned with psychology than with ethics. The last words give an idea of the quality of the book. "This work being completed, I see I must go back to myself. . . . I must return from the outward utterance of words to the council chamber of the heart" and "returning to myself within, putting aside the leaves of words, and the branches of sentences, when I look closely at the very root of my intention I find that I specially desired to please God thereby. And yet the desire of human praise in some unknown secret way blends itself with this desire to please God." Our evils are purely evil, and the good things

63

which we believe we possess never purely good; and so this book, into which he has put everything he has, is not only an exposition, it is also a confession. It is literal introspection, carried out ruthlessly and *au fond* by completely objective standards, and attaining complete detachment; the passage quoted is almost the only place where St. Gregory mentions himself personally. Of all the people whom I have "met" he is the person who I feel was most completely conscious of himself and of his actions. He was conscious of the whole world of his time in the same light, to an extent which seems to me unique in history. It is this consciousness that is the peculiar quality of his sanctity.

The world of his time was at a singularly depressing crux in history. The Roman tradition was battered and obviously decaying but still essentially intact; and no other form of civilised life was conceivable. St. Gregory was a Roman, born of senatorial family, passionately devoted to his city. He spoke and wrote Latin as his native tongue; he was the last great writer to do so. He inherited the full classical tradition, being educated at the University of Rome in the study of language and letters. He would not, however, have taken the view that the Roman tradition could be equated with Cicero and Virgil, he had none of the medieval respect for these authors; for him the great period of Rome was in its second great flowering in the fourth, rather than in the first century, and the food he found for his mind was in the Latin fathers, not in pagan poetry; he thought the former more relevant to life, he was never an escapist. It is typical that he deliberately rejected the elaborate and nostalgic literary Latin of earlier sixth-century writers. For him the primary object of writing was intelligibility, but his style also reveals a highly sophisticated and educated mind. The most vivid image of the Roman tradition as he knew it is, I suppose, the great mosaic in the church of SS. Cosmo and Damian, commissioned by one of St. Gregory's own ancestors, Pope Felix IV (526-530), about ten years before his own birth. The great figure of Christ has all the old Roman qualities, stability, material presence, vast scale, and added to them the Christian revelation of supernatural power and demanding charity.

But like the writings of St. Gregory this mosaic is the last of its kind. Political circumstances were making any sort of civilised life or activity more and more precarious. At the beginning of the century the greatest Romans of their time, Boethius and Cassiodorus, had put their faith in Theodoric and had hoped that the Gothic dynasty would transmit and revive civilisation. The reign of Theodoric brought thirty years' peace to Italy, from every other point of view the dream proved disillusioning. The great king left no effective successor; he himself ordered the execution of Boethius, and the nation remained heretic Arian. The possibility was finally killed when the Emperor Justinian ordered the reconquest of Italy. St. Gregory has no good word to say for the Goths, no word at all to say of Boethius, or of Cassiodorus, who retired to found his monastery at Squillace about the time of the saint's birth, four years after the beginning of the war; but then he looked forwards not backwards.

The reconquest of Italy for the Empire took seventeen years and affected the population of the country in much the same devastating way that the Thirty Years War affected Germany. And in the end reunion also brought disillusion. Constantinople was now the capital of empire, Italy was only an impoverished province and Rome not even the centre of the Imperial administration, which was at Ravenna. A certain amount of reconstruction was put in hand, the university for instance was reopened in Rome. But in general the government's chief concern was to recoup itself for the expenses of the war; and rapacious tax collectors descended on a ruined country. We read of places where parents sold their children in order to meet their demands, or preferred to leave their homes and live under barbarian rule. Certainly many of the great landowners abandoned their estates where the margin of profit may have become negligible, some to enter monasteries, some to take up their residence in Constantinople; so that the dwindling educated class was further diminished. In 565 the great Emperor Justinian died, to be succeeded by the mad Justin II.

In 568 Italy was invaded by a new barbarian people, the Lombards, "cities were laid waste, fortified places overthrown, churches and monasteries reduced to ruins, and populous centres turned into dreary solitudes." Surely a world without hope. St. Gregory was then about twenty-eight.

He seems to have had a happy childhood, perhaps in the way that many children have had a happy childhood during our two wars. He was devoted to his parents and to his home, and though many of his class lost their money in the war, his family was still wealthy and important. We do not know whether they were in the city for the terrible year-long siege of 545 which ended in its capture by the Goths, but even if he had no personal memories it must have darkened those of the circle in which he grew up. Possibly he was evacuated for some years to his parent's great estates in Sicily, probably he was back in Rome by 549, and no doubt like a child accepted as normal the uneasy peace which arrived when he was about fourteen. He would then have begun to attend lectures at the recently reopened University. There he found himself far the most brilliant student; a position of intellectual pre-eminence which he retained all his life. Exhilarating perhaps at first; but very lonely.

It was a very strange Rome in which he grew up. To us the Imperial city would have seemed virtually intact. The most conspicuous traces of the sacks of 410 and 455 were the ruined palaces on the Aventine which had never been reoccupied. The great baths were still complete, furnished with their mosaics, frescoes, and statues, but unused since the Goths had cut the aqueducts in 537, since when of course the fountains had been dry. The last games in the Circus Maximus had been in 549, but the buildings were there, so was the Colosseum, magnificent as when it was built, but abandoned; the great edifices on the Palatine had been restored not so long before, but only a little corner was lived in by the few official who administered Rome. The pagan temples had not yet been turned into churches; they stood as always, but with closed doors. It must in its way have been an incredibly beautiful city, for the great churches were already built, adding their different beauty, old St. Peter's, St. Mary Major, the Lateran with the papal palace beside it, all the seven basilicas and the eighteen titular churches with their marble wall-coverings and great mosaics intact and unrestored. But the streets were empty, almost all the shops closed, whole quarters uninhabited, masonary might hit you on the head from buildings visibly growing ruinous. The vast population of statues lay about fallen and broken. The city built for about a million people was now inhabited by a dwindling population of about 40,000.

Still Gregory's career took a fairly normal course. His father had been *Regionarius,* that is, probably the officer responsible for the administration of one of the Regions of Rome. His son may have held a similar office; anyhow by about 573 we find him Urban Prefect, that is, holding the highest secular office in the city. No doubt he filled the office very well, he had all the gifts of a first-rate administrator. No doubt also he enjoyed the work. He wrote later that for "late and long I declined the grace of conversion," that even after he had been "inspired with heavenly affection" he persuaded himself that it was better for him to stay in the world, believing that he could do so in semblance only, until he found the semblance growing into a reality. Then at last he made the break. He sold all his great possessions giving the proceeds to the poor, and for the foundation of six monasteries in Sicily; and his home, the palace on the Celian Hill, he turned into a seventh monastery, where he became a simple brother. It says much for his parents and the happiness of his youth that he found it possible to leave the world by transforming rather than by abandoning his home. He had their portraits painted on the walls of the atrium.

The next three years were the happiest and perhaps the most important in his life. It must have been a house of fervent spirit; St. Gregory tells various stories of some of the other monks for whom he had a great veneration. Certainly he loved the austerity of the life, though it was already too much for his health. He tells how bitterly he minded the fact that he could not fast on the vigil of Easter, "when not only old persons but even children fast," because he was continually fainting and in pain, "unless I did continually eat something my vital spirit was going away." One year to his delight the prayers of a holy monk enabled him to fast like other people. But above all he loved his monastery, and looked back to its life, after he had been forced to leave it, with unutterable longing, because it was there that he experienced the contemplation of God. "When I lived in my Abbey my soul was superior to all earthly matters, far above all transitory and corrupt things, it did usually think upon nothing but heavenly things; and though it was enclosed in a mortal body, yet it did by contemplation pass far beyond earthly bounds, and penetrate to the very height of heaven." His time was very short. In 578 he was called upon by Pope Benedict I to be seventh Deacon of the Roman Church, that is to superintend one of the seven regions. In the next year he was sent as Papal Nuncio to the court of Constantinople, with the special mission of securing military help for Rome, which was now in a very precarious position. It was imminently threatened by the Lombard kingdom in the north, which reached as near as Viterbo; on the east, always menacing communications with Ravenna and the Imperial deputy, the Exarch, was the Lombard duchy of Spoleto; on the south was the Lombard duchy of Benevento. Ringed round by Lombard swords, it was inadequately garrisoned by a few irregularly paid imperial troops.

St. Gregory spent seven years in Constantinople. Looking back he saw their compensations. He was accompanied by several monks from his monastery and he was able to share part of their regular life which he felt was like "an anchor on the firm shore of prayer." It was to them that he originally gave the sermons which years later he revised and published as the *Morals on the book of Job*. Here too he enjoyed the company of the most intimate friend he ever had, Leander, Archbishop of Seville, who was at court in the interests of his convert the Visigothic prince Hermanigild. Leander came to his sermons and together they talked, and prayed, and made music. Leander was himself a composer, and to him St. Gregory poured out the story of his early life and all his inmost thoughts and aspirations. They never met again and were both too busy to correspond much later, but passages in the letters which do exist are touchingly affectionate, "the image of thy countenance is pressed forever on my inmost heart." One has the impression that St. Gregory was naturally very affectionate and demonstrative, but in Italy there can have been very few to whom he could talk as an equal. There is one to whom he writes, Venantius, a man of his own class and education, a Sicilian, perhaps a neighbour to his own paternal estates and a childhood's friend. Like Gregory he too became a monk, but to his friend's bitter grief he abandoned his vocation, left his monastery and married. St. Gregory maintained the connection, writing very affectionately to his daughters after the death of his friend. In Constantinople there were more congenial people and Gregory made numerous friends, with the Empress, Theodore, the Emperor's doctor, Anastasius, formerly patriarch of Antioch: he also found Romans, perhaps family friends or relations, who had taken up residence in the East. But there was another side to his life. He was ill, suffering from intermittent fever and digestive disorders. His mission was unsuccessful, the Emperor was fully engaged in his Persian wars and was not prepared to do anything for the West. He found himself out of sympathy with the Greek ecclesiastics and their interests. Though he was forced into one controversy while he was there, which he was considered to have won, it was not his line. He was far more interested in the heretic than in the heresy; it seemed to him that the champions of orthodoxy were often creating heresies, in order to have something to attack. A futile occupation; but so much of the life in Constantinople must have seemed futile to him when he thought of the desperate straits of the abandoned city which was his home. The contrast must have been with him continually as he walked through the streets of New Rome, bustling with crowds engaged in the manifold business of a capital city, trade, intrigue, sport, fashion, politics, a city of immense wealth and luxury, in which he kept himself a stranger. He never learnt its language.

In 586 he was at last relieved and able to return to his monastery, where he was shortly elected Abbot. He was still, however, the Pope's close adviser, probably his secretary, certainly a public figure. It is probably at this time that he saw the English slaves in the market-place, and became aware for the first time perhaps of the peoples outside the dwindled Roman world. The experience must have been a sort of revelation to him, for he not only remembered it long afterwards, when he was overwhelmed with pressure of other business; but at the time he himself set out on the mission. He was recalled after three days' journey by a papal messenger withdrawing permission, and by his own sense that he had misinterpreted the call. But it must have been a very urgent call which made him feel he must leave his much loved monastery and city.

In 590 the real call came. It was a season of disasters, there were terrible floods throughout Italy. In Rome the main store of corn was ruined. They were followed by the plague, mortality was appallingly high and among the first to die was the Pope, Pelagius II. The clergy and people, with whom the election rested, turned unanimously to St. Gregory. And he was appalled. He knew exactly what was involved, exile from the detachment and the vision of God for which all his soul longed; for life. He wrote to the Emperor imploring him to withhold his consent. In the meantime he set himself to lead his fellow-citizens in their terror. In a great sermon in the Lateran he summoned the entire population to take part in three days' penitential procession. Each estate in the city was to assemble at a church in a different region and proceed to St. Mary Major and there to acknowledge and beg pardon for their sins. A deacon from Gaul, a friend of Gregory of Tours, who was present in Rome, saw the seven long processions, the clergy, the abbots and monks, the abbesses and nuns, the laymen, the married women, and the children, each making their way from different quarters, many dropping down dead as they went; and the bishop-elect leading and exhorting them. It was on the third day that St. Michael was seen on the top of the Mausoleum of

Hadrian, since known as the Castel Sant'Angelo, sheathing the sword of God's anger.

It is said that when the messenger bringing the imperial confirmation arrived, St. Gregory tried to hide; and if one imagines the terrifying responsibility and unremitting strain of the rest of his life it is easy to understand his fear, not only at the loss of his own peace, but lest he should fail in his great office. It is typical that when he saw that he was not meant to escape he set himself the task of writing the *Pastoral Care,* that is of formulating his exact duties and setting before his own eyes and those of the world a standard of perfection by which he should be judged. The book became the accepted manual for all bishops and priests for centuries, and exercised incalculable influence; one can also see how St. Gregory wrote it as it were to himself. He was frightened of the absorbing interest in affairs, which can so busy the mind that "it is as though it were so preoccupied during a journey as to forget what its destination is." One can almost hear him telling himself that he had no right to refuse to use the gifts, of which he cannot but have been aware, in the service of his neighbour, in order to gratify his own desire for a life of prayer. Or again telling himself to fear the devotion with which he was no doubt surrounded "everything at his service, his orders quickly executed to suit his wishes, praised for what he has done well but never criticised for what he has done amiss, he must never forget to judge himself inwardly, he must not believe himself to be such as he hears himself outwardly proclaimed." And again, his fear of elation after preaching a good sermon, "when the devil comes and enumerates all he has done well and aggrandises him with thoughts about his pre-eminence over all others."

Preaching was in his eyes a primary duty, and as long as he was able he preached regularly to his people, appointing the stational churches for different feasts, where they should meet and hear him. His sermons made an immense impression, the great basilicas were crammed, he was called "golden mouth," and his words were taken down and circulated, so that he was obliged to issue a standard text. When he was too ill to preach himself he still dictated sermons which were read to the people. He also wrote for their encouragement, his *Dialogues,* a charming book of stories of holy men of their own time to show them that for all the scourges they suffered God was still with them. There is another duty on which the *Pastoral Care* insists, that of personal contact with his people; the government of souls, "which is the art of arts," the cure of "the wounds of the mind that are more hidden than the internal wounds of the body." There is no record of this work of his, but one cannot doubt that he did it, with infinite understanding. What is difficult, however, is to imagine how he could possibly have found the time. For as he says the pastor cannot expect his people to listen to his spiritual admonitions unless he is also solicitous for their physical needs. And no one else cared for the physical needs of the people of Rome, or indeed of most of Italy, which were very great. St. Gregory took it all upon himself. When he heard that a man had died of starvation in one of the common lodging-houses of Rome he blamed himself as if he had killed him with his own hands, and for some days would not allow himself to say Mass. Every day he sent out cooked meals to the poor. To those who had once been rich with infinite tact he sent a dish from his own table. Centuries after there was still preserved at the Lateran Palace a great papyrus volume with the names and circumstances of all those in need to whom he sent not just money, but food or clothes or bedding.

The distress was due to chronic conditions of war and insecurity, with such wealth as there was drained out of the country. Shortly after his accession the crisis became much more urgent. The Lombards were on the move and a full-scale attack on Rome seemed imminent. Refugees poured into the city, some of them cruelly mutilated. No doubt everyone anticipated a repetition of the terrible sieges of the Gothic war which older inhabitants would have still remembered. The garrison were too few, and were unreliable; the Exarch would do nothing, he would neither defend the city nor make a peace. We find St. Gregory forced to take charge, writing to military commanders giving them instructions, finally going out to meet the Lombard leaders and making peace with them himself.

St. Gregory thought that the end of the world was very near, all evidence seemed to point to it, not least the plight of the city of the Apostles, "this old and grievously shattered ship." One might have expected him under these circumstances to have abandoned all except the most immediate material consider- ations, all attempts to work for a better order for the future. Instead of that he fought ceaselessly for peace and against corruption and injustice. Just as he rejected a nostalgic use of Latin, so in secular affairs he never looked backwards, but took a completely realistic view, and worked himself, as he con- tinually urged all others to work, remembering always that he must answer for his actions at the judgment seat of God. And so actually his work was immensely fruitful for the new, post- classical world which he could not imagine, but did not refuse to envisage.

We get an extraordinarily vivid and circumstantial picture of his work outside the city from his letters, of which more than eight hundred survive from the fourteen years of his pontificate, and the register is not complete; a full-time job in itself. The Roman Church was a great landowner; its scattered estates may have comprised 1,800 square miles. It was from the revenue of these lands that St. Gregory was able to dispense his great charities. He also used it to ransom captives from slavery, and to buy off the Lombards, as well as for the ordinary administrative costs. But the estates had to be run; he had agents but they were not all trustworthy, and in any case required supervision. I wish I had room to quote from the letters. He knew everything that went on; one sees him righting old wrongs. "I will not have the purse of the Church defiled by base gains." Seeing that the peasants have justice, for instance, that each shall be given a written assessment of his tax liabilities so that they shall not be tricked when Gregory is dead. Asking whether particular wills have been carried out, or mortgages redeemed; always following up his orders. And throughout constant commissions of kindness and charity, a cloak with a double nap to be sent to the bishop who feels the cold, wheat for certain impoverished ladies, beds and bedding to be arranged for a home for old people as far away as Sinai, and carriage to be paid.

There were also his specifically ecclesiastical cares. Everywhere there were disorders and troubles, difficult questions of discipline, questions of relations with secular powers, resurgent paganism, shortage of clergy, unsuitable clergy; St. Gregory took cognisance of it all. The last difficulty was perhaps the worst. There are endless patient letters and some for which perhaps he set himself penance for "reproof that blazed forth immoderately" to some of his exasperating brethren. Saddest of all was his conflict with the patriarch of Constantinople, who in 595 began to style himself "universal bishop." "By this unspeakable title the Church is rent asunder and the hearts of all the faithful are offended. . . . It is the last hour; pestilence and sword rage throughout the world, nation rises against nation . . . all that is foretold is coming to pass. The King of Pride is nigh at hand and—inexpressible shame—priests are serving in his army." On every side the remnants of the civilised world are threatened by the barbarians; the duty of priests is to do penance, instead their sins are the allies of the enemy. His great cry was reiterated to the Patriarch, to the Emperor, to the Empress. They were unmoved. In ecclesiastical as in political matters Constantinople was indifferent to the point of view of the Pope.

It was probably in the same year that St. Gregory remembered the English boys in the market-place and began to plan his mission to them. One wonders whether he was beginning to see a new interpretation of that great impression which he had experienced long before; whether he now saw it as a message to bring into the Christian comity not only those unknown romantic barbarians but the known repugnant ones. The Lombards were not noble savages, they were cruel and greedy and faithless, "men whose promises stab like thorns." He used earlier to call them "unspeakable," *nec dicendum.* The

Franks were no better, except that they were Catholic not Arian, but for many of their rulers religion was merely superstition, quite unconnected with thought or morality. The natural thing would have been for Gregory to have regarded these people as anti-christ, as the scourges foretold. Instead during the greater part of his reign all his efforts were directed to making peace with them, and mediating for them with the Emperor. And the peace he sought was not a political peace but a real one. "In loving peace you have proved that you love God, who is the author of peace," he wrote to the Lombard king. He wrote in the same strain to the Frankish princes, including the formidable queen-grandmother Brunhild, accepting them as Christian kings and urging upon them their duty as such. Finally from that Rome which was "falling into decay of itself," he sent out missionaries to a country which had been an outpost even of the Empire in its heyday, and was now inhabited by unknown savages. It was an extraordinary act of faith—one which even St. Augustine found it hard to follow except in blind obedience.

One might have thought that having set his servant such a colossal task God might at least have given him health. St. Gregory seems to have been constantly ill. To the ailments of his earlier life was added the torture of gout, a disease of the period. Already in 600 he wrote "now it is a long time since I was able to rise from bed . . . at one and the same time a burning pain racks me, and mind and body fail me"; that was four years before his death. In 603 he wrote to a fellow-sufferer, "I beg you pray for me, that I may be the sooner led forth from this prison house of the flesh, and that I be no longer tortured by such agonies." Over and over again too he reiterates his aching cry for the contemplative life he has lost. "Either very rarely or not at all does the wing of contemplation raise my heart aloft, my sluggish soul is torpid." At the beginning of the *Dialogues* his secretary found him "drowned in a dump of sorrow." He loved music, he loved simple people, he was an emotional, demonstrative, quick-tempered man. The life he was called to lead was an unremitted struggle to fulfil every duty, to commit every action, to speak or write every word in the presence of God, to live supernaturally, but one might also say entirely rationally, and that not on a personal plane, but on the widest political stage.

St. Boniface

675-754

Christopher Dawson

AFTER TWELVE HUNDRED YEARS it is high time that we remembered St. Boniface. For there is no doubt that he has been most shockingly neglected by his own countrymen. There is no standard English edition of his works; there has never been an adequate English biography of him and he was not even included in Newman's lives of the English saints where, at least, one would have expected to see him treated with especial care as the great representative of Anglo-Saxon missionary action. Yet there can be no question of his greatness both as a saint, a missionary and historical figure. As I wrote twenty-two years ago, he was "a man who had a deeper influence on the history of Europe than any Englishman who has ever lived," and though this seemed to some a paradox or an exaggeration, I still believe that it is strictly and literally true. No doubt he was no hero in Carlyle's sense. He was entirely lacking in that daimonic quality which the romantic historians and men of letters prized so highly. He was a servant rather than a master of his age—*servus servorum Dei*—but it was just because he was a faithful servant, accepting every charge that was laid upon him and never attempting to impress his personality on the course of history that he achieved such a great and enduring work, so that he deserves to be named with St. Benedict and St. Gregory the Great as the creator of medieval Christendom.

And the neglect of St. Boniface is the more astonishing

because of all the men of his age, he is the one of whom we have the fullest, most personal and most intimate record. His letters, as Sir Frank Stenton has written, are "the most remarkable body of correspondence which has survived from the Dark Ages." This is not only because that part of the correspondence which deals with his relations with the Papacy and with the Frankish rulers is an authority of the first importance for the history of his age. Even more remarkable is the correspondence with his friends in England and in Germany which reveal the rich background of personal relationships on which his work and his character were founded and which are also of the highest value for the history of Anglo-Saxon culture. Even men whose business it has been to study the history of that age have seldom appreciated sufficiently the character and achievement of that culture. What could be more surprising than this sudden flowering of Christian culture—even, one may say, of Christian humanism—in the midst of a barbarian society which had been pagan and illiterate and divorced from the higher culture of the Byzantine-Christian world only a century before? No doubt it was an aristocratic society. Boniface himself was of noble birth, perhaps the scion of one of those lesser tribal ruling families which had been absorbed by the growth of the West Saxon kingdom—and alike in Wessex and Northumbria and East Anglia the kings and princesses of the ruling families played a leading part in the development of the new culture. It was also a monastic society, which owed its high culture to the confluence of the two streams of monastic influence which flowed from Ireland to Lindisfarne and Malmesbury and from Rome to Canterbury and Jarrow and Ripon. The interest in culture and the apostolic spirit which inspired St. Boniface were common to both traditions, but it was the Roman tradition and the Benedictine spirit which gave the new Anglo-Saxon culture its distinctive character and made it a creative force in Europe. It was St. Willebrord and St. Boniface who took up the work of St. Gregory and St. Augustine and established that bond between the Papacy and the new Christian society of Western Germany and the Netherlands which was the corner stone of medieval

Christendom. And they could never have accomplished this task unless both of them, but especially St. Boniface, had been not merely individual missionaries but creators and organizers of a great social movement which transplanted the new spiritual culture that had grown up in the Benedictine monasteries of Northumbria and Wessex to the barbarous lands and peoples beyond the Rhine.

It is clear from his letters that St. Boniface was a man with a genius for friendship who saw in every personal relationship an opportunity for the enrichment of the Christian life.

Thus at every stage in his career he associates his friends and relations and the church of his native land with his mission, and they repaid his affection with interest. Whatever the obstacles he met with—and we know that he suffered greatly from a sense of discouragement and frustration—his countrymen never let him down. For once the prophet was not without honour in his own country. And the letter which the Archbishop of Canterbury wrote to St. Lull on hearing of his martyrdom shows how the whole English church united to recognize his greatness and to canonize him as their patron along with St. Gregory the Great and St. Augustine of Canterbury—an almost unique example of the public and official cultus of a contemporary figure.

And yet his contemporaries cannot have realized the full significance of his achievement. They saw him as a great saint and a great missionary, but they could not have realized the extent to which his work was destined to change the face of Europe and the future of the world. There has never been an age in which the Western civilization and of Christianity itself seemed darker. Christendom was being attacked from every side and it seemed in danger of losing its internal cohesion and its power of resistance. During the generation before the birth of St. Boniface the whole of the Christian East had been conquered by Islam and the very existence of the Byzantine empire was in danger. During Boniface's youth conditions steadily deteriorated and the Christian world was sinking into a state of anarchy. Nor was the situation any better in the West.

When Boniface was a monk at Nursling in 711-713 Spain was being conquered by the Saracens, and while he was beginning his mission to Germany the Saracens were beginning their invasions of France. The death of Pepin II, the protector of St. Willebrord in 714 had left the Frankish realm without a master, and it was only after years of civil war that his bastard Charles Martel had succeeded in overcoming his rivals and their allies, the pagan Frisians, and was in a position to defend the West against the pagans of the North and the Saracens in the South.

Now Charles throughout his career until his death in 741 was the protector of St. Boniface in his missionary enterprises. He was no doubt acting in his own interests as the ruler of the Franks, while St. Boniface was obliged to work under his protection if he was to work at all. But beyond that the two men had nothing in common. Charles was essentially a warrior, a man of blood from his youth, like the heroes of the *chansons de geste*. But he was ruthless and unscrupulous in the extreme in his dealings with the church, confiscating ecclesiastical property and using bishoprics and monasteries as fiefs to reward his relations and his captains like Milo, a good soldier, who received the bishoprics of Treves and Reims in payment of his services. But St. Boniface was a Christian after the manner of St. Paul who was entirely absorbed in his mission and who found the whole atmosphere of the court with its secularized bishops and greedy courtiers antipathetic. The more successful he was in creating a new Christian society among the northern barbarians based on the Anglo-Saxon monastic colonies, which were centres of culture as well as schools of the Christian life, the more glaring was the contrast with the moral and canonical anarchy of the Frankish church. Unless this process of corruption were checked, it must inevitably infect the new Christian society, and how could this be done, while the churches and monasteries of Southern Gaul were being ravaged by the Saracens so that the very existence of Christendom was in question?

In this dilemma St. Boniface turned to the Papacy as the only centre of stability and unity and order. From the beginning to the end of his career it was to Rome that he looked and throughout his correspondence we see how the intimate sense of his personal bond with the Apostolic See penetrated his whole work. The oath which he swore to Pope Gregory II in 722, which was the regular oath of a suburbicarian bishop of the Roman diocese, was to him no formality but a solemn personal obligation to which he remained faithful at all costs and in all circumstances during his mission of more than thirty years.

Here I think we can see the action of that new spirit which was to transform the Christian Empire into medieval Christendom. The old Roman pattern of hierarchy and law and obedience remained intact, but it was renewed and transformed by the conceptions of homage and loyalty and fidelity which were so deeply rooted in the heroic age of the Northern Germanic and Celtic peoples. St. Boniface had become the "man" of St. Peter, and he was bound in honour to set the interests of his lord before all else. Hence it was not enough for him to carry out that missionary vocation on which his heart was set. He forced himself against his natural inclination to undertake the vast and ungrateful task of the reform of the whole Frankish church, when the death of Charles Martel at last opened the way to a new order in church and state. Charles' successors, Pepin and Carloman, were men of a different type from their father, especially Carloman who now ruled Germany and the East Frankish Kingdom and was prepared to do all in his power to forward the work of St. Boniface. It was at his request that St. Boniface held the first of the reforming councils in 742, and thenceforward the prince and the saint worked together to carry out a far-reaching programme of ecclesiastical reform and to bring the Frankish Church into closer unity with the Papacy. In 744 the movement was extended with the co-operation of Pepin to the West Frankish kingdom, and finally in 747 the work was completed by a great council of the whole Frankish Church, the proceedings of which are described in St. Boniface's letter to Archbishop Cuthbert of Canterbury.

The work of these five years is of decisive importance in the history of the West, for they laid the foundations of that threefold alliance of the monastic reformers, the Papacy and the Frankish monarchy which was the basis not only of Carolingian culture but of medieval Christendom itself.

As soon as the West Frankish Church was also committed to the principle of reform, Carloman resigned his kingdom to his brother and became a Benedictine monk at Soracte and Monte Cassino, while St. Boniface turned back to his missionary vocation and to the development of Fulda as a centre of Christian culture for the new lands. The work which Boniface and Carloman had begun passed to Pepin and to the Papacy which was now fully aware of the importance of the Frankish alliance. The change of dynasty which inaugurated the Carolingian kingdom and Empire was not the work of St. Boniface, though his English disciple St. Burchard played a certain part in it. But I think it is possible that the new ceremony of coronation and unction, which was performed by St. Boniface himself in 751, may have also been due to him, since it is not of Frankish origin while it has an obvious affinity with the spirit of St. Boniface and the Anglo-Saxon culture which were deeply permeated by Scriptural tradition and imagery. On the other hand it is extremely unlikely that St. Boniface had anything to do with the policy of Frankish intervention on behalf of the Pope against the Lombards, a policy to which his patron and disciple Carloman was actively opposed.

Ever since 747 St. Boniface had been withdrawing from public affairs in the Frankish kingdom and turning back to the field of his original missionary activities.

Thus when Pope Stephen crossed the Alps to conclude his alliance with King Pepin, Boniface had already washed his hands of temporal affairs and set forth on his last missionary journey to Frisia. He had already written to Pepin's adviser Fulrad, the abbot of St. Denis, begging him to secure the protection of the king for the Anglo-Saxon monks whom he was leaving behind him: "almost all strangers, some of them priests set in many places to minister to the Church and the people, some monks placed in cells to teach children their letters, some of them old men who have lived and laboured with me. For all of them I am anxious that they should not be lost after my death, but may have your counsel and royal protection and should not be scattered like sheep without a shepherd, and that the peoples who dwell by the pagan frontier may not lose the law of Christ."

He went on his last missionary journey fully conscious that there would be no return, commanding his disciple and successor St. Lull to send his shroud with him in the box of books which was his most precious possession. Finally before his departure he sent for St. Lioba, the abbess of Bischofsheim on the Tauber, who of all the English missionaries was nearest to him in spirit and culture. He charged her not to return to England after his death but to remain at her post as long as she lived, commending her to the protection of St. Lull and the abbey of Fulda and asking that she should be buried with him in the same grave, so that "as they had served Christ with the same desire and affection during their lives, so their bodies might await the day of resurrection together."

This last request is very typical of the consideration and affection which St. Boniface always showed in his personal relations. But it is more than that. It was also an acknowledgement to posterity of the help that he had received from his fellow country-women in his apostolate. Today we regard it as a matter of course that nuns should play an important part in all missionary activities. But it was not so in the past, either in antiquity or in the Middle Ages or in the missions of the sixteenth and seventeenth centuries. Thus the part taken by the Anglo-Saxon nuns, like St. Lioba, St. Walburga, St. Thecla and the rest, in the conversion and teaching of the German converts is almost unique. They brought to the German lands that high tradition of Christian feminine culture which had been formed during the preceding century by the great royal abbesses of Whitby and Ely and Thanet, and Barking and Wimborne, a tradition which was to live on in the abbeys of the Carolingian and German Empires after the Anglo-Saxon monastic culture had itself been swept away by the Danish invasions. In this tradition St. Lioba herself holds a central place, for she became the close friend of Queen Hildegard, the wife of Charlemagne and the mother of Louis the Pious, so that the authentic Bonifacian tradition of spirituality and culture was carried on into the Carolingian age.

But St. Boniface himself had no thought even for post-humous success. His whole mind was concentrated on the culminating point of his apostolate. For him there could be no turning back and no resting on his achievement. Therefore his martyrdom near Dokkum in Frisia on 5 June, 754, was the only appropriate conclusion to his career. All his life he had prepared himself for such a consummation. Years before, he had written to St. Lioba asking her to pray that God would give him the spirit of a chief, so that when the wolf came he would not fly but would give his life for the sheep. And so when he and all his great following were massacred by a pagan mob, the Christian world received the news not with horror and dismay, but with a sense of triumphant achievement.

I have already mentioned the letter which Cuthbert, the Archbishop of Canterbury, wrote to St. Lull on this occasion, and we may well recall his words today. "We give thanks to the unspeakable goodness of God that the English people which dwells in Britain has deserved to send forth to spiritual conflict before the eyes of all men so great a scholar and soldier of Christ with the disciples that he trained and educated, for the salvation of many souls . . . wherefore, after the apostles and the evangelists, we hold and venerate him among the greatest doctors of the orthodox faith. And so in our general synod we have decided to celebrate the day when he and his companions suffered martyrdom by a solemn annual feast, since we hope and trust to have him, together with St. Gregory and St. Augustine, as our special patron before Christ the Lord, Whom he so loved in his life and Whom he has so glorified in his death."

St. Thomas of Canterbury

1118-1170

Leslie Macfarlane

IN TERMS OF POPULAR APPEAL, St. Thomas of Canterbury was undoubtedly the greatest English saint of the Middle Ages. With a swiftness unusual for a canon lawyer, Alexander III canonised him within twenty-six months of his murder in the late afternoon of 29 December 1170, although the common people, abandoning prudence to the four winds, had long since acclaimed him to be among the blessed. Within twenty-five years, the name of St. Thomas of Canterbury was invoked throughout the length and breadth of Christendom. Stone, stained glass, frescoes and illuminated manuscripts told of his martyrdom across Europe, and beyond to the Holy Land itself. His tomb, later installed behind the high altar of his own cathedral, rivalled in splendour and popularity the Spanish shrine of the apostle James, and the track to it, which winds through the Kentish countryside to this day, brought to Canterbury for three and a half centuries the hopeful, the curious, and the grateful of every Christian nation. No one could deny the unprecedented and almost violent popularity of his cult throughout the Middle Ages.

Why was this so? Was it because of the dramatic circumstances of his death, the splendid courage which he showed at the last when surrounded by armed violence? Certainly this would have caught the popular imagination, for acts of physical heroism always compel admiration, and this was particularly true of the age in which he lived and died. Was it because of the miracles and the legends which came to be associated with his name in an age supposedly more credulous than our own? These too must have played their part. These factors alone, however, would not account for his continued popularity. The truth is, of course, that St. Thomas rapidly became identified with the cause for which he died, namely, the assertion of ecclesiastical liberty. Not that the people who flocked to his tomb from every corner of Christendom whiled away their pilgrimages discussing the finer points of current politico-ecclesiastical thought. Geoffrey Chaucer can tell us pungently enough the sorts of topics more likely to have been discussed on the road to Canterbury. Nevertheless, underneath the banter, the credulity and the excitement, most pilgrims were aware, in however garbled a manner, of the stand which archbishop Thomas Becket had made against the growing encroachment of the Crown in ecclesiastical affairs. For most of them, at any rate, he symbolised the Church's right to be free to act according to its own laws, where the laws of the land were considered to violate human rights and the law of God. Thomas, in fact, had struck at the very roots of secular totalitarianism, or any other form of government which denied the Church the right to uphold its own laws, and to protect its members from tyranny and injustice. This is why devotion to him endured. To the medieval, Augustinian mind, the problem of dual allegiance, of where ultimate authority lay, was an ever-present one—incapable of solution, perhaps, in a world recognisably fallen, but nevertheless a real and live issue. For them, at least, Thomas epitomised one side of the never-ending struggle of rendering to both God and Caesar.

The truth of this can be seen in the petulant violence of Henry VIII's action in 1538, whereby the tomb of St. Thomas was desecrated, and his name ordered to be removed from every liturgical book in the country. For the opposition to Henry's ecclesiastical claims by men like Thomas More and John Fisher, who had recently gone their own stubborn way to the scaffold, was proof enough to the king that Becket's cause was still very much alive, and that it was still capable of providing a rallying-point fraught with the possibilities of popular insurrection. Henry's vigorous suppression of Becket's cult, was, in fact, a measure of his political acumen. At any rate, within a century, St. Thomas had slipped into a hagiographical limbo, from which he was rescued only in comparatively recent times, when the Latin texts of his contemporary biographers were re-edited, and the details of his remarkable career were brought once more to the notice of the general public. This great quarry of information has provided most of the material for those modern studies in prose, drama and film, by which he is best known today. It is a strange and pleasing thought that television and the rest, have made the details of his life more widely known than they were seven hundred years ago; more widely known, that is, but perhaps much less understood. For it must be admitted that unless we are very young and romantic about the past, most of us, when we can bear to think about them, regard our medieval counterparts with a mixture of superiority, pity and repugnance. We find it difficult to realise that many of their problems have a direct relevance for us today, and that in our rush to exist, few of us are able to command the detachment and clarity of vision to both see and solve those problems. This is why the facts of his life are worth recalling. They help us, at least, to see his dilemma, and to recognise that in greater or less degree, it is our own.

Thomas Becket was born in London of Norman parents in 1118, on the feast of St. Thomas the apostle, after whom he was doubtless named. His father Gilbert was well connected, and at the time a prosperous business man. His mother Matilda, gentle and pious, was seemingly ambitious for her son, as many mothers are. Thomas, however, does not appear to have been either an ambitious or an unduly pious boy. We may take it that his childhood was conventional for a boy of his social background—school at Merton Priory, holidays with his parents and sisters, and the occasional thrill of a hunting and hawking expedition with a Norman friend of his father's. At the age of twenty he was sent off to complete his studies in the Schools of Paris, but drifted back to London in the following year to take up the threads of training for a business career. By now his father's fortunes were impoverished, and the home made empty by the death of his mother, to whom he was deeply attached. Having neither the aptitude nor even the enthusiasm for a career in the City, it must have been with a sense of great relief that, with influence, he obtained an entrance into the household of Theobald, archbishop of Canterbury. He was now twenty-four years old, seemingly mediocre, and lucky to be in the select company of cultured men at the very centre of English ecclesiastical affairs.

It was in these early years in Theobald's curia, however, that Thomas found himself. Not for him could there be a dazzling career in the Schools, to be followed by a bishopric, or some other ecclesiastical reward for merit. But as he travelled about the archbishop's business, it was clear that he had a head for detail, a flair for doing things and for getting things done. He could execute the commands of others with a thoroughness and an efficiency beyond the normal, and above all, with tact and great charm. In this way Thomas soon attracted the attention of the archbishop himself, and indeed, accompanied him to Rome on business in 1143, and to the Council of Rheims in 1148, where he must have met St. Bernard. Four years later Theobald delegated to him the delicate task of persuading Eugenius III to accept the young Henry of Anjou as successor to Stephen, king of England, a mission which Thomas successfully accomplished. Promotion swiftly followed, and after a short spell at the famous law schools of Bologna and Auxerre, he returned to take up an important administrative appointment as archdeacon of Canterbury. In 1155, the young Henry, doubtless grateful for Thomas's part in his recent succession to the English throne, but also strongly attracted to the character of his archdeacon, decided to appoint him chancellor of England, the highest secular official in the land. Thomas's success had been meteoric. Trusted and liked both by the old archbishop and the young king, he had become, within thirteen crowded years, one of the greatest men in the realm. He was thirty-seven years old.

Like most people given the opportunity, it did not take Thomas long to adapt himself to magnificence. He accepted greatness gracefully and gratefully. Freely he had been given, and freely he was prepared to give. Just as the young king lavished gifts of all kinds upon him as a proof of royal friendship, so Thomas gave him in return loyal and efficient service, and gave generously also to those of his own large and splendid household, and especially to the poor. His smallest actions had the touch of magnificence in them. Theobald, who knew better than anyone in the realm the hazards involved in high office, kept a shrewd but kindly eye upon his protégé, and cannot have failed, at times, to fear for him. It was not that Theobald objected to the show of splendour, although his own tastes were simple; rather he must have feared that, engrossed in secular affairs, Thomas the cleric would become unduly contaminated by them, and so give cause for scandal. This is probably why, as he lay dying in the year 1161, Theobald sent for Thomas, in order to give him some final counsel. But Thomas never came, and just over a year later, at the king's instance, Thomas Becket the chancellor was nominated archbishop of Canterbury.

There is no reason to doubt the sincerity of Becket's dismay on hearing the news of his nomination. He had none of that false modesty about him which would have formally protested but secretly rejoiced at the news. He knew himself to be quite unworthy of the office. He was neither priest nor scholar, his career had been devoted almost entirely to secular affairs. Furthermore he was aware that the monks of Christ Church, Canterbury, whose privilege it was to elect their archbishop, had been subjected to royal pressure in order to secure his election, and could hardly have viewed their "choice" with enthusiasm. Henry II alone must have been content. As chancellor, Thomas had shown himself to be his faithful servant and personal friend, and there was every reason to believe that he would remain so as archbishop. With his co-operation, indeed, Henry would now be able to regain the hold over the Church in England which the Crown had lost since the days of his grandfather, Henry I. For during the interim of anarchy, the Church had loosened itself considerably from royal control. The development of canon law, the growing independence of ecclesiastical courts from secular jurisdiction, the freedom of appeals to Rome, in short the ability of the English Church to put into effect the reforms of the more recent Church Councils, told heavily against royal autocracy. Henry II was not the kind of man to allow this trend to continue. He argued that his Norman ancestors, the Conqueror and his sons, had never allowed so large a measure of ecclesiastical independence within the realm, and he looked to Becket to help him re-establish what he considered to be his proper rights over the Church in England.

Undoubtedly Becket knew precisely what the king wanted of him when he was nominated to the archbishopric of Canterbury. He knew Henry intimately. A man of action himself, he admired Henry's dynamic energy, the singularity of purpose which drove him around his vast dominions to subdue, unite, and control. He was also fully aware of the dignity and the responsibilities of the office which had been offered him, and it can be shown that when the proposal was first put to him, he warned Henry that the kind of co-operation expected of him would not be possible. The king refused to take the matter seriously, however, and with much heart-searching Thomas was ordained priest on 2 June 1162, and consecrated archbishop of Canterbury the following day.

The bitter and protracted quarrel which soon broke out between the two men, to be terminated only by the archbishop's murder eight and a half years later, is one of the most celebrated in the history of medieval Christendom. In order to throw the full force of his energies into spiritual and ecclesiastical affairs, Becket's first move was to resign the chancellorship of the realm. It was also a public demonstration of his break with the old ways, and Henry never forgave him for it. We may not suppose, however, that this reorientation of his career, sudden as it was, brought any basic change to the character and personality of the newly created archbishop. The command of detail, the old flair for magnificence remained, although few but his closest companions knew now of the vigils, the nights spent in prayer, the fastings and scourgings, his struggle for self-mastery which, for all who take the road, is never done. It is at this stage that many of his later critics, unable to reconcile these facets of his nature, have seen in his mortifications an extravagance bordering on the theatrical, another proof of the instability of his true character. That is as may be, but those who knew Becket best had only admiration for the harsh penances he inflicted upon himself as he surrounded himself with splendour. For not only have we to consider that his age sought remedies to subdue the flesh which the more comfortable world of our own day finds repellent and excessive; we have also to reckon on Becket's own determination to live up to the standards which he considered the highest ecclesiastical office in the land demanded of him. One can never escape this sense of efficiency in Becket, this urge to accomplish successfully each task which came to hand. Previously, that task had been in the sphere of secular affairs, which he had mastered as had few chancellors before him; now, as the chief shepherd of his flock, however he had come by the office, his task was to bend his irrepressibly masterful nature to conform to the pattern demanded of him by the Good Shepherd. It was this challenge of perfection, and not a sense of "theatre," or an inborn vulgarity of mind which sought the ostentatious, that made him accept the discipline, the hair shirt, and the rest. Indeed, it is characteristic of his real humility that these mortifications went along with the outward show of magnificence, the generous gesture and the smiling face, and were, in fact, known only to a few of his own household while he lived.

There were several minor brushes with the king before an open breach occurred between them at a Council held at Westminster in October 1163, over the thorny problem of criminous clerks. Henry insisted that clerics who had been convicted of crime should be handed over to the secular arm for punishment, as the recent customs of the land had allowed. Becket opposed this as a violation of canon law. Certainly there was no easy solution to a problem which, at the time, lay in a jurisdictional no-man's-land. Before long, the issue had broadened into a general discussion on the laws of the land. The archbishop finally gave his verbal assent to the king's customs, but only after it had been put to him privately that violent opposition of this sort at a public council caused acute embarrassment to the king, who had no desire to press such cases in actual practice, but who, nevertheless, could not afford to lose face before his own secular vassals at these assemblies.

In the following January the king summoned his Council to meet him again, this time at Clarendon. Without a doubt, his purpose was to force Becket publicly to accept the customs of the realm, and after him, the entire episcopacy. After some days of bitter argument, Becket was persuaded to take the oath, and urged the bishops to do likewise. When he saw the constitutions drawn up in writing, however, and realised their significance, he refused to put his seal to them, although the remainder of the hierarchy present did so. Returning from Clarendon, Thomas was plunged in gloom, and wept when one of his monk companions, in a burst of frankness, accused him of selling the pass. Swift to excuse others, the archbishop saw himself as a false shepherd, one who, in the hour of crisis, had wavered and fled. This was not entirely true, but he must have realised that his actions at Clarendon had left his episcopal brethren confused and disunited as rarely before. He must have realised too, if he had not already long since done so, that Henry was now his implacable enemy, bent on his ruin.

Henry did not have long to wait. Failing to answer a royal summons over a dispute in a case which the archbishop considered to lie within his own jurisdiction, Thomas was ordered to stand trial for contempt of court at Northampton in October of the same year, 1164. His position was now much weaker; legally the king had a case against him which did not involve the rest of the hierarchy, who were nevertheless constrained to be present in order to pass judgment on him. For several days Becket withstood the sustained attacks of both the secular barons and his own episcopal colleagues. Looking now at the evidence of this trial, which has been preserved for us in graphic and minute detail, it is difficult not to admire his iron self-control in the face of violent threats on his own person by the lay barons, as well as the subtler and crueller arguments of his brethren, most of whom urged him to submit unconditionally to the king's judgment and to resign the archbishopric lest he bring ruin to the Church in England. It broke down only on the eighth day of the trial when, forbidding his colleagues to pass an unlawful sentence on him, he marched out of the judgment hall and heard, above the uproar and confusion, the king's illegitimate brother leer the word "traitor" at him. "You bastard," shouted back Thomas, as he stumbled over some faggots near the door, "If I were a knight these hands of mine would prove you a liar!"

His escape from Northampton Castle, his flight through the Fens disguised as a lay brother, and his perilous journey across the Channel in an open boat would seem to belong to the realm of pure fiction were they not authenticated fact. Making his way through Flanders to Soissons, where he was sympathetically received by the French king, Thomas pressed on towards Sens, where he hoped to find Alexander III and lay his case before him. Meanwhile, Henry had acted swiftly. Finding that Thomas had escaped the country, he sent a delegation of bishops immediately to Sens, to present his case. With great skill they put it to the pope that the English king was a reasonable man who had no wish to disobey the Holy Father's injunctions, but that Becket's defiance of royal justice, together with his mishandling of ecclesiastical affairs, had brought grave disunity to the Church in their country. It was hinted that Becket's appointment to the archbishopric had been an unfortunate one, since it was clear that his background and personality made him unsuitable for the office. Finding that neither honeyed words nor bribery could move the pope, who said that he must hear what Thomas had to say before giving judgment, the bishops returned to England.

Thomas then saw Alexander. It seemed to the archbishop that to have placed his seal to the constitutions of Clarendon would have given the king potentially, if not actually, full control over the Church in England, and that the rights of the papacy itself were involved in this controversy. Once more he begged to be relieved of his office; firstly because of his initial hesitation and attempted compromise before he realised the danger of such a course, and secondly because in defending the rights and dignity of his office, it seemed clear to him that he was unworthy of it.

One cannot fail to be struck by the contrast between the façade of confidence displayed by the contingent of English bishops on this occasion, who fought their case on personal grounds, and their troubled, unhappy archbishop, who strove to rise above personal issues and to argue the case on matters of principle. It says a great deal for Alexander III, who had his own troubles, that he condemned most of the constitutions of Clarendon, reconfirmed Thomas in his office, and with sympathy urged him to accept the offer of French asylum until the worst had blown over. Accordingly, the archbishop, with a few companions, went to live with the Cistercian monks at Pontigny. With some difficulty, though with equal determination, he fashioned his life to their austere discipline, so that his general health began to suffer. There was to be little peace for him there. Before long his own relations, besides a number of his monks at Canterbury, were outlawed from England and forced to present themselves to him, miserable and destitute, as a measure of the king's vindictiveness. Henry then brought such pressure to bear on the monks at Pontigny, that for their sake Thomas moved to the French monastery of St. Columba at Sens, where he was to remain for four years.

There can be little doubt that this period of exile schooled Thomas for the supreme test which lay ahead. Rebuked by one of his friends for his preoccupation in the study of canon law (by which means he had hoped to fortify himself in present and anticipated litigation), he devoted himself instead to the study of the Sacred Scriptures, and threw himself once more into an austere routine of mortification and prayer. The correspondence of this period shows him to have been heavily involved in litigation following his excommunication of some of his enemies at Vezelay in the summer of 1166, at which the constitutions of Clarendon were also once more publicly condemned. He was now in open enmity with several of his bishops, who continued to defy him, but who nevertheless feared his power to excommunicate them. The rift between himself and the king, which Thomas had made some unsuccessful attempts to heal by correspondence, seemed now irreparable. Delays and subterfuges in the process of his case, prolonged by the pope's own unhappy position at the time, brought him to the edge of despair. We cannot tell what "cliffs of fall" his mind must have experienced during these years of sorrow, self-doubt and disappointment, but some of his bitterness occasionally reveals itself in the letters written towards the end of his exile. As the seasons passed, he must have realised that with all their kindness to him, the community with whom he lived were, by now, weary of his stay; an awkward guest, he had long since worn out his welcome, especially after January 1169, when the French king's efforts to reconcile the archbishop to his king at Montmirail had ended in failure. Slowly it began to dawn on him that the only way to break through the impasse was to return to his See, come what may. For too long the sheep had been scattered and harried, without their shepherd. Once his mind was made up, his spirits rose. He did not doubt that the future was dark and uncertain, but for him, who had fought out his soul's battle in the silence of his cell at Sens, the conflict was over. He would return to Canterbury.

In the summer of 1170, Henry's eldest son was crowned at Westminster, a feudal practice which was performed during the king's lifetime in order to ensure the peaceful succession of his son to the throne. From time immemorial, however, it had always been the prerogative of the archbishop of Canterbury to perform this solemn act, and its performance by Becket's old enemy the archbishop of York, in the presence of several other

English bishops, was a move of calculated defiance. It brought a
sharp rebuke from Alexander III, who empowered Thomas to
suspend York and to excommunicate the recalcitrant bishops.
Thomas hesitated, and wrote for further instructions. At the
end of November, however, as he was about to embark for
England, he heard that the archbishop of York and other
bishops under threat of excommunication were about to join the
king, then in France, in a further act of defiance. Thomas
therefore sent ahead the dreaded letters of suspension and
excommunication, which news the unnerved bishops immediately conveyed to Henry. Incensed by what he considered to
be a fresh insult to the Crown, the king spoke wildly of Becket's
having lived long enough. Four of his knights at court did not
wait for his temper to cool; they had heard enough.

   Thomas landed at Sandwich on 1 December 1170. Already
the news of his impending return had spread, and as the boat
carrying his archiepiscopal cross at the masthead entered the
harbour, many of the excited jostling crowd rushed into the
water to greet him as a saviour and hero. His biographers tell us
of scenes of tumultuous welcome as the archbishop, gay as
never before, made his slow triumphant progress towards
Canterbury; we read of his confirming large numbers of
children in the lanes and byways, of his abandoning himself to
the demonstrations of love which the common people made as,
scattering his benedictions, he passed them by. As a gesture of
peace, Thomas then made his way towards Woodstock in order
to pay homage to Henry II's crowned son, but had not
proceeded far beyond London when he was told that the young
king had no desire to see him. Finding that his enemies
continued to insult his office by despoiling his lands and
submitting his tenants to further humiliations, Thomas took up
the challenge, and on Christmas Day, in his own cathedral, then
crammed to the doors, he publicly excommunicated those
responsible for the latest outrages. His sermon on this occasion
echoed his longing to forgive old wrongs, his desire to live at
peace with his enemies. But since their malice towards him was
seemingly irreducible, he had decided to fight them with all the

power and authority his office could command. There can be no doubt that he realised his danger. Reminding his congregation of the martyrdom of one of his predecessors, St. Elphege, he added: "Soon enough you may have another. . . ."

Four days later the four knights burst in on him as he sat discussing ecclesiastical matters with some of his companions after Mass in one of the rooms in his palace. Sharply Thomas asked them to state their business. They commanded him to free from suspension and excommunication the archbishop of York and the other bishops under censure, and with many violent words repeated all the old charges against him— treachery, pride, rebellion, contempt for the king. With some difficulty Thomas mastered the indignation which welled up fiercely within him. His thoughts ranged over the long and bitter struggle, the years of exile which he had never found easy to bear. But all that was over. "It's no use threatening me now," he said quietly. "If all the swords in England were brandished over my head your threats could not budge me from keeping God's justice and obedience to the pope. Long ago when intimidated, I fled. But I did not return here to flee again; anyone who wants me will find me here. Foot to foot you will find me in the Lord's fight. If I may be allowed to hold my office in peace, well enough; if not, may God's will be done. . . ."

The knights left him to arm. When they returned, later in the afternoon, the monks, thoroughly alarmed at the uproar, pleaded with and finally persuaded their archbishop to go into the Church to hear vespers. Thomas seemed reluctant to go, and insisted on having the Church doors left open, although the monks and servants had already bolted and barred all the entrances to both the Cathedral and the house. Shouting after him in the gloom, the four knights came across Thomas by a pillar between the altars of St. Benedict and the Blessed Virgin, as he was making his way up to the chapel of the Holy Trinity. Rushing at him repeating their threats and insults, they were overawed and fell back as he turned to face them. Gently but firmly the archbishop remonstrated with FitzUrse, their leader, who was his own liegeman and therefore doubly under his obedience. It was too late for argument however. But as FitzUrse snatched at the archbishop's cloak, the old Thomas momentarily revealed himself. "Keep your hands off me, you pander," he shouted as he wrenched himself free. Then seeing the others close in on him with raised swords, he commended his soul to God, the Blessed Virgin and other saints, and bowed his head, awaiting their blows. Staggering under their repeated strokes at his head, he was heard to murmur, "I am ready to accept death for the name of Jesus and the defence of the Church." He fell at last, and lay on the flagstones, as one of his monks afterwards wrote, as if in adoration or prayer.

But that was long ago. That the archbishop's stand had been heroic, hardly a person in Christendom was prepared at the time to deny, and few would deny even today. And yet, if we exclude the personal factors involved in the quarrel—the clash of personalities, the background of the times and so on, we are disturbed to find that its pattern is just as familiar to us now as it was seven hundred years ago. One need search no further back than our own century to find distressing parallels of this struggle between the Church and the State over the problem of ecclesiastical liberty. One has only to think of the persecution of the Catholic Church in Mexico in the 'twenties, in Germany in the 'thirties, in China, Hungary and Poland in the 'forties and 'fifties, to realise that the issues at stake are basically identical with those defended by St. Thomas; only the enemy has changed. In the case of Hungary, their primate, too, was singled out from the rest of the hierarchy long before his arrest, and subjected to every kind of subtle pressure which the State could contrive. The actual issue at stake was the nationalisation of denominational schools, a dispute which was chosen, like the criminous clerks clause in the constitutions of Clarendon, merely to mask the secular government's real intention, namely, to subject the Church, in the last analysis, to its own control. Cardinal Mindszenty was not deceived and the case he presented to the world in his last pastoral letter before his arrest, written 18 November 1948, put the issue in its true, if stark perspective:

The country is condemned to silence [he wrote], and public opinion has been made a mere frivolous jest. If a man dares to raise his voice in contradiction, he is dismissed from his post or punished in other ways. With regard to the fact that between Church and State no agreement has yet been reached, it is well known that when the Church was at last invited to negotiate, the main point—the problem of the schools—had already been settled by the State, and the Church had to play the role of scapegoat. Of my predecessors in office, two were killed in action, two were robbed of all their possessions, one was taken prisoner and deported, one was exiled. However, such a systematic and purposeful propaganda of lies, time and again disproved and time and again repeated, has never been organised against the seventy-eight predecessors in my office. I stand for God, for Church and for Hungary. This duty was imposed on me by the fate of my nation which stands alone, an orphan in the whole world. If I am compelled to speak out and to state the facts as they are, it is only the misery of my people which forces me to do so, and the urge for truth. Here I stand, waiting to see what is going to happen to me.

In twelfth-century England, a royal despot, in twentieth-century Hungary an atheistic tyranny; and the essential tragedy of this never-ending struggle between Church and State is that those who strike at the Church, strike at the only power in the world designed to protect their personal rights and liberties; that the authority they seek to ruin was destined from the beginning to bring them the happiness which, in their dark perverted ways, they thirst to attain. Few of us are called to represent that authority and to make the right decisions in moments of crisis, as St. Thomas of Canterbury was called to do, and as many after him have been so called. But we ought never to forget our debt to him, the protomartyr of all those servants of God throughout the ages who have had the clarity of vision, when their moment came, to resist the unjust claims of secular authority. That clarity of vision, certainly for St.

Thomas, was no sudden gift from heaven. Behind it lay long nights of prayer, mortification, the agony of doubt, self-mistrust, remembrance of humiliations, loneliness, tears for past failure; but once resolved, self-mastered, Thomas kept his courage to the end. This is why he was the most popular English saint of the Middle Ages, and why, in a very real sense, he deserves to be so today.

St. Hugh of Lincoln

1135-1200

Renée Haynes

NOW THAT POLITICAL ACTIVITY is regarded as one of the chief
duties of man, it is normal to live preoccupied with problems of
power. To exert it in some administrative capacity is a common
way of earning a living; to sit on a voluntary committee is an
agreeable recreation for the many who enjoy it. Power is there,
like water in a tap, which must be turned on by all kinds of
people, elected or appointed or promoted or co-opted, responsible, careless, or rule-bound. This entails a constant necessary
exercise of decision, and a consequent inevitable pull not only
towards the grosser sorts of civic dishonesty but also towards
personal pomposity, self-inflation and ever other evil sum-
marized in the axiom that all power corrupts.

There are in fact twin problems: how can it be ensured that
statesmen and administrators shall use power with completely
disinterested justice; and how, even if they do this, can they
avoid the corrosion of habitual pride. They are very old
problems, though the managerial revolution has involved in
them more people than ever before. Among the solutions
propounded for the first are that rulers should be specially
educated, as in Greek theory and Spartan practice; that they
should be kept apart from the sly infectious stupidity of those to
be ruled, the common herd, the *lumpen-proletariat,* as in Wells's
Samurai theory and in Indian caste practice; and that they
should be imbued with impersonal devotion to an abstract idea

of the common good, as in Utopian theory and totalitarian practice. To the second problem only Plato adumbrated an answer; that the philosophers, to whom power meant nothing, should be Kings: but how could men of this temperament and discipline be induced to assume such a harassing and distracting burden?

To these questions the life of St. Hugh of Lincoln is startlingly relevant; it exemplifies the curious unexpected twist with which sanctity seems to fulfil human theories by transmuting them.

His youth and his manhood till he was forty he devoted to stripping himself of self-will by vow, rule, and daily detailed habit, in order to be fit for the contemplative life. His remaining years were spent, in obedience to a general command, precisely in the constant exercise of will, judgment, decision, authority in a most turbulent age; and he was a man who wanted above all else to be alone with God, if God so willed, in that blessed state he had once known:

> *O beata solitudo*
> *O sola beatitudo.*

He was the last of the three sons of William, a knight who had in his youth thought of entering religion, but had fought in the wars instead, married a lady called Anna, and lived with his family in the castle of Avalon in Burgundy. Anna died when Hugh was eight. Her husband divided the inheritance between the three boys, left the two older ones to run the property, and took the youngest, and his share of the estate, to enter with him the small community of the Canons Regular of St. Augustine at Villars-Benôit. In his old age St. Hugh told his chaplain, the Benedictine monk Adam of Eynsham who wrote his Life, that his father had always regretted his decision to spend his manhood in the world, and had made up his mind that this small boy should have the happiness of dedicating the years of his strength to God. "I needed no persuasion," said St. Hugh, "to renounce pleasure of which I knew nothing, and to follow him as a fellow soldier in the spiritual army."

The child could make no formal vows until he was fourteen, but he was offered to God. He was tonsured, and given an unconsecrated Host and Chalice to carry until after the Gospel had been read at Mass: then he was brought to the Prior, who clasped his hand under the altar cloth, and afterwards clothed him in the habit of the Order. Where, as occasionally happened in the later Middle Ages, this ceremony was used on an uncertain child the procedure was, of course, nauseating. Where the child was eager for it, like young Hugh, it must have been inexpressibly moving. It is touching enough today to see the awe and generosity with which a small boy will treat the little rite of becoming a Wolf Cub, sworn to "do his best and not to give in to himself"; how much more this innocent gift of a whole lifetime. There is now so keen a sense of the problems of human beings at one temporal stage or another—the infant, the "toddler," the adolescent, the elderly—that it may take an effort of the imagination to realize how fully our ancestors acknowledged the eternal in them at every age. Where we regard a child primarily as something in biological and psychological transit, and diminish his present human value by emphasizing his potentiality for the future instead of his significance now, they saw him as an immortal soul, capable of choice and of sanctity.

The Canons educated a few boys from neighbouring families, with whom Hugh did some of his lessons. He learned to write, to read the Latin classics, and to study Scripture and theology. He had never cared about games, even at Avalon, and no one forced him into their primitive distractions now. His tutor, indeed, kept him back when the others ran off to play—they were to live in the world again after their schooling—saying gently, "Let them do as they want, it is all right for them. . . . *Hugonete, Hugonete,* little Hugh, little Hugh, I am bringing you up for Christ; ragging about is not for you."

At fifteen years old he took his first vows, and his place in the community. He was put to nurse his father, now very old and frail; he looked after him lovingly, and was with him when he died. At nineteen he was ordained deacon and set to preaching, which he did very well; then he was charged with the little parish of St. Maxime, now St. Maximin. He was allowed to have an old priest with him, but carried on the active work himself. It was his first contact for eleven years with the everyday world, unfocused and undedicated. It became apparent, from his handling of the lands and vineyards, and his care that they should have honest energetic tenants, that he had a good head for business. His dealings with his parishioners were sane, gentle, and marked by that "authoritative innocence" which Ruskin saw as his chief characteristic. It seems to have been here that he first knew the strength of the physical desires he was vowed to sublimate. After a year, he asked to return to the community, and did so, living there for some while.

It is normal for the young to leave the place and people that nurtured them, for something new. The time for Hugh to do this came when he accompanied his old tutor, now Prior, on a visit to the Grande Chartreuse, remote in the mountains. Above the clearing where the monastery stands all is forest and rock; below sounds "the boom of the far waterfall like doom." Of the life there its founder St. Bruno wrote: "As to the blessing and sweetness of solitude and silence, let those who have chosen them tell their fascination. . . . It is there that generous men can enter into themselves, and dwell with God alone in the very centre of their souls. . . . It is there that perfect rest accompanies labour, and action does not hurt the peace of the soul."

The young man was drawn to it at once, and asked the Prior, Dom Basil, for leave to enter. He was put off, as the Rule demanded, by a most discouraging picture of Carthusian life, and told he was not strong enough to undertake it. His own Prior, much distressed, hurried him away, burst into tears, asking how he could have the heart to leave him in his old age, and extorted a vow that Hugh would never forsake him as long as he lived. Presently it became plain to Hugh that his vocation was indeed to be a Carthusian, and that he could not be false to it; that the vow, made under emotional stress, was not binding; and that he must go. He put everything for which he was responsible in order, and silently returned to the Grande Chartreuse. This time he was admitted as a novice. He was twenty-three years old.

For ten years he lived the bed-rock life of a Carthusian, praying, walking, reading, writing, cooking, eating, chopping wood alone in his house, from whose garden could be seen soaring into the sky beyond the enclosure wall the peak of the Grand Som. He practised the austerities of the Order, the fasting, the perpetual abstinence from meat, the wearing of the hair shirt like incessant nettlerash, and the complete obedience. His solitude, intense as that of the Desert Fathers, was yet buoyed up on the recurrent communal rhythm of the liturgy sung at midnight, morning, and evening in the monastery church by voices which used ordinary human converse only between Noon and Vespers on Sundays and great feasts. "Everything in the life of a Carthusian," runs Fr. Thurston's English edition of the great French Life of St. Hugh, "is so arranged as best to dispose his soul to recollection, to meditation and, if grace calls him to mount higher, to that state of more perfect prayer . . . which is a foretaste of the Beatific Vision." It seems probable that Hugh used a book on prayer written by Dom Guigo, who succeeded Dom Basil as Prior, called the *Scala Claustralium*. Up its four rungs, reading, meditation, prayer and contemplation, the monk was to climb every day until, as Richard of St. Victor wrote, "the soul reaches the last stage, transforming vision. . . . It practises virtue in an heroic degree; it longs to suffer for God; it loves sinners as He loves them, and longs for their salvation; it becomes intensely apostolic, yet is ever in peace." There could hardly be a more accurate description of St. Hugh in his maturity.

That maturity ripened in time and pain. Ordinary life, with its succession of details, talk, people, habit, interruption, noise and disturbance, might seem precisely calculated to keep the heart from considering ultimate truth, to shield it against the impact of *"le silence éternel de ces espaces infinies."* To be confronted continually with these things, in loneliness and deep quiet, might almost crush a man; in whom this loneliness and this quiet must also sharpen to an intolerable, an ineluctable brilliance, temptation, which must be fought direct, since in such a life there can be no distraction from it. Hugh suffered for a long time, physically and imaginatively, from lust which would have become almost unbearable but that, as he wrote, "in the midst of darkness I still heard Thy voice speaking in the depth of my soul."

Presently he was given an aged sick monk to look after, who could not leave his cell. It was he who prepared the young man to be ordained a priest as he longed to be. Later Hugh was given charge of an old Cistercian Archbishop ultimately canonized as St. Peter of Tarentaise, who used to come and stay at the Grande Chartreuse. Hugh waited on him, washed his feet, traced quotations and found books for him in the library, took him for his slow walks along the mountain paths, and sat talking with him on a plank nailed between two pine-trees as a seat. In 1173, in his thirties, he was made Procurator of the monastery; he was responsible for the lay brothers and their work of tending crops and cattle, he had to occupy himself in administration, to welcome and entertain guests, and to give alms to the poor people of the neighbouring villages when there were any alms to give. When the cupboard was bare, he could at any rate listen to people's troubles, remember them, and comfort as best he could. He was loved not only by humans, but by the birds and squirrels which came in at his window, and foraged round his kitchen. The Prior, who thought they might distract him from prayer, forbade him to give them crumbs.

He longed to return to his solitude—this theme recurs throughout his life henceforward—but he was not allowed to give up his work, and had to be content, every time he left "the lower house" where business was conducted, for the monastery church, to take off his cloak and say to his anxieties and preoccupations, "Stay here with my cloak, and when Office is over I will take you all up again." At forty he was for a time terribly tortured once more by lust, and was almost at his wits' end when at last his deliverance came in a dream one night that Dom Basil, the Prior who had received him and was now dead, came to him and blessed him. He was never troubled in this way again. Only a few days after this last great struggle came his summons to the outer world.

In penitence for his part in the murder of St. Thomas Becket, Henry II had vowed to found two Carthusian monasteries in England. The first, inaugurated in 1178 at Witham in Somerset, had been extremely unsuccessful, because no preparations had been made to receive the colonists from the Grande Chartreuse. The site allotted to them was occupied by the huts of serfs bound to work on the royal demesne; they were feared as potential usurpers, hated as foreigners. They had had to set up little wooden structures in the forests. In two years Witham had had two Priors; the first broke down, the second died. Rather piqued by this, the King took advice from an anonymous "nobleman of Maurienne," who told him to demand as a new Prior Hugh, "who carries the whole human race in his heart, and loves all men with perfect charity." The Prior of the Grande Chartreuse opposed the request, the Chapter was divided, Hugh said that as he could not govern his own soul he was not fit to govern others; the Bishop of Grenoble, himself a Carthusian, over-ruled all, and told Hugh under obedience to go, saying "The only Son of the Eternal Father, quitting . . . ineffable tranquillity . . . clothed Himself in our human nature for the salvation of the world. You too must make the sacrifice of your quiet cell, and of the companionship of the brothers you love."

Hugh took at least one of the lay-brothers, an indomitable old monk named Aynard, with him on the long journey by mule-back down the mountains, through France, over the sea which he had probably never seen before, through a strange land to settle among a hostile people. At Witham he called the serfs together and offered them either a transfer to comparable holdings on other Crown manors, or freedom and leave to settle wherever they liked. He also arranged with the King, who combined genial elusiveness with an infinite capacity for rage if he were pinned down, that they should receive compensation for all the huts they had put up. Henry tried his usual delaying tactics, but his new Prior refused to settle in Witham till this had been done. Delaying tactics were tried again over the money which had been promised for building materials for the monastery and builders' wages; this time they went on till Hugh, with Aynard and another lay brother, Gerard, journeyed across England to see the King. They were met with further agreeable promises but no money, and no definite date for its arrival. Gerard exploded, told Henry what he thought of him, and said they would all return to France. Henry, on the verge of one of those volcanic furies supposed to run in the line of his demon-ancestress Melusine, asked Hugh whether he was going too. The Prior said gently, No; he was sorry for the King in all his anxieties, and he was sure he would keep his promises in the end. Henry embraced him, gave him the money and cemented a sometimes embarrassing friendship by coaxing from St. Swithin's monastery a beautiful Bible the monks there had made for their own use, and giving it to Witham. After some months Hugh by chance discovered what had happened, and gave it back to St. Swithin's as a present, promising that Henry should never know of its return.

For six years he governed the Witham Charterhouse. Then came the last separation from the cloister to which henceforward (in spite of repeated appeals to the Pope to be allowed to return) he would come back only as a guest to draw strength again each year from a month's retreat in the old solitude, silence, prayer and manual work. (He is said to have taken an innocent pride in his talent for washing-up.) In May 1186 Henry appointed him Bishop of Lincoln. Hugh wrote to the Dean and Chapter telling them that this meant nothing, they alone could elect to the vacant See. They elected him. His last hope was gone when the General of his Order commanded him to accept their offer. Under obedience he rode to Westminster to be consecrated, with attendants a little ashamed of his shabbiness. A Bishop, he rode on to St. Catherine's Priory outside the walls of Lincoln. At dawn, after a night's prayer, he went barefoot to the Cathedral, which he later helped to rebuild, carrying stones and mortar with the workmen. He caused offence by refusing to give money to the archdeacon who enthroned him; the Lateran Council had just forbidden this practice. He gave, however, a great feast of roast venison to the poor of Lincoln, telling his steward to kill three hundred deer from his park for them, "and more if that is not enough."

His diocese was enormous, his duties crowded innumerably upon him. They included, in addition to the work of a Bishop to-day, the administration of justice in the Courts Christian (which dealt with wills and matrimonial disputes), and the maintenance of a running fight with the civil power, in the persons of three highly temperamental and arbitrary Plantagenet monarchs, to rebut encroachments of all sorts on the province of the Church. Throughout the long journeys that all this necessitated he kept himself so deeply recollected in prayer that someone had to ride in front of him for his horse to follow. If another rider passed between him and his guide, the horse would quite frequently follow the wrong leader until the right one, finding himself alone, galloped back to look for his charge grumbling "Mercy on me, they have stolen my Bishop again." (Was a leading rein, which seems the obvious device for this situation, considered undignified?)

Once arrived, however, the Bishop was very much on the spot. He did not fall back on his authority without having first tried every means of reasoning, persuasion, sometimes even a gentle guile. In his face to face conflicts with Henry II and Richard I there occasionally flashed out a certain *enfant terrible* quality. It served him well at Woodstock one day, where he was angrily summoned after he had excommunicated, without consulting Henry, the atrociously cruel head-forester Galfrid, and had followed this up by refusing to allow royalty to appoint a layman to a vacant prebend at Lincoln. When he arrived, he found that a vast snub had been organized to greet him, a snub comic to modern eyes but potent in an age of highly ceremonial etiquette. The King and his court were sitting on the grass with their backs to him, refusing to speak. The Bishop nudged a courtier to move up, and joined the silent circle. Tension grew and muscles stiffened. After a time, as an excuse to fidget, Henry asked a servant who was standing by to fetch him a needle and thread, and began to stitch a piece of linen round a cut on one of his fingers. Hugh remarked sedately, "You know, you look exactly like your great-great-grandmother of Falaise." (It will be remembered that William the Conqueror was the bastard son of a girl belonging to a tanner's and glover's family there; an ancestress probably seldom discussed among the pedigree-proud.) Henry was startled into a burst of laughter, and in the subsequent relaxation took quite reasonably the reminder that spiritual decisions did not come into his province and that only priests ought to hold church benefices.

Hugh as steadily opposed Richard's various claims on his diocese for presents, for cash, for armed men and for canons to serve as ambassadors at their own expense. Incidentally, in so doing he created more than one constitutional precedent for resisting unjust taxation. When the Archbishop of Canterbury advised him to keep on the right side of a King who "thirsts for money as a dropsical man thirsts for water," he replied pointblank, "If the King does suffer from dropsy I have no desire to be the water he swallows to ease it," and continued to refuse unlawful demands, even when Richard published an edict confiscating all his episcopal possessions. As St. Hugh had already declared excommunicate all who seized Church property no one could be found to execute this; so deep was the awe aroused by his authority on the rare occasions when he exerted it.

In general he was, to quote the opinion of the usually rather acid Giraldus Cambrensis, who knew him well, "a pleasant companion, full of talk and fun, bright and cheerful as though his mind were free from cares, easily roused even upon a small occasion; brusque, full of enthusiasm, and a strict disciplinarian." His habitual asceticism—he never abandoned Carthusian austerity—did not make him stoical, unsympathetic, or embittered. Because he was able "to rejoice in God as misers do in gold and Kings in sceptres," he could "enjoy the world aright"; and perceive created things with a clear and sharply-focused vision undimmed by self-involvement, undistorted by self-regard. He was vividly aware of the glorious and intense significance of the body; and was accustomed to tell women they should remember that while "no man could say he was the Father of God, a woman was truly God's Mother." He was careful of the health of his clergy, and profoundly compassionate to the sick. Many, both before and after his death, traced their cure to his prayers. He was called to one of them, Roger Colhoppe, by an excited crowd, as he was riding to Waltham Abbey; the man, a sailor, had been seized on board ship with terrifying fits during which he tore at himself with teeth and nails. He had been bound and brought home. The Bishop, appalled and pitiful, found him twitching violently on the floor, his hands made fast to two stakes, his feet to a post; and restored him to calm, health and sanity. Another patient was a young man met crossing a bridge over the Medway. He was tormented physically by infected ulcers and spiritually by despair over his sins, had already twice attempted suicide and was planning a third attempt. Hugh took him with him to Canterbury, blessed him, prayed for him, and sent him off, healed, on a pilgrimage to Rome. He ended his days in peace, a Cistercian lay brother.

Like a man sailing a dinghy, instantly responsive to the pressure of wind and current yet keeping his course, buoyed up on the depth of the sea, St. Hugh responded without impatience to the unforeseen meetings, the urgent demands, the unexpected needs that came his way, buoyed up on the deep peace of recollectedness. He did not, of course, exert himself for casual contacts alone; he regularly visited the leper hospitals of his diocese, especially one close to him in Lincoln, and washed and comforted the patients there just as he remembered his mother tending lepers when he was a child at Avalon. He did not even shrink from the physical contact of a caress, which they must so sorely have missed in their isolation; and when someone said, perhaps as a dig at him, "You know, St. Martin's kiss healed a leprous body," replied instantly, "But the leper's kiss heals my soul." He helped them to understand and use their misery by reminding them that they could offer it with Our Lord's disfigurements and sufferings all that long last night and day of His Passion. He kept at the same time a strong sense that whatever was to be offered to the active service of God must be physically unblemished, and refused, for no immediately apparent reason, to ordain a young man, who proved a few months later to have leprosy upon him. It was probably from his lively sense of the meaning of the unique, tangible, individual created things that Hugh derived his strong devotion to relics, of which he made a large collection. He gave a silver reliquary containing most of them to the Grande Chartreuse on a happy unexpected visit there the summer before his death. From the same source sprang his care for corpses, then too often left to lie helplessly abandoned in town back alleys or on wild commons. For their souls he prayed every day, saying that the dead of his diocese were as much his children as the living; their bodies he buried with reverence, doing the last service he could to each "loved creature of God." Indeed, to the horror of his clergy—as he was always in conflict with the Crown over matters of principle, surely he should not be found wanting in ordinary courtesy—he risked being extremely late for the ceremony of homage to Richard Coeur de Lion on this account; for, finding in the street on the way there the body of someone killed in the previous night's rioting, he insisted on taking it to be buried at once, conducting the funeral himself. He was in fact extremely late; but Richard was later still. Perhaps again it was his love of God in His creatures that drew intuitive, sub-rational beings towards him; the squirrels of the Grande Chartreuse, the goose that visited him for three years at Witham, the six months old baby that laughed and jumped for joy when it saw him at Newark, the nephew of the same age that cooed so volubly in his uncle's unknown arms in Burgundy, the fierce wild swan that would fly up to his house at Stow days before his return, guard his sleep, eat bread from his hand, and "bury its head and long neck in his wide sleeves as though it were plunging them into limpid water." St. Hugh's simultaneous relationship in harmonious unison with the worlds of instinctive creatures, of humanity and of God is most clearly shown in the traditional pictures of him with the swan beside him, the chalice in his hand, and a Child smiling in the Host above it; an allusion to a vision known only because someone once shared it with him, and was told to speak of it as a pledge that God had sent him.

One of St. Hugh's sayings was that in the cloister or the world to be a true Christian a man must have purity of life, love in his heart and truth on his lips. His personal concern for the first two has already appeared; his quiet passion for the last expressed itself not only in speech but in determination to discover and maintain essential truth. Dying, he replied to a question about his legal decisions, "I cannot remember that I have ever consciously deviated from justice." Living, he discouraged alike superstitious practices, such as well-worship and changing babies' names to change their luck, pious fusses over trivialities, and undue concern with "signs and wonders"; he refused for instance to go out of his way to see a "miraculous" bleeding Host, saying that no miracle could surpass that of the consecration at Mass every day. His desire accurately to establish the facts of a case led him rigorously to investigate popular devotion to a pseudo-martyr, a man who had plundered the Jews in a riot at Northampton, rushed off to Stamford with his loot, and was robbed and killed there by an acquaintance, who threw his body over the city wall. It was assumed that the Jews had murdered him, and pilgrimages were organized to his tomb bringing in considerable profits to the local people, who were much annoyed when the Bishop discovered the truth and suppressed the cult.

It is sad that the potent anti-Semitic propaganda story of the apocryphal Little St. Hugh should have arisen in the very See of his great namesake, fifty years after the latter's death, for the Carthusian several times risked his life to protect this alien people in his diocese from the triply pleasurable hatred of their neighbours, who detested them because they were ineradicably foreigners; because, being for the most part forbidden to make their living in any other way, they were usurers; and because, belonging to the race which killed the cause and flower of its own being, Our Lord, they were ideal scapegoats on whom Christians could project with fatally enjoyable rancour the guilt of their own betrayals of Him. In the fierce racial riots of 1190 and 1191 Hugh's calm courage finally prevailed as, bareheaded and unarmed, he remonstrated with furious laymen and clerics in Lincoln Cathedral itself, in Northampton with the townspeople shouting and clashing weapons, with armed knights in the lovely grey stone town of Stamford, and at Holland with a milling crowd, one of whom raised a sword to kill him. His cousin William of Avalon snatched it away and would have cut down the attacker but that Hugh forbade it. It is not surprising that the Jews wept in the streets of Lincoln at his funeral, crying out that "this was a true servant of the Great God."

After a journey through France, where King John sent him to witness the signing of the Peace of Andelys, and where he saw Avalon, and Villars-Benoit, and St. Maxime and the Grande Chartreuse again, he returned to England feeling ill. He endured two months of increasing weakness and pain, and died in November 1200, lying as he had wished in his Carthusian habit on a cross of ashes spread on the floor. They were saying Compline in his room and had just begun *Nunc dimittis.* Administration was over, decisions were done with; he could depart in peace to know eternally the peace of God which had shone through all his actions in time.

St. Dominic

1170-1221

Sheila Kaye-Smith

IT WOULD BE hard to find a bigger contrast than the lives of those two friars who brought light and learning into the Church towards the close of the twelfth century. St. Francis and St. Dominic were contemporaries, they were, though working apart, leaders of a great religious revival, and they founded two religious Orders that have lived fraternally ever since. Yet one could scarcely imagine two men whose characters and lives were more unlike.

St. Francis has about him a glamour that the other entirely lacks. His careless youth and striking conversion, the romantic, indeed adventurous beginnings of the Order have made him a well-known, well-beloved figure even to many outside the Church. On the other hand, St. Dominic—moving from a pious childhood through a studious youth to a narrowly ecclesiastic middle-age and thence on to a theological battlefield—is little known even to Catholics. It might be said of St. Francis that his personality eclipsed the Order that he founded, whereas St. Dominic the man has been largely swamped in his own achievements, and is certainly outshone by his great son St. Thomas Aquinas, and indeed by his two daughters, St. Catherine of Siena and St. Rose of Lima. Finally, St. Francis has this distinction in the popular mind, that he preached not only to men but to birds and animals, while St. Dominic in that same mind is tarred with the brush of the Inquisition.

Yet during his life he was as much loved by his followers as the beloved beggar of Assisi, a man of charm and humility, goodness and gaiety. He was also a man of power and faith. The founding of the Dominican Order was no fortuitous collection of sympathizers, but a bold act intellectually conceived and efficiently organized in the face of many difficulties. It has carried his work down to the present day with a continuity and unity that few religious Orders have achieved. The Preaching Friars are doing the same work as they did seven hundred years ago. Conditions and methods have changed, but the work is the same—the defeat of error and the proclamation of truth by preaching, study and prayer. *Contemplata aliis tradera.*

St. Dominic came of the noble Spanish family of Guzman, and was born in the little town of Calaruega, where his parents were royal wardens. It is common knowledge that the vast majority of saints have come from what might at least be called good Christian homes. The flower on the dunghill is not unknown, but numerically it bears no relation to the flower grown in well-tended soil. St. Dominic's home was something more than that. It might even be described as sensationally Christian, for surely it is sensational for three members of a single household to have attained acknowledged sanctity. Dominic himself, the youngest, is the only canonized saint, but his mother, Jane of Aza, was beatified and her festival is kept by the Order three days after her son's. Also beatified was his brother Manes, and the eldest of the three, Anthony, though no ceremony confirmed his eternal blessedness, is known to have led a most exemplary life of sacrifice and devotion to the poor. All three brothers were priests.

In such a household a saint would make a flying start, and we are not surprised to find that little Dominic played at being a monk in much the same way as modern children play at being gangsters. He also started at an early age his life-long habit of spending at least a part of every night on the floor. He was fond of study, too, and showed remarkable abilities to his tutor and uncle, the parish priest of the neighbouring town of Gumiel. Precocious even for a time when a boy became a man some five years earlier than he does today, he was only fourteen when he went to take his arts degree at the University of Palencia.

This degree was compulsory. The medieval youth was not allowed to specialize, and for six years young Dominic must study the sevenfold "arts"—grammar, rhetoric, logic, arithmetic, geometry, music and astronomy—before passing on to his own special subject, theology. This occupied him for four more years, at the end of which his education might be considered complete. The date of his ordination is uncertain, but after the custom of his time he was performing various ecclesiastical functions for some years before it. In order to support themselves, theological students were allowed to accept benefices, and Dominic was even before his ordination a member of the Cathedral Chapter at Osma.

He was now twenty, and his life from earliest childhood had flowed in a quiet unbroken stream of study and prayer. It was to continue the same for another thirteen years. Until he was thirty-three he remained a Canon of Osma, finally attaining the dignity of sub-Prior. It was a life of complete retirement, and we know very little about it except that it was also a life of great austerity. He denied himself the accepted comforts of a bed at night and a glass of wine at his meals. On the positive side of sacrifice, he sold his library for the benefit of the poor at Palencia.

This might not seem so big a sacrifice to us today as it must have seemed to his contemporaries. We might forget that he lived some hundreds of years before the invention of printing and that his books were all inscribed by hand on hand-made parchment or the specially treated skins of animals. A book once sold could not be restored in another copy, and Dominic had bidden his cherished books farewell for ever. "But I could not bear to prize dead skins when living skins were starving and in want." After this episode it is not so surprising to hear that he twice attempted to sell *himself*. He offered to go into slavery in exchange for some wretched captive of the Moors, as was occasionally done by holy people, who offered themselves as substitutes for the fathers of families or for weaker brethren who might be tempted to apostasy. We are not told why his offer was refused, but possibly the Cathedral authorities intervened.

Shortly before his birth his mother had dreamed of her child as a little dog with a blazing torch in his mouth. His godmother also had dreamed of him, as a child with his forehead lit by a star. A torch and a star . . . both are now familiar Dominican blazons, but in the year 1203 they must have seemed merely the emotional fantasies of two women who expected too much. Dominic was good and holy and beloved by all who knew him, but he certainly had not shown himself either a burning brand or a guiding light.

Our saint is a striking instance of the falsity of the idea that a life hidden with God in the cloister necessarily unfits a man for playing his part in the world should he ever be called upon to do so. Where such unfitness is shown it is nearly always the result of defects that existed *before* the subject's retirement. Quietly as he had lived for over thirty years, Dominic had already shown himself a man of courage, and with study and prayer he had laid up an arsenal of mental and spiritual weapons that for the last eighteen years of his life were to make him a mighty warrior against the Church's enemies.

The call to battle came unexpectedly, and from an unexpected quarter, since it was in the first instance a call of romance. Few saints can have lived more remote from romance than St. Dominic, yet but for a certain royal romance, humanly speaking, there might have been no Order of Preachers. King Alfonso IX of Castile wished his son Ferdinand to marry the daughter of a certain "Lord of the Marches"—probably a Scandinavian prince, though there is nothing known certainly about him. In accordance with the procedure of his day, he sent a deputation of knights and clerics to ask for the young woman's hand. As the head of this deputation he appointed Don Diego, Bishop of Osma, who invited to accompany him the sub-Prior of his Cathedral, Canon Dominic.

It is a curious gap in our knowledge that we do not know where their journey took them or the scene of their negotiations. All we know is that their way led through France, through the territory of Languedoc, and the city of Toulouse; and it is here that what was in intention a diplomatic mission, an affair of courtiers, suddenly became something very different and a turning point not only in the life of St. Dominic but in the history of the Church.

For Toulouse was at that time the heart and hot-bed of the Albigensian heresy, that medieval version of the gnostic error which for more than half a century had been eating into the Body of Christ. Most of the principal men of the city were heretics, and the Bishop and his sub-Prior, putting up at the principal inn, found a heretic in charge and ready for dispute. Theological debates were part of the general education of the time and St. Dominic's training in rhetoric and logic must have stood him in good stead. On the other hand his adversary was well-instructed in his own errors, also eloquent and persuasive in their defence. The Canon and the innkeeper were evenly matched and spent the night in argument. But when morning came it was the Canon who had triumphed and the innkeeper who was on his knees, asking for reconciliation.

I doubt if the saint was as much surprised as the heretic. He knew too well the strength of his own side and the powers that sustained it. But I think that he was disappointed—because he could not stay and watch over the fruits of his victory. The strong man had been driven out, but his conqueror had had no time to do more than sweep the house to which with seven other devils he might return. It was hard for Dominic to ride away, to sink his triumphant memories in the chatter of courtiers and the dry shop of ecclesiastics, and for the rest of the journey his thoughts and prayers must have been with the innkeeper of Toulouse, left to prove his steadfastness in an apostate city. In his conversion the Lord's hound had, as it were, first tasted blood, and though no one yet knew it the great world-wide hunt of the *Domini Canes* had already started.

The mission was successful. The "Lord of the Marches" gave his consent to his daughter's marriage, and back the deputation came, only to set out again a short while later to escort the young bride to her new home. An unknown girl, of unknown country and parentage, is not a tool we should expect to find in the armoury of God. Yet it was through this girl that the Dominican Order came into being. All she herself did about it was to die. The records are as incomplete as ever. We do not know what caused her death, whether she suffered or whether she was mourned. But the news of it was brought to the cavalcade of knights, clerics and courtiers when it was some way on its journey. There was nothing to do but to turn back, and the company was halted and disbanded.

Though Bishop Diego had been so much and so recently away from his diocese, he does not seem to have felt any immediate call to return there, but took instead the road to Rome, still accompanied by his sub-Prior. The Bishop must have been as much struck as the Canon by the shocking state of affairs in Languedoc, for we find him bringing it into discussion with the Pope. Innocent III had some time earlier put the campaign against the Albigenses into the hands of the Cistercian Order, but the arrangement was not working well and the monks seemed powerless to stem the flood of heresy. The Pope must have been impressed by the zeal of his two Spanish visitors, for their next move, with his encouragement and blessing, was to the Cistercian headquarters at Cîteaux.

Here they found strangely opposed conditions. The religious life of the community and the beauty of the ceremonial in the monastery church were so impressive that Diego actually asked to join the Order. But the monks who had set out in bands to convert the heretics had hopelessly failed, not only because they had been outshone by their opponents in preaching and in argument, but because their manner of life—owning extensive and valuable property, and travelling comfortably with all the pomp that Canon Law allowed—compared unfavourably with the austere, self-sacrificing lives of the leading heretics.

Externally heresy varies with every generation and each new one that springs up shows a face that suggests something bright and new. But under the surface they are all akin, for all—no matter what outward form they take—are fundamentally an attack on the Incarnation. The attack may be made—as it generally is today—through a denial of Our Lord's divinity, or—as it was in St. Dominic's day—through a denial of His human nature, or it may take the form of a denial of the goodness or the reality, of the world He made and in which we live; but beneath all these denials is the same opposition of matter and Spirit, of the dualism that sees evil in corporeal substance and regards the created world as sin. Albigensianism was the direct descendant of Gnosticism, Manicheism and the more exaggerated forms of Neoplatonism, just as it was the direct ancestor of Puritanism, Theosophy and Christian Science. But its period and its setting combined to carry its teaching to logical conclusions which had been mainly ignored by its ancestors and are certainly not accepted by its descendants.

Since matter and the created world were sin, it was the duty of the sons of Light to do all in their power to bring them to an end. Hence marriage was sinful, for it led to the birth of children and the continuance of the race. On the other hand suicide was heroic and to be admired as the speediest way out of a world in which it was impossible to eat or drink or carry on business without doing the devil's work. There would be no resurrection of the body which it was a degradation for the soul to inhabit, and which Our Lord had never known, wearing only an appearance of flesh and in no physical sense born of Mary. This vile body must be treated with the greatest austerity by those who had not yet acquired the courage to destroy it altogether.

It may well be believed that these doctrines were not likely to make a popular appeal, and the flourishing condition of the heresy, which had taken possession of most of southern France and had resisted all attempts not only ecclesiastical but military to suppress it, was due to the division of its adherents into two groups—an inner circle of the Perfect who lived lives of monastic asceticism, refusing to engage in business, abjuring matrimony and denouncing in their diet not only flesh meat but eggs and cheese, and an outer ring who contented themselves with abjuring the Church and the sacraments, but otherwise lived a normal life in the world, with the added attraction that as concubinage was no more sinful than marriage they were free to indulge in it without censure.

It is interesting to note that a sect not unlike the Albigenses appeared as recently as the nineteenth century in the district of the Surrey and Sussex borders. The Cokelers, as they were called, forbade marriage to their adherents and also business for profit, while their lives were austere to the point of allowing no recreation except in prayer and religious reading. They were, however, entirely free from the antinomianism of the earlier heresy, and not a breath of scandal ever attached itself to the young farmers who, denied a wife, engaged a Cokeler "sister" to keep house for them. The sect was still in existence at the end of the first World War, but has apparently failed to survive more recent changes and catastrophes.

The Cokelers were simple and ignorant people. Not so the Albigenses, who supported their error with a weight of learning. They were fond of public disputations, in which hitherto they had had things far too much their own way, and both Canon Dominic and Bishop Diego saw that it was necessary to meet them on this ground with a better equipment than had hitherto been brought to the defence of the Church.

They had sought and obtained the approval of Rome for a new campaign against the Albigenses. The attack was to be two-fold, intellectual and ascetical. From the beginning Dominic had seen the need for this double assault. Not only must the Catholics be able to defeat the Perfect in argument, but the austerity of their lives must at least equal if it did not exceed that practised by the heretics, since even by the rank and file who lived as they chose austerity was admired as a sort of spiritual athleticism. They were like a modern football crowd, watching and applauding a game they would never attempt to play, and the Catholic side were lost unless they were able to tackle their opponents on this ground as well as on the higher levels of argument.

As for Dominic, all he had to do was to let his ordinary manner of life become public knowledge. Hitherto he had practised mortification in secret, but now the austerities he had

concealed at Osma and Palencia were openly displayed. He beat
the Perfect at fasting by living on bread and water for the whole
of Lent. He always slept on the floor—in the church if one was
available—and without a covering. For food he had little more
than bread and soup, though he would occasionally accept a
couple of eggs, never more, from charitable ladies. These
rigours he endured while living a strenuous life of preaching
and public disputations, moving from town to town in the Midi,
from Cîteaux to Servian, from Servian to Béziers, from Béziers
to Carcassone, finally setting up his headquarters at Fanjeaux.
But it was at Pruoille, some miles from Fanjeaux and a hitherto
unconquered fortress of error that he achieved the crowning act
of his warfare. For it was here that he established the
congregation of women which was eventually to become the
Dominican Second Order. The Albigenses were largely supported by women, many of whom had formed themselves into
religious societies and erected convents which they used as
schools for the dissemination of heresy. A counterblast was
needed, also a place of refuge for women who had abjured
Albigensianism and were in consequence denied the protection
of their own homes. Moved by a sudden appearance of light
over the forsaken church at Prouille, Dominic was inspired to
choose that spot—now known as the Signadou or Sign of
God—for the site of his new enterprise and here he gathered
together nine women, the first Dominican nuns.

From the first they were strictly enclosed—apart from other
considerations, their safety demanded it; nevertheless their
presence was felt in the renegade Midi. For one thing, they were
all women of birth and position, the daughters of well-known
men, and they had all been heretics, so it is natural that their
change of religion and manner of life should create something of
a stir. They were also a school to which children could be sent to
be brought up as Catholics, and a refuge for women converts
who had been turned out of their families. They wore a habit
very like that worn by the Order today, a white robe under an
outer cloak of unbleached wool. Jordan of Saxony wrote of
them: "The life they lead in this place sanctifies them and

edifies their neighbour, rejoices the angels and consoles Our Lord."

There has been some uncertainty as to the date of the foundations of the friars; but as Humbert de Romans speaks of the nuns' spiritual welfare being confided to "the friars of his Order outside the enclosure," we may gather that Dominic had established an institution more common in his day than it is in ours, that of the double monastery. This indeed is a primitive model and at one time was fairly widespread—all the Gilbertian foundations in England were double monasteries—and at Prouille the arrangement had obvious advantages. The presence of the friars was a protection to the nuns in such a hostile neighbourhood, where also there might have been difficulties in the way of their spiritual provision had no order of priests been close at hand. The friars and the nuns both had their separate convents, yet they joined in a common life under their Prior, who in this case was Dominic himself.

The Saint had now been working for four years in the country of the Midi. Bishop Diego had returned to Spain, but his former Canon and sub-Prior stayed on among the heretics. Albigensianism still flourished—indeed it was far too firmly established to be overthrown in many times four years and actually survived till the end of the following century—but some powerful inroads had been made on its strongholds and its power was shaken. The weapons used by Dominic and his Order, as well as by the now reformed Cistercians, had been entirely spiritual and intellectual—prayer, penance, preaching, informal debates and public disputations (let us keep in mind that printing had not been invented, so that the written word was not the useful weapon it became later). *Fides suadenda, non imponenda.* As if to illustrate these words of St. Bernard the friars wore rosaries dangling at their hip, where the laymen carried his sword. St. Dominic has been credited with the invention of the rosary, but all the evidence points to its existence and use at a much earlier date. The same can be said of another less approved invention alleged to be his, that is the Inquisition.

This tribunal of inquiry was already in operation as early as

1198, a period when Dominic was living quiet and unknown at Osma, so he certainly had nothing to do with its creation. Its establishment against the Albigenses followed an unfortunate sequence of events which brought (not for the first time) the secular arm and the knightly sword to settle a theological controversy. The "crusade" under Simon de Montfort (the elder) followed directly on the assassination of the Cistercian legate, Pierre de Castelnau, and led to a confused war of religion in which politics and private grudges became involved with noble causes. It resulted in a temporary triumph for Catholicism, but terrible deeds of treachery and violence were done by both sides. Dominic, caught as it were in the very heart of the fire, did all he could to abate the fury of the crusaders. This did not, however, prevent him becoming a close friend of de Montfort and helping the Catholic armies with his prayers, to which indeed their leader attributed his most notable victories. No doubt the saint was sufficiently a child of his day to believe that war could help spread the kingdom of God. Indeed in our own times clerics of all denominations have believed it could spread the cause of freedom and dethrone a tyrant without establishing, like William Blake's "Monk of Charlemagne," another tyrant in his stead.

But most certainly St. Dominic did not instigate the Catholic resort to arms, nor was he responsible for the establishment of the Inquisition. This department of the Holy Office was instituted with a view to removing the trial of heretics from the secular to the ecclesiastical courts. Heresy had always been regarded as a crime against the state, but it was suspected that certain rulers, notably the Emperor, Frederick II, had used it as a pretext for getting rid of a number of their political and personal enemies. It became necessary therefore to place these trials in the hands of men who were incorruptible judges as well as trained theologians, and the Dominican friars, who were becoming well known as preachers and debaters, seemed the very Order to be entrusted with such a reform. They were, however, by no means the only Order involved. The Franciscans also became active as inquisitors, especially in Italy. It was not till very much later that the Dominican Thomas Torquemada gave the Preaching Friars their bad name. Indeed the Inquisition in Languedoc in the early thirteenth century was a very mild affair compared with its sixteenth-century developments in Spain. The death sentence was very rarely inflicted, and punishments, while they sometimes took the form of imprisonment or sequestration, were more usually on the same lines as the penances of the early Church and of an entirely ecclesiastical nature, such as a temporary exclusion from the sacraments or the order to undertake a pilgrimage.

St. Dominic was undoubtedly for a time attached to the Inquisition in the capacity of advising theologian, but his personal warfare against heresy was carried on in a very different manner. He still engaged in verbal contests with the leading Albigenses. The popular taste was all for public debates and disputations, an intellectual version of the knightly jousts. Both the sides were mental athletes, skilled in rhetoric and logic as well as in theology. As a debater, Dominic won many triumphs—indeed he went in peril of his life, so great a danger had he become to those whose creed did not forbid assassination; he was also, we are told, a "torrential preacher." But his main work was achieved by means of his Order, by the bands of nuns and friars he was able to send out carrying the torch of truth into every cloud of darkness; and finally by the Third Order of men and women living in the world, which he founded to maintain what the friars had won and to which he gave the title of *Militia Christi*.

The constitution of the friars had brought him many difficulties. Rome had recently passed an edict forbidding new rules for religious Orders, since there were already too many of these. It was therefore necessary to choose a rule from those already existing, and Dominic no doubt was wise to base his on that of the Augustinians, which out of them all had most flexibility. The main distinction between an Order of friars and an Order of monks is the former's mobility. The life of a monk centres on his monastery, of a friar on his work, which may take him to the world's end. St. Dominic forbade his Order to possess property in the form of religious "houses"—a restriction which later conditions have necessarily modified. No doubt he remembered how greatly wealth and property had prejudiced the cause of the Cistercians in Languedoc, and his first act as a religious founder was to disperse his tiny band of followers—seventeen all told—all over Europe. It was not his wish to establish a monastery but a body of men who like himself were wanderers, preachers and debaters.

Their founder realized, however, from the start that his friars must be learned. The thirteenth-century heretic was a much more formidable antagonist than his successor today, in the sense that he was a man of wide general education (not a specialist surrounded by whole fields of ignorance) and he had a thorough knowledge of his opponent's case as well as his own. For this reason one of Dominic's first acts was to make a foundation in Paris, close to the University. Having done so, he made another at the University of Bologna; indeed throughout Europe his custom was to establish his Order at the various seats of learning. Even in England, where he did not go himself, but sent Gilbert Ash as his deputy, the Black friars made their first settlement at Oxford. He believed error has very little chance of spreading where true knowledge really exists, and indeed the story of the rise of Albigensianism is the story of the decline of theological training in the various dioceses. St. Dominic's great work was to link up once more religion and learning, and to defeat heresy not by the negative violence of repression but by the positive activity of truth.

The ignorance of our present time has associated his name with repression and bigotry. No doubt our attitude—even the attitude of Catholics—towards heresy has changed. We find it hard to picture the days when not only the clergy but the whole lay population hated and feared it. There are records of lynchings that have no parallel except in the American "deep South"—of frenzied mobs attacking gaols where heretics were incarcerated and dragging out their wretched victims to burn them alive, because they feared they might be dealt with too leniently by the ecclesiastical authorities. Tolerance is a virtue that has emerged late in human history. It has sometimes been spoken of as if it were another name for indifference, and no doubt indifference is a soil that favours its growth, or we should not find it flourishing to such an extent in the religious field, where it seems outrageous that a man should ever be called to die for his faith, though we have no scruple in putting him to death for high treason.

In the Middle Ages a heretic was regarded as a criminal from whom the public must at all costs be protected, and St. Dominic was doing a work that was not only godly but humane when he persuaded men and women that the most effectual weapons against error were not those of princes and armies but of the mind and spirit.

To this work he gave his life, not only in the figurative sense of spending the whole of it either in preparation for his mission or in its fulfilment, but in the sense that he died at a comparatively early age, worn out by his labours. When we think that in less than fifteen years he made over thirty religious foundations in different parts of Europe, when we realize the exhausting and dangerous conditions of travel at that period, and remember that throughout it all he was not only putting forth the full strength of his mind in sermons and public disputations, but also subjecting his body to constant and severe penances, we are less surprised at his dying at the age of fifty-one than that he lived so long.

He died at Bologna, where he had gone—already gravely ill—for the second general chapter of his Order. It was fitting that he should die in the midst of his work, for in his work we seem to have lost him long ago. During his life he was deeply loved, but those who loved him—unlike those who loved St. Francis—have done little to put his personality on record. When he died he was already reputed a saint, but that was no reason at all why he should be today so little known as a man. Doubtless his chroniclers are at fault—unlike many lesser characters he has not been well "presented." He lived almost entirely among ecclesiastics and it is perhaps understandable that in their records of him they should have overstressed his spiritual qualities to the exclusion of those endearing personal oddities, those precious idiosyncracies that he *must* have had or he would not have been human, and undoubtedly St. Dominic was very human, or he could not have been a saint. But only once do his biographers allow the man to look out from under the friar's cowl and that is on his deathbed.

As he lay dying at Bologna he spoke of his vow of chastity and thanked God for having preserved him in it. But then he added: "though God's grace has preserved me from all stain until this moment, I must confess that I have taken much more pleasure in conversation with young women than with old ones."

It is not much—a mere flash—but perhaps it is enough. I doubt if he would wish us to see more, for he was a man of the deepest, most retiring humility and a preacher who throughout his life was a lover of silence. He has not even given us a glimpse of his personality in a book. Many saints have bequeathed themselves to us in their writings, but St. Dominic's pen was his tongue, and his legacy to the world was the Order that he founded—one as much more valuable than books as "living skins" must always be than the "dead skins" of his original sacrifice.

His Order still carries on the work for which he started it, though its methods no doubt have changed. The Prior of Oxford is not likely to challenge the Archbishop of Canterbury or the editor of the *Daily Worker* to a public disputation, for the printed rather than the spoken word is the chief Dominican weapon in these days. Unlike the weapons of secular armies the weapons of religious warfare have become more suave, and the fight against heresy is now a constructive rather than a destructive campaign. As knowledge spreads into popular misunderstanding and specialists rashly take upon themselves to dogmatize on matters outside their own field, it will probably consist more and more in providing a plan and the "cement of faith" for that edifice which the modern world is trying to construct out of a wilderness of loose stones.

St. Francis of Assisi

1182-1226

Douglas Hyde

ST. FRANCIS was the son of a well-to-do business man who had married a daughter of an aristocratic family. The age into which he was born was one when men lived keenly, with a great zest for ideas. It was also one of successive wars and revolutions. It was an age of conflict. He was a conscript at the age of twenty, then a prisoner of war: then after his release and return to civilian life he seemed something of a playboy, who apparently succumbing to the escapist post-war mood, spent his nights in the gayest company in the town. Later, when he had worked his war-time experiences out of his system he would have to consider the question of a career, and if his parents had their way this would be in the Diplomatic Service—for what could be more suitable for a young fellow with such a background? Meanwhile he was getting all the fun he could, often in rather doubtful company, whilst nonetheless somehow succeeding in keeping his dreams and remaining clean. He was that curious mixture of rather wild, pleasure-seeking, ambition and essential decency which one finds at times in most classes, but particularly among young ex-officers who have still to settle down to normal civilian life.

That was the young Francis Bernardone early in the thirteenth century, a type perhaps more easily recognizable and nearer to our age and mood than the Francis who, to all too many of his admirers, was just a little man who lived seven centuries ago in Assisi and was temperamentally so remote from

131

his fellow men either of his day or our own, that he could spend his time preaching to the birds when he wasn't patting the head of fierce Brother Wolf.

The fact of the matter is that it is reasonable to assume that Francis Bernardone at that time felt much the same as do plenty of young men of the same age today. His experiences had been much the same: so, too, were his reactions to them. Of course the differences between his age and ours are enormous. The wars of his days were puny little affairs as compared with our world conflagrations. The social disturbances and revolutions which were such a feature of his day changed no more than the regime of some little city-state, not like that in the Russia of 1917, which changed the face of one-sixth of the world, or that in China which thirty years later brought another 400,000,000 people under similar rule.

The battle of ideas, too, was a more restricted one, kept most of the time within the limits set by the Church or, as with the fight against Islam, when it went outside them, within the confines of belief; not like that of today which is between the men of belief and those whose aim it is to erase the very memory of the name of God from the mind of man. Yet, subjectively, for the man who dragged himself bowels in hands across a lonely deserted battlefield to die under the night sky, whether it was in the Italy of the thirteenth century, the Flanders of 1914 or the Normandy of 1944, his war seemed the biggest, most important and most dreadful of all time. The man who escaped such a fate and got through the war with his skin still intact was just as surprised and relieved to find himself still alive and just as ready to go along with all the others of his age group who were also trying to forget. The p.o.w. dreamed then of home as he does today. And the men engaged in fighting the great battle of ideas felt with good reason then that upon its outcome hung the fate of Christendom, just as we know that the fate of mankind for centuries ahead is being settled in the current struggle for man's mind and soul.

In short, no matter how huge the differences between his age and ours, one can legitimately draw close parallels between how the men of his day felt about their times, and their experiences, and how men feel today. This is important if we are to attempt to understand the mind of the man who in time came to model his life so closely on that of Our Lord Himself, and if we are to judge how far his message is applicable to our own times.

The colossal change from the high-spirited, adventurous young dreamer to the saint who was destined to inspire millions over the ages, began as he was about to set out for the wars once again. And it began with a dream. Full of ideas of fame and glory, he had been equipping himself with suitable magnificence in order to join the wars, in response to the call of those seductive propagandists the troubadours. But as he slept he dreamed that someone called him, took him to a great palace, residence of a beautiful bride, and told him that it was for him and his followers. He took the dream as indicating that he would be a great prince, and, inspired by that amibition, set out next day. But again he dreamed. This time the voice challenged his proud ambitions and told him to go home and wait for the meaning of his dream to be revealed. At some point most men's material ambitions are challenged but not all men respond. Francis accepted the challenge, returned home, dropped his dreams of glory and waited.

Until then his career had seemed little different from that of many another essentially decent young man. But in recognizing the spiritual challenge when it came, and acting upon it, he showed himself to be exceptional.

Whilst he waited he became increasingly aware of the poor who were all around him. Enjoyment of his revels and his social privileges was spoiled by the beggar on the corner, the poor woman in her hovel. When his comrades noticed how he no longer shared their mood, even though he still accompanied them in their search for pleasure, they not unnaturally said "The poor chap must be in love." And to that, one day, he replied: "Yes, in truth I am thinking of taking a wife more noble and richer and beautiful than any you have seen." They sniggered, but he was thinking of the bride of his dream. Francis Bernardone was on the way to accepting the social challenge, the challenge of poverty.

In the period of spiritual anguish which followed he lost his ambition for material success, lost his pride and took on instead a great humility. He lost his love of extravagance, his desire for a costly good time. Instead, the suffering of the poor became his suffering, their wretchedness made the comfort of his own life seem obscene. He went on a pilgrimage and outside St. Peter's, in Rome, borrowed a beggar's clothes, took his place outside the church all day, and learned first-hand something of the life of the poor.

He was not the first young man suddenly to become aware of the iniquity of poverty in the midst of plenty, to be revolted by it and to change his whole way of life under its challenge. Men still do it. That is why there is a wholly disproportionate number of young men of middle-class origin in leadership of almost every Communist party in the world today. They, too, revolt at the sight of poverty, seeing their whole lives challenged by the social injustices which exist around them. But, despite all their crusading they are proud, arrogant young men. Francis was saved from becoming one of their type because when he responded to the challenge of poverty he had already accepted the spiritual challenge and had rid himself of pride. The consequence was that he did not set out to attack poverty with a sword in his hand, and hatred in his heart. He identified it as the bride of his dreams and made her his own instead. He married the Lady Poverty.

Having met the challenge of poverty in this way he did much the same with that of suffering, too. The problem of pain in a God-made world, like that of poverty, had been a stumbling block for many a sensitive man. Francis did not revolt against it. He made the pain of the sufferer his own instead. Just as his new attitude to poverty was symbolized when he took beggar's clothes for a day, lived the beggar's life, then returned to his companions at night so, too, his attitude to the suffering of mankind was symbolized when he took the appallingly disfigured leper, whose appearance had sickened his very soul, into his arms and received his kiss with joy. Indeed it was there, in the arms of the leprous beggar, compound of pain and poverty, that he plighted his troth to the lady of his dream. He had longed for chivalry and romance and he got it. It was, of course, just about as unlike what he had at one time hoped for as was possible. It happened to be God's idea of romance, not the average man's. Yet it set the heart of Francis Bernardone on fire, made his head swim and his tongue sing until years later he was known all over Christendom as God's troubadour.

Each time the voice came he responded. He believed that he was being guided by the Divine Will. So when, having on an impulse gone into a crumbling, all-but derelict church he heard the voice again, this time telling him to "go and repair my Church," he knew that that voice was the voice of God. And having answered "Gladly, Lord, will I repair it," he suddenly felt a new love for the crucified Christ such as he had never felt before.

Young men in love are not noted for their discretion. Francis was indiscreet this time, as he was by ordinary standards on so many subsequent occasions, but it was the indiscretion of the man whose head is in a whirl because he has seen a vision of God, hanging in self-accepted poverty and pain upon a man-made cross. He went off, piled some of the contents of his father's store upon his horse, sold the goods, and, for good measure his horse as well, then offered the entire proceeds to the priest, which the good man, being also a prudent one, rejected. Francis thereupon threw the money on to a window sill and left it there. But the priest accepted his request to be allowed to live with him so that he might be of service in rebuilding the premises.

There have probably been few odder ways of starting a church rebuilding fund. Certainly there has been no decision to restore a tumbledown church in a poor country parish which has had more far-reaching consequences. For the method of his first attempt at doing it, and the fury of his father when he discovered what his strange son had done, matter little as compared with the fact that when the unexpected request came he recognized whose was the voice and accepted the command as one to be obeyed.

So it was from then on. Often his actions were strange, unexpected ones. Some were of a type which, coming from another man, might seem indiscreet, eccentric, absurd, or even exhibitionist, and there were undoubtedly men who at one time or another called him all these things and more. But that was not the way the mass of those who met him came in time to think of him, nor how history remembers him either.

Looking back across the years it is difficult for us to see the Francis of that time except against the background of his sainthood. Inevitably we see his life in reverse and the saint gets in the way when we try to imagine what were his feelings and those of his erstwhile comrades at that time. What they saw was the gay, overdressed young blood of a few months before collecting with his own dirty hands the stones required for the rebuilding of first one little ruined church and then another. They saw him, dressed in the roughest clothes, associating with lepers and with beggars, and apparently enjoying the company of these derelict creatures even better than once he had enjoyed their own, for if he had sung loudly before, in the army, in jail, and at their gay parties, he sang even louder now. To us, he was obviously engaged in the imitation of the Christ, whose name both they and he bore. To most of them he seemed to have gone off his head. But not to everyone. For before long he had acquired a most unlikely pair of followers for one whose apparent eccentricities were shocking all the best people in his small home town.

One was Bernard Quintavalle, a rich and highly respectable man who, sensing the very essence of the Franciscan spirit, which was the spirit of the Gospels, sold all that he had and gave it to the poor. The other was Peter Cattano, doctor of laws and a canon of the Church, as solid in his learning and in the ecclesiastical world as was Bernard in the world of merchandise and material prosperity. Neither was of a type from which one normally expects dramatic conversions. And off the three of them went, the once gay young spark, the solid burgher and the respected canon, to build themselves a den adjoining the local leper hospital, where they could live together the lives of beggars and tend the men whom no one else dared care for. It was no wonder that the ridicule of the townsfolk from whom they begged each day, came in time to turn to wonder and then to awe, for such things are not easily explained in human terms.

After them came Brother Giles, a small farmer, who left his little piece of land to join with Francis—and for a peasant to leave his holding is as great a wrench as it is for a merchant to leave his gold.

And then, one after another, under the influence of "the itinerant minstrel of the Lord" they came, Philip the Long, Sylvester the priest, Morico the nursing brother from the leper hospital, Angelo and the rest, to be gentle knights of the Lady Poverty and to head a band which grew and grew until it became a great army of men of every type and class.

Those early days of the brotherhood were probably Francis' happiest ones. The men who came did so under the direct influence and example of Francis himself, inspired by the Gospels, knowing all, or most, of what was involved, ready to be sent to the four corners of the earth with neither purse nor scrip nor stave. Later, when their numbers had grown to scores, then hundreds, there were men who joined simply because this was the latest movement which was causing such a stir, or for whom the Franciscan spirit was something acquired only at second hand. That was why, as the years went by, it was possible for some of the Brothers to reveal by their actions that they had had only the barest understanding of what it was really all about and for things to be done by the Friars Minor, almost as a whole, in the absence of their leader, which were entirely out of harmony with all that he desired.

For him it was essential that this band of happy mendicants should be backed by as little organization as possible and no property at all. That was easy enough when they were a tiny group with pretty much of a common mind and purpose, more difficult by far when they were a force to be reckoned with in the land in which was the See of Peter itself.

In those early days they lived together in huts, built close enough together for all to be able to gather at the Portiuncula, the Chapel in the Wood, and to share the company of the little beggar man who, as they walked the roads together, sang them songs of his own composing, expressing the joy which had come to him since he had accepted the challenge of the Crucified. He talked to each one, shared with them his own treasure, infected them with his own spirit to such an extent that one of them, Brother Juniper, not content that all had already given everything they possessed to the poor, collected up their few communal possessions, including the sacred vessels themselves, and gave them away as well.

Francis' own approach to things was almost as direct and uncomplicated as that of Juniper. His purpose was to convert the world to the wisdom and the beauty which he had seen in the face of his Crucified Lord, and had seen again each time he looked into the faces of the poor and suffering. He was no organizer. Every mistake which could be made was made by Francis. Yet, so long as he was around, the inadequacy of some of his followers, the different views which they held as to the role and nature of their movement, were concealed. It was only when he left them for his missionary journeys that they began to show. Typical of his disregard for the organizational needs of the moment was the timing of his mission to convert the infidel with whom Christendom was then at war. For he made his decision just when a first serious clash between the brethren was coming to a head.

His mission to the Islamic Sultan is one of history's magnificent failures. And only a man of the spiritual calibre of Francis could make it magnificent. Undertaken by anyone else it would have seemed absurd, not only to the men of his own day but to ours as well. There was something about Francis which made magnificent everything he touched. We all know of the strange old men and women who stand in public parks with birds perched on their heads and hands. They impress few people, they influence no one. They are just seen as cranks. Francis preached to the birds, and it seems the most natural thing in the world that he should do so. We know, too, of the people who talk to their pampered pet dogs as though they were human, and they are a source of embarrassment to those who hear them. Francis could talk to Brother Wolf and his conversation has become part of the folklore of the world. George Lansbury, the British Socialist politician, set out at the end of his days, and on the eve of war, to convert Hitler, Mussolini and Stalin to his own Christian pacifism in order to stop a world conflagration, and the charitable explain away the story of that particular failure by asserting that by then the kindly old politician had taken to thinking exclusively with his heart instead of with his head.

But Francis' mission provokes neither embarrassment nor malicious mirth, for once again he had accepted a challenge which had been with men through the ages and is with us yet, the problem of war. He had met the spiritual challenge by accepting Christ as few if any others have done: he had met the challenge of Poverty by making her his own, met the challenge of pain by identifying himself with the most tormented among sufferers, courting the risk of literally joining their ranks. Now he met the challenge of war by going to the enemy, who for years had been driving at the very heart and mind of Christendom, and seeking to convert him.

The spirit which animated the best of the crusaders was epitomized in the comment of the old soldier who, hearing once again the story of the Crucifixion, declared: "Had I been there with my henchmen I would not have permitted them to crucify my Lord." Yet the grizzled old campaigner's proposed method, magnificent though the spirit was that prompted it, was not that of Our Lord. It was magnificently heroic, but the situation called for more than heroism.

Christendom today would be the stronger were there more who felt as deeply and in as uncomplicated a fashion the desire to go out and fight and, if need be to die, for their faith. Yet

Francis by his attempt to convert the Crusaders' enemy showed that he realized instinctively that the lasting answer to the threat of Islam was not the physical extermination of Mohammedans, not the breaking of their temporal power, but the conquest of their hearts and minds.

That was a hard lesson for the statesmen and the soldiers to learn. Even to attempt it on a national scale calls for a faith and a courage greater than that required for its military alternative. Today, in North Africa, where missionaries labour for a generation without a single convert, the attempt to convert Islam after seven hundred years of consolidation, is one of the most heroic and superficially unsuccessful labours of our day. But in the end the attempt had to be made. The story might have been different had there been an army of St. Francises to follow his example.

But the practical consequences at the time of Francis' actions matter least, and in one sense he failed at every turn. But his failures had about them the quality of the failures of Our Lord Himself. Each act of his asserted a principle, underlined a lesson that mankind has even yet to learn. One of the most appalling, damning commentaries on the crazy age in which we live is that all over the world today there are good men who long for war—war with all its horrors—which will liberate their lands from the enemies of Christ. Yet, in the end, it will be to the methods of Francis Bernardone that men will have to turn. The only certain way of defeating your enemy is by converting him to your side.

Nor did Francis make the mistake of thinking that the fight for the conversion of the men of his day, professing Christians and pagans alike, was simply a battle of the mind. "That which is not formed by reason cannot be destroyed by reason," said Dr. Johnson, and to that St. Francis would, one imagines, have said "Amen," for he saw that most men's "difficulties" are first of the heart rather than of the head, they are moral rather than intellectual.

That was why, though he had a profound respect for learning and for the written word, he resisted so passionately those who sought to establish Franciscan schools which would make the Friars Minor famous for centres of learning able to compete with others of the day. He did not reject study and book-learning, but he valued heart-knowledge still more in the task which he wanted his followers to perform. That was why, though he rejected the proposals for such schools, he welcomed his disciple Anthony of Padua as a kindred spirit, for his was a combination of great learning and simple faith, of eloquence and humility.

In 1224 it was granted to the man who for years had modelled his life on that of Our Lord to experience something of His passion and His death, for upon him, sealing and confirming all that he had striven to do, was conferred the honour of the stigmata. On Mount Alvernia, high up in the Apennines, after days of prayer, fasting and meditation upon the Passion, he came nearer to the love of God than even he had ever been before, and he came so near that a being like a crucified seraph seemed to hang over him. And when it had gone he found in hands, feet and side the very marks which once his Lord had borne. Francis had travelled perhaps as far as any man could travel on the road to God. He had set out dreaming of success and of the romance of wearing knightly armour. His romantic dream was realized when he was privileged to wear in his flesh the stigmata, the uniform of Calvary.

Two years later, in the Chapel in the Wood, he met his last challenge, the challenge of death. And he met it in the way that he had met all the others which had preceded it—he defeated it by conversion, by greeting that which men have most feared with the words: "Welcome, Sister Death."

Archbishop David Mathew, writing of the huge problems in mid-twentieth century Africa, recently declared: "The Catholic Church is in great need of a new St. Francis who would come to serve the Africans in their industrial setting. He would come freed from every privilege and would bring with him the charity of Christ."

That is indeed true of that continent whose fate hangs in the balance and where racial and social problems present themselves in their sharpest form. But it is also true that a new St. Francis, or many men with the spirit of St. Francis, is needed to shame the rich nations of the world into accepting responsibility to aid the poor and under-developed ones; to shame them into thinking and working along the lines of a creative Christian peace; to shame us into identifying ourselves with the wretched of the earth wherever they may be, and so freeing ourselves, as did the rich little beggar man, of every privilege that we may bring with us the charity of Christ.

St. Louis of France

1215-1270

Sir John McEwen

IT IS THE FASHION of this day and generation to pay particular honour to the peasant saint. Nor need we be ashamed of so doing. But we do well to remember that not shepherds alone, but kings also, came to the Manger, and that among the glittering company of the saints are to be found not only those who have triumphed over the temptations inherent in poverty and obscurity, but likewise those who have surmounted the no less insidious temptations which beset such as Almighty God has called to walk in the high places of this world.

Of those who have so walked King Louis IX of France remains one of the most outstanding examples of all time. He was born in 1215 and died in 1270. His life therefore spans that marvellous century of which it has been said that it saw the evolution of the most Christian society in history. This was the age in France of the guilds and the universities; of the founding of the Sorbonne; of the bridge-builders; of the first light-houses; when food-giving plants and fruit trees were imported from Spain and Sicily; when the vine was cultivated as far north as Normandy and Flanders. Above all this was the Age of Faith, when the great cathedrals began to rise. Then, as we read, "every time that great blocks of stone were drawn from the quarry the people of the country, and even those from neighbouring districts, gentry and peasants alike, had the cords attached to their arms, chests or shoulders and drew loads along like beasts of burden." And at the head of it all, ruling, inspiring and directing every effort on the part of his people, was the King himself, the pattern of all chivalry, the finest flower that the age produced.

Of what manner of man he was we have ample evidence, and even through the mists of seven hundred years he stands out as a vivid, live and captivating personality. In appearance he was tall and of a spare figure, with fair hair and blue eyes. Of a serious and determined expression in repose, his features, when he smiled, conveyed a charm and *bonté* that were irresistible. He had a liking for fine clothes, was a good horseman, and was generous to a fault. He feared God but no man, and was no great respecter of persons.

Louis IX came to the throne while he was yet a child, and his youth was spent under the tutelage of his mother, Blanche of Castile, who was Regent, a lady of strong character and great integrity. Queen Blanche has sometimes been harshly judged, but at least it can be said of her that she was a successful mother, for every one of her children grew up to be a credit to her. She was, first and foremost, pious. The story is told of a German youth, a son of St. Elizabeth of Hungary, who visited the Court. Him "the Queen kissed upon the forehead for devotion's sake, for she knew that his mother must ofttimes have kissed him there." That was her admirable side. She had another, less admirable, side to her character however. She was over-jealous and possessive as a mother. The chief sufferer from this weakness was her eldest and favourite son. When the young king married Margaret of Provence his mother did her best to see that he and his wife—they were little more than children— never met or spoke to one another all day. The only time they were allowed to meet was when they went to bed together at night. For this reason, Joinville tells us, the King ever preferred Pontoise to all his other castles as there he and his wife lived in rooms which were situated one above the other and joined by a communicating stair. On this stairway the couple would meet while their servants would give warning at the outer doors to enable the pair to be back in their several chambers by the time the Queen Mother put in an appearance.

Queen Blanche was never a popular figure in the country of her adoption. Like many another Queen of France after her she suffered in the eyes of her subjects from being a foreigner and, more particularly, a Spaniard. It was a sign of the growing sense of nationality then beginning to develop. Louis IX was the first king to call himself King of France instead of, after the hitherto prevailing Merovingian custom, King of the Franks. Which latter title, oddly enough, was to be revived six hundred years later as an isolated instance by King Louis-Philippe, in 1830. Nevertheless St. Louis was deeply attached to his mother and remained for days inconsolable when the news of her death reached him in the Holy Land in 1254. One valuable lesson at least she taught him (it was one in any case which was in keeping with the traditions of his line) which was that the Crown should look for support from the people and the bourgeoisie as against the power of the nobles. This was to remain the wise tradition of the French monarchy up to the death of Charles IV and the accession of the Valois dynasty in 1328. It was the House of Valois that, in defiance of their saintly predecessor's advice, chose to lean exclusively on the nobility for support and thus called down on their own heads the later disasters of the Hundred Years' War. During a revolt of some of the vassals of the Crown which took place in the early years of the reign, we are told that the common folk thronged round the little king as he passed, wishing him long life and victory, thus affirming the alliance between them. This lesson the King never forgot. Nor were his partners in the alliance any less faithful to it than he. Later, in 1251, when the news reached France that the King had fallen into the hands of the Infidel, bands of men, women and children—the *Pastoureaux*—rose up in the northern provinces, avowing their intention of going to his rescue and capturing Jerusalem. The fact that under ignorant leadership they fell into evil ways and had to be suppressed by force in no way detracts from the significance of the movement which they started.

The Court was patriarchal in character. It was perpetually on the move from one large monastery to another, mostly in the neighbourhood of Paris, never remaining long in any one place. From Vincennes to St. Germain, then on to Fontainebleau, Poissy, Montargis and Vernon; such was the usual round. Apart from the personal holiness of the monarch himself, the sacerdotal nature of the monarchic office was much in evidence. Nor was it for nothing that the cloister rather than the palace was the customary royal residence as can be seen from the following description of the King's daily routine of devotion: "Every day he heard his Hours with music, and a Requiem Mass without music, and then the Mass of the day or the holy day, if there fell one, with music. Every day he rested after meat on his bed. And when he had rested, the Office of the Dead was said privately in his chamber between him and one of his chaplains before he heard Vespers. At night he heard Compline." Beyond this he was tireless in seeing to the affairs of his kingdom, making known to all and sundry by word and deed his passionate desire for peace abroad with all Christian kings, and justice as between man and man for all his subjects at home. Any individual from the meanest to the greatest could bring his or her plea in person before the King. And so it is that we see him, as tradition has fondly pictured him ever since, sitting beneath the oak tree at Vincennes and administering impartial justice to his people. And if ever there was a just man it was he. "If a poor man quarrels with a rich one," he says in his famous Testament, addressed to his son, "support the poor man more than the rich, until the truth is discovered." Here is no mere courting of the common man; no precept based on flattery of the vulgar. "Until the truth is discovered": upon that discovery must all justice be based. To his brother, Charles of Anjou, he said: "There should be one king in France and one king only. Think not therefore, because you are my brother, that I shall spare you against right and justice." And, while well known for the particular love he bore to all "who serve God and His Blessed Mother," yet he did not hesitate to rebuke the representatives of the Holy Church when he considered that their conduct deserved it. Even to the Pope himself he was prepared to speak out on occasion, and in such a way moreover as left no room for misunderstanding. Yet for all his independence of mind and moral courage he was far from trusting exclusively to his own personal judgement. On the contrary, when faced with any decision of importance, he would always be most careful to consult with his advisers upon the matter beforehand; then having carefully digested their advice he would make his own opinion known, which, having been stated, was final. But it was above all his humility which forms one of his most endearing characteristics. Joinville tells of how the King, being newly come to land after his first Crusade, was offered by, and accepted from, the Abbot of Cluny the gift of two palfreys, one for himself and the other for the Queen. While making the presentation the Abbot remarked that, with his majesty's permission, he would return on the morrow and speak to the King "of his needs." The next day, the royal consent having been readily obtained, the Abbot returned and remained closeted for a goodly space of time with his sovereign.

When the Abbot had gone thence [Joinville goes on] I came to the King and said: "I would ask you, an it please you, if you have listened to the Abbot with a better grace since yesterday he gave you those two palfreys?" The King thought for a long while and then replied: "In sooth, aye." "Sire," said I, "I commend and counsel you that you forbid all your sworn councillors when you shall come into France that they take aught from those that have business to bring before you, for be you certain, an they take it, they will hear more gladly and more diligently those that have made such gifts, even as you have heard the Abbot of Cluny." Then the King summoned his Council and recounted to them forthwith what I had said to him. And they said that I had given him good counsel.

Such was the good King's nobility of mind that it would not occur to him to impute unworthy motives, but the flaw in his behaviour having been pointed out to him, such was his complete lack of vanity, that after giving it careful consideration he makes full and generous acknowledgment of the justice of his critic's remarks. God, we are told, loved King David, and it surely permissible to conjecture that He loved King Louis for very much the same reasons: for in many respects those two great kings were very much alike.

The saintly King, however, when the occasion called for it, could be severe enough. It happened, for instance, that on the voyage home from the Holy Land at the Queen's behest he sent two galleys into Pantellaria to obtain fresh fruit for the royal children. The King's ship was already past the island but no signs were there of the galleys returning, and hopes were expressed that they should hurry on and leave the galleys to their fate since, situated as they were between the unfriendly kingdoms of Sicily and Tunis, they feared for the safety of the King and his family. He, however, would not hear of it and insisted on turning back. So back they went and presently met the truant galleys on the way. They explained that six children on board had landed and had become so taken up with the delights of eating the various fruits they found on the island that they had not returned to the ship at the hour prescribed.

> Then the King ordered that for punishment they should be put in the ship's boat. But they began to cry out: "Sire, for God's sake, fine us all that we have but put us not there where thieves and murderers are put, for ever afterwards it will be a reproach to us." The Queen and the rest of us did all we could to beg them off. But to no plea would the King listen, and there they were put and remained until we came to land. Moreover [the chronicler adds] it served them right, for their gluttony did us such harm that we were delayed a good eight days because the King had the ships turned about.

It may be suspected, however, that neither the delay which they had caused him to suffer nor their sinful gluttony was the true reason of the King's severity towards these offenders. For if there was one sin more than another that he detested it was that of swearing. To him it was a form of blasphemy, and he never could abide it. "I had willingly," he once remarked, "be branded by a hot iron if by that covenant all evil swearing might be banished out of my realm." Joinville asserts that in all the twenty-two years he was in his company he never once heard the King swear "by God, or by His Holy Mother, or by the saints, but that when he was of a mind to affirm aught he would say 'Truly it was thus' and 'Truly it is so.' Nor did he ever name the Devil save it were in some book when it behoved him to name him." Another saintly leader of the nation one hundred and fifty years later, St. Joan, was to feel no less strongly on this very point than he.

The King, as has been said, was a man of peace. He would defend himself at need (and did so highly successfully at one time against the English), but as a general principle he abhorred the thought of war between Christian men. "Keep thyself from beginning war," he warned his son, "without grave deliberations, against a Christian Prince, and if wars and dissensions arise among thy subjects, make peace between them as soon as lieth in thy power." There was, however, one cause in which he held that all men should be proud to take up arms, and that was against the Infidel. It is perhaps difficult for us, looking back, to realize how passionately men felt in the Middle Ages—even the least pious of men—about the city and Holy Places of Jerusalem. The fact that they were in the hands of unbelievers was a continual challenge. It was as if every man's mother was in captivity and crying aloud to him for rescue. And St. Louis, who had seen to the placing of the sacred Relics of the Passion, purchased at a great price, within the splendid chapel he had built for their reception in Paris, was of all men most likely to feel the reproach as a slur on the very honour of Christendom. And so it was that in 1244, to mark his recovery from a serious illness, he took the Cross, and four years later, after elaborate preparation, set sail for the East.

Into the complicated details of the ensuing campaign it is not necessary to enter. Suffice it to say that a landing was effected at Damietta in Egypt in the face of a large enemy force drawn up on the shore. The noise they made with their drums and

Saracen horns was horrible to hear, the Sieur de Joinville tells us. However, in spite of their formidable appearance they were unable to withstand the French onslaught and retired inland, leaving the Damietta in the invaders' hands. After this there followed many months of intermittent warfare composed of forays and charges, in all of which the King played a leading part. Eventually, cholera and dysentery having decimated their ranks, the Crusaders were defeated at Mansourah when the King, together with all his surviving knights, was taken prisoner. He was by this time a very sick man and was treated with great harshness by his captors, who kept him in strict confinement and threatened him with torture if he would not renounce his faith. His proud and steadfast bearing in the face of such menaces and under the burden of his misfortunes became a legend throughout the Christian world and called forth even the admiration of his Saracen foes, who at least agreed to accept a sum of 250,000 crowns for the deliverance of the army, and the return of Damietta for the deliverance of the King's own person. For as he himself proudly said, "he was not of such a sort as should be bought back with gold."

All that remained of the once great host, an impoverished and fever-stricken remnant, now took to their ships and sailed up the coast as far as Acre. There they took up their quarters, fortifying the castle and the town, until such time as they should have sufficiently recovered to renew the war.

It is interesting to note that neither the failure of the expedition nor his own capture by the enemy had in any way diminished the authority or prestige which by this time had become so universally attached to the King's name. On the contrary his fame now stood higher than ever. One day, while the army lay at Acre, an Armenian pilgrimage making for Jerusalem under safe-conduct from the Saracens reached the camp. The leaders of the pilgrimage made special request that they and their followers might be allowed to see "the saintly King." The Sieur de Joinville accordingly went to the King, whom he found sitting on the ground at the entrance of his tent, and said, " 'Sire, there is without a band of many folk from

Great Armenia that are going to Jerusalem, and they pray me that I show them the saintly King: but I have no wish as yet to kiss your bones.' And the King laughed aloud and told me to go seek them; which I did. And when they had seen the King they commended him to God, and he them." That his plans should have miscarried was sad indeed; but it was the will of God. What mattered was how he had borne himself in the face of his misfortunes; and that, God be thanked, was a cause of rejoicing to all Christian men wherever they might be.

It happened about this time that a message came from France from Queen Blanche urging her son to return home, as the situation there demanded his presence. The King was sorely put to it to know what to do. On the one hand it was on his conscience that he had been away from his kingdom for so long, and he felt in duty bound to comply with his mother's wishes. In which direction also his brothers and all his Council were urging him. On the other hand, his power was daily growing and he might yet hope to achieve his heart's desire and take Jerusalem. So he called together his Council and asked them for their opinion. They all advised an immediate return to France. Two voices only were raised on the other side, and one of them was Joinville's. But the story throws so much light on the King's character that it is best told in the Seneschal's own words:

Which answer did I make, not because I would not have gone with him very willingly, but because of a saying of my cousin, the lord of Bourlemont, that he made to me when I was setting out across the seas. "You go oversea," he said; "now take heed to your coming back. For no knight, whether rich or poor, can come back without dishonour if he leave in the hands of the Saracens the meaner folk of Our Lord in whose company he set forth." The Legate now asked me, very wroth, how it could be that the King could hold the field with so few men as he had. And I answered, as if wroth likewise: "Sir, I will tell you, an it please you. They say, Sir (I know not if it be true) that the King hath not yet spent any of his own moneys, but only the moneys of the clergy. Let the

King disburse his own moneys and send beyond the seas to seek knights. And when they hear the news that the King payeth well and generously knights will come to him from all parts, whereby he may hold the field for a year, if God wills. And by his staying will the poor prisoners be delivered who have been taken captive in God's service and his, who will never come out if the King go hence." Then the King said to us: "Lords, I have hearkened to you and I will make answer to you of what it shall please me to do, in eight days from now." When he had gone thence the assault upon me began from all sides: "Now, Lord of Joinville, is the King a fool that he gave heed to thee against all the Council of the realm of France?" When the tables were laid the King had me sit next him at meat, where he used ever to have me sit if his brethren were not there. But never did he speak to me as long as the meal lasted, which was not his custom, for he used always to take notice of me while we were eating. And I thought truly that he was wroth with me for that I had said that he had not yet disbursed his moneys and that he should spend freely. As the King was hearing grace, I went to a barred window that was in an embrasure; and I put my arms through the bars and thought that if the King went back to France I would go to the Prince of Antioch (who counted me kin) until such time as another expedition should come whereby the prisoners might be set free according to the counsel that the Lord of Bourlemont had given me. At this instant the King came and leaned upon my shoulder and held me with his two hands upon my head. And I thought that I was my Lord Philip of Nemours, who had given me annoyance enow for the counsel that I had given the King, and I spake thus: "Leave me in peace, my lord Philip." But at the turning of my head the King's hand fell across my face and I knew it was he by the emerald he wore upon his finger. And he said to me: "Keep you quiet, for I would ask you how you are so bold that you, who are but a young man, didst dare to counsel my staying against all the great and wise men of France who counselled my going." "Sire," said I, "had I evil in my heart I would not advise you for aught to do it." "Say you that I should do evil were I to go?" "God help me, Sire, aye." Then he said to me: "If I stay will you stay?" And I said, "Yea, if I can, whether at mine own expense or another's." "Then be you content," said he, "for I owe you thanks for that which you counselled me. But tell no one all this week."

So he stayed for another year and more. But apart from one or two small feats of arms no great thing was accomplished. Much building of towers and ramparts was carried out at Acre, Jaffa, Sidon and other towns, and we have a glimpse of the King at one such place "carrying a hod upon his back, among the workmen, for the remission of his sins." The sort of action in a commander that Napoleon would have appreciated, although without even beginning to understand the motives which in this case prompted it.

It was probably the death of the Queen Mother in 1254, who had been acting as Regent during her son's absence, that made the King's return home imperative. In any case the following spring saw him, with the Queen and his family, once more in France. He was still a young man, but the hardships and anxieties of the past five years had told upon his health and he now looked older than his years. It was noted also "that after the King was come back from beyond the seas never again did he wear ermine or miniver, or scarlet, or gilded stirrups or spurs. His robes were of grogram or of watched cloth; the furs of his coverlets or of his robes were of wild goat or lamb." Temperate as he had been all his life in the matter of eating and drinking, his strictness in this respect became even greater. These increasing austerities were, however, of a purely personal nature and were not imposed upon the Court at large. Like the great gentleman that he was he was even prepared to abate the rigours of his own private way of life in the interest of good manners, for, we are told, "when any rich strangers ate with him he was good company to them." But ever on his conscience lay the weight of that all-important task which yet remained to be accomplished. It was to him a wholly unbearable thought that those walls which had maybe echoed his Saviour's voice, the ground that had been drenched with his Redeemer's most precious Blood, should remain alienated and in non-Christian hands. Was it possible that so plain and ringing a challenge could by any true heart be ignored? And yet he could see that so far as his councillors were concerned the prospect of taking the Cross for a second time made small enough appeal. "Tell me, Seneschal," he said sadly one day, "why it is that a man of integrity is worth more than a devout man." If he could not persuade men to go for the love of God, surely by appealing to their honour he could move them. And by one or other means move them he did. Not all, however; for the faithful Joinville excused himself on the grounds that it would be to the grave hurt and harm of his people were he once more to leave them. Of this last Crusade, he says, he can tell us nothing since, he adds with that mixture of piety and common sense that endears him as much to us as it ever did to his royal master, "I was not there, thank God." One thing yet remained to do. In case he should not return he must endeavour to indicate to his son the lines of behaviour which a Christian king ought to follow. So was written what came to be known as the Testament of St. Louis, surely one of the great Christian documents of all time.

Beau fils [it begins], the first thing is to set thine heart to love God, for without this can no man be saved. . . . It were better to fall into all manner of torments than to fall into mortal sin. . . . If God send thee adversity, receive it with patience, giving thanks to Our Lord and bethink thee that thou hast deserved it and that He will turn it to thy profit. If He give thee prosperity, thank Him for it with humility, that thou be not the worse by reason of pride. For one should not contend against God with His gifts. Confess thyself often, and choose a worthy man for thy confessor that will know how to teach thee what thou shouldst do and refrain from doing. Bear thyself also in such wise that thy confessor and thy friends also will dare to reprove thee for thy misdeeds. Hear thou the services of Holy Church with devotion and pray to God . . . especially at Mass when the sacring is done. Be tender and pitiful towards the poor, the wretched and the afflicted; comfort and help them according to thy power. Support the good customs of the realm and suppress evil. Be not a greedy ruler. Burden not the people with taxes and tolls unless it be for thy great need. . . . Take heed that thou have men of worth and loyalty about thee and speak though often with them. Let no man be so bold before thee as to speak ill of another behind his back, neither suffer any vile speech concerning God or his saints to be spoken in thy presence. Be thou righteous and steady with thy people, turning neither to the right hand nor to the left. If thou holdest aught that is another's . . . if the matter be certain, restore it without delay. . . . Give the benefices of Holy Church to men of virtue. . . . Keep thyself from beginning war . . . but if it behoveth thee to do it, protect Holy Church and those that have done naught wrong therein. . . . Be diligent to have good judges. . . . Take heed that the expenses of thy household be within measure. . . . And finally, most sweet son, have thou Masses sung for my soul and prayer made throughout thy realm, and grant me an especial and open part in all thy good deeds that thou shalt do. . . .

In face of this Testament, as one historian has justly observed, the civic wisdom of the ancients, from Solon to Marcus Aurelius, fades; for these are words of one who through experience of faith and hope has won to peace and to the possession of that charity which is greater even than they.

All was therefore now in order, and in the early summer of the year 1270 the King left France for the last time. They set sail from Aigues-Mortes and at Tunis, for reasons that still remain obscure, the army disembarked and laid siege to Carthage. Within a week or so of landing, plague broke out in the ranks of the besiegers. The King's health was in any case precarious. For many months past he had been too weak to mount a horse, while the jolting involved in travelling in a cart was almost more than his strength could stand. It is not surprising therefore that he fell an early victim to the epidemic. The end was not long delayed. He received the Last Sacraments and was able to repeat the alternate verses of the penitential psalms as the priest recited them. In the midst of his sufferings he was heard to call many times on St. James, and also upon St. Denis and St. Geneviève whom, as protectors of his country, he would naturally hold in special devotion. Shortly before the end he asked to be laid on a bed of ashes on the ground; and so, with his hands folded peacefully upon his breast, he died. Some say that at the last moment, raising up his eyes, he said in a loud voice, "Hierusalem! Hierusalem! ecce ascendimus"; that is, "Jerusalem! Jerusalem! behold, let us go up thither." And it may well be so: for what more likely than that a vision of the New Jerusalem, a greater and holier than that which he had aspired to win, should have been granted to him in foretaste of that Heaven towards which his eyes had, all his life long, been turned.

St. Catherine of Siena

1347-1380

Alice Curtayne

NOT TO BE ACQUAINTED with this saint is to miss a fascinating personality in Christian history, one of the greatest figures of the fourteenth century and certainly the foremost woman of her own day. Six volumes of her letters and one strange mystical book, *The Dialogue,* have come down to us, forming a significant contribution to medieval classical literature. She succeeded in bringing to an end a supreme crisis in Christian history by actually guiding the Church out of it in a personal intervention.

Born in 1347, her name in life was Catherine Benincasa. Her father was a wool-dyer and she was one of the younger members of a very large family. The old-time hagiologists were bemused by the convention that their subject had to provide a contrast between either humble birth and nobility of soul, or else noble birth and humility of character. The *via media* did not fit into the conventional opening to a career in holiness, so Catherine came to be ranked as of humble birth. In actual fact her father was able to maintain his large family in the kind of comfort we nowadays associate with middle class, slightly upper. He owned the large house in which he lived and the workshops in which he ruled over a number of apprentices; he also had a farm and vineyard outside the city. He was a man of standing and good repute among his fellows. Not to be of aristocratic birth was an advantage rather than otherwise in the social thought of his environment. When his children were growing up, the

Commune of Siena had been living under the People's rule for nearly seventy years. Under the rule of the Nine, from which nobles were excluded and which lasted for sixty-three years, Siena reached her peak period of prosperity and glory. It was the People's day. Catherine was born into the class that ruled the city. In the succeeding government by the Twelve, a brother of hers was one of the Twelve Governors of the Commune and was invested with the resounding title of *Magnificent Lord, Defender of the People.*

True, in the light of her achievements, her status does appear humble. Who was she to give advice to the crowned heads of Europe? There is no human explanation of why they should have sought it from her. Speaking again from the human point of view, she was a person of no account to take the guidance of the Church into her daring hands in a passionate affirmation of its divine origin. It is doubtful whether noble birth, or wealth, or great material influence could qualify her for such an action, but anyhow she had none of them. She had not even maturity, or that wisdom commonly said to be the fruit of age and experience.

After a childhood normal in every respect except for a tale of one vision, she became a solitary at the age of sixteen. Even among the saints, she is immensely singular in this isolation. In the vital formative years, without the help of either a spiritual director, or community life, she trained herself in asceticism until she could live on a spoonful of herbs a day and a couple of hours' sleep at night. She acquired self-mastery by living thus in entire seclusion in her own room for three years. True, she was a Dominican tertiary but this was no help to her at the beginning, except for the convenience and protection of a religious dress. The spiritual foundation of her amazing career was laid in those years of solitude during which she never went out except to go to the nearby Dominican church and she never spoke to anyone except her confessor. He was a young, inexperienced priest to whom she was a huge embarrassment and who was afterwards emphatic in saying that he was completely incompetent to guide her. He expended much spiritual energy in trying to hold her back, to persuade her to take the "normal" way of girls of her age and time.

The greatest opposition to the life she had chosen came from her own family and especially from her mother, Monna Lapa: a hardworking woman, a great wife and mother, who coped most successfully with her very large family, giving them a great example of energy and industry. When obedience was reluctant, she compelled it in shrewish outbursts and violent language. To a woman of her practical common sense, Catherine was just a problem; the girl's craving for solitude just another of the troublesome "vapours" of adolescence in which Monna Lapa was certainly experienced. She considered it her first duty as a mother to restore Catherine to normality. She took her away for a course of curative spa water; arranged a most advantageous marriage for her; expostulated, cajoled, caressed; pursued her with food; and insisted on sleeping with her when she discovered this strange business of "vigil." She also tried the usual family expedient of pinning the troublesome daughter to an endless succession of household chores and, when Catherine still held out, she punished her heavily.

The rest of the family supported Monna Lapa in the view that if Catherine would not obey in this matter of a "good" marriage, which would help them all, she should take herself off to a convent. Surely it should be either marriage or the cloister? But Catherine was equally opposed to both courses. She would not surrender her freedom. Against all opposition, she clung to her self-imposed solitude until she was nineteen. Then, much against her own will, but under divine direction, she returned to family life, took her share in the work of the home and began to do voluntary nursing in the city hospitals.

Immediately Siena became aware of her and, in a matter of months, she became so heavily involved in ecclesiastical and communal affairs that the reader will have to forgive a digression into history in order to explain her action. Before she was a year old, Europe had been overwhelmed in a terrible catastrophe, the epidemic disease called the Black Death. Among other effects, it had badly shaken the external organisation of the Church by sweeping off thousands of priests and religious. In order to carry on the sacramental life of the Church, new candidates for the priesthood had been hastily recruited and ordained without the usual careful selection and training. Twenty years later, the evil results of this expediency were only too evident in the corruption among clergy and laity, from which even the Papal Court was not immune. There was general agreement on the need for reform, but there was also a serious obstacle in its way.

The Church appeared to have lost her independence, because the Papacy was then resident in Avignon for sixty-five years with the exception of one little inconsiderable interlude. The fact that the Papacy was under the control of France was a continual exasperation to the rest of Christendom. Just as the need for reform was self-evident, so was the truth that effective reform would have to begin with the restoration of the Papacy to Rome. Dante with passionate invective and Petrarch in milder cadences had implored it. All the *élite* in Christendom concurred that this was the first essential move towards a new life.

But the time had begun to lend its sanction to the Avignon captivity. The whole shape of contemporary affairs seemed set against even the hope of bringing it to an end. The reigning Pope and the majority of the Cardinals were Frenchmen who preferred to live in their native country. They looked on the Romans as barbarians. The Church was heavily in debt to the French king, who was determined to keep the Papacy in Avignon as a matter of French prestige. Financial considerations also kept the Head of the Church chained to Avignon. The transfer of the luxurious and imposing Papal Court would be a costly business. Then again ecclesiastical Rome was in ruins, its spiritual significance wellnigh forgotten. As a detail, there were cattle grazing around the altar of St. John Lateran's. The renovation of the churches alone would cost prohibitive sums. France would not finance it. There was complete public apathy.

Returning to Catherine, she now began to fill the role of leader among a growing circle of followers, who were a motley band of men and women, anxious to serve her devotedly in return for what she could teach them about the true Christian way of life. They wrote letters at her dictation, provided the parchment and found couriers, undertook works of charity under her direction and tried to spend some time with her every day. The plain people of Siena did not care for this novelty, especially in the quarter where Catherine lived. Here, they said in effect, was Monna Lapa's daughter, a kind of a nun, said to be holy, yet who went about freely with numbers of young men, who were in and out of her house at all hours of the day. Whoever heard of such a novelty? Holy people did not live like that; they led a retired life. So they nicknamed her derisively "The Queen of Fontebranda"; and the young men, whom they averred she had bemused, they called the *Caterinati*. This was the *soubriquet* thrown after them when they passed through the streets.

Indeed they had many names. Catherine lovingly called them her Family. Their own humorous epithet for themselves was the *bella brigata*. Jeers did not succeed in dispersing them and public disapproval did not even cloud their gaiety. Ecclesiastical history has rewarded this strange club with the noble title, *School of Mystics*.

The group included university students like Neri, a young poet then enjoying considerable fame in his native city. He was skilful in taking down her rapid dictation and was an efficient secretary. Later, he brought to the circle his friend and admirer, Francesco Malavolti, member of one of the five great Sienese families. He was a social celebrity with beautiful manners, but a worldling whose conversation always turned on women, horses and falcons.

When Malavolti first called at the Benincasa home, he was divided between pity for Neri, who he thought had fallen under some strange delusion, and contempt for himself in visiting such a place. As they walked through the streets, he kept saying to himself: "If she preaches to me about the soul . . . and as for Confession! She'll get her answer from me." When they entered Fontebranda, which was the district where tanners and dyers plied their trade, he stiffened at the contrast between his own gorgeous person and his prosaic surroundings. Glancing around him disdainfully, he sniffed with fastidious repugnance the acrid, pungent odour of tanned hides spread out in the sun to dry. But when he confronted Catherine, all the smart things he had ready to say died away on his lips. Such a trembling seized him that he almost fainted. When she spoke, he underwent such a change of heart that he hastened to Confession and immediately re-ordered his ways. True, he had occasional lapses afterwards, but in the main he succeeded in keeping his life oriented towards God. Henceforth, nothing amused him more than to see other people going through his own experience. There was always scope for plenty of fun of this kind in the *bella brigata*.

His boon companions did not let him escape from them without a struggle. There were two of them especially ribald at his expense, both of them having shared in his former episodes of gallantry. Whenever this pair sighted him on the street after his conversion, they bore down on him to abuse Catherine, and they had blistering tongues. One day they stung him to such effect that he challenged them to meet her, saying: "If it has no effect on you, I promise to go back with you to the old life. But I know that the moment you see her, you will be converted and go to Confession." "Confession!" Their howls of derision startled the street. "Why Christ Himself couldn't do that!" But of course they'd meet her and they'd tell her . . . Malavolti walked between them, listening to a flood of indecencies. He led them in and quietly murmured their names, waiting for the promised crash of verbal assault. But no word came. They stood there like stockfish, their mouths open, staring at Catherine. She took the initiative and energetically reproached them for what they had been saying on the way. (Who, in God's name, could have told her such a thing?) The gallants reddened; then, to their own disgust, the tears fell from their eyes. "Tell us what to do," they sobbed. "Just tell us what you want us to do." Catherine turned to Malavolti: "Take them to Confession," she said. He led them up the hill to St. Dominic's.

There were some people of every rank and age in that group. Solid personages like Ser Cristofano di Gano Guidini were a foil to the young and giddy. Cristofano was a notary from a little village outside Siena, practical and level-headed, somewhat older than the other men. He had wanted to be a monk, but he had been obliged to remain with a widowed mother of whom he was the sole support. His way of approaching marriage was a joke among the younger men. He had no less than three damsels in mind whom he considered suitable and he wrote out their advantages at some length and then asked Catherine to help him choose! At first, she waved aside the request with the plea that she did not know any of the three ladies. But when he persisted, she indicated a name. In the end he married someone else. Perhaps all three on the first list had refused him!

There was even an Englishman in the group, a monk named William Flete, who was a famous controversialist and ascetic. The only drink he ever took was water "flavoured" with vinegar. He had permission to leave his monastery every morning for a retreat in the woods where he spent the day in meditation and writing. Once he complained to Catherine because the Prior asked him to say Mass now and again for the community. He thought this a great hardship. She told him roundly that he should say Mass every day for the community if that was the Prior's wish and she went on to reprove the scholar for what she called his "ignorance": she pointed out that he was lacking in compassion and was far too self-centred and too harsh in his judgment of others.

The circle also included Sano di Maco, an influential merchant; Fr. Santi, an aged hermit; Simone da Cortona, a young novice; Andrea Vanni, the artist; Stefano Maconi, a soldier, who became one of her most devoted disciples; many women from among the Dominican tertiaries and several priests. Most interesting in its diversity, the group was distinguished by a charming camaraderie. There was little elegance in these assemblies, for they had to accustom their noses to the reek from the tanners' yards and sessions were always open to interruption from the explosive energy and shrewish tongue of Monna Lapa. But on the other hand, they were delightfully free from the stuffiness and worldly intrigue characteristic of the later literary *salons*, which were mainly intent on providing a platform for every unworthy carpet-bagger of half-baked philosophies.

Catherine in the midst of the *bella brigata* certainly succeeded in making holiness attractive. She was typically Sienese in her gaiety, that quality which distinguishes her compatriots from among the Italians even to the present day. The possessor of torrential emotions, she kept them in perfect control. She had complete contempt for convention, but profoundly respected asceticism. Compassionate towards all humanity, it is clear that she was accessible to everyone, condescending even to the fool and the bore, yet it has to be added that even to her most intimate friends she remained tantalisingly elusive. Outspoken, volubly eloquent, with a blasting power of invective, she had reserves too that no one could penetrate. She never once, for instance, committed herself to a description of her visions: "It would be like proffering mud in place of gold" was her defence of this silence.

During those years of her early apostolate in her own city, Catherine was the occasion of many spectacular conversions. One of the best known is the case of Niccolò di Toldo. The Communes of Siena and Perugia had been at war in 1358 and relations between the two powers had been strained for twenty years. Niccolò di Toldo was a young Perugian aristocrat who, at a public banquet in Siena, had made a contemptuous reference to the Sienese Government. For this he was arrested and condemned to death. There was commotion in the city over the severity of the punishment, considered too extreme even by the Sienese. The Perugian Papal Legate intervened on behalf of his misguided young compatriot, but in vain. The Government's answer to the numerous petitions for a reprieve was that they had to protect themselves.

As for the unfortunate young man, first he raged powerlessly in his dungeon and then he despaired. When hope of a reprieve had to be abandoned, several priests visited Niccolò to help him to prepare for death, but he threw them out with fierce blasphemies and even assaulted one of them. Finally, appeal was made to Catherine, who went at once to the prison. She managed to persuade Niccolò to go to Confession and Communion. Later she told the whole story in one of the best-known of her epistles, written to a priest friend:

I went to visit him of whom you know; whereby he was so comforted and consoled that he confessed and prepared himself right well. And he made me promise for the love of God that, when the time of execution came, I would be with him. And so I promised and did. Then, in the morning, before the bell tolled, I went to him and he was very glad. I took him to hear Mass and he received Holy Communion for the last time. His will was attuned and subject to the will of God and there alone remained a fear of not being brave at the last moment. . . . He said to me: "Stay with me and do not leave me. Thus I cannot be other than well and I die content." And he laid his head upon my breast. Then desire increased in my soul and, aware of his fear, I said: "Be comforted, sweet brother, for soon we shall come to the nuptials. You shall go there, bathed in the Blood of the Son of God, in the sweet name of Jesus, which must never leave your memory. And I will be waiting for you at the place of execution." Just think, Father, his heart then lost all fear, his face was transfigured from sorrow to joy. He rejoiced, exulted and said: "Whence comes so much grace to me that the sweetness of my soul will await me at the holy place of execution?" You see what light he had received when he called the scaffold holy! He said: "I will go there all joyous and strong and it will seem a thousand years to me before I reach it, when I think that you are waiting for me there." And he spoke so sweetly about God's goodness that I could scarcely bear it.

I waited for him therefore at the place of execution . . . in continual prayer and in the presence of Mary and Catherine, virgin and martyr. I besought Mary for the grace that he might have light and peace of heart at the last moment and that I might see him safe in God. My soul became then so filled with the sweet promise made to me that I could see no one, although there was a great crowd there.

Then he came, like a meek lamb and, seeing me, he laughed. He asked me to make the Sign of the Cross for him. I did so and said, "Up to the nuptials, sweet brother, for you are soon to be in everlasting life." He knelt down with great meekness and I stretched out his neck and bent down over him, reminding him of the Blood of the Lamb. His lips said: *Jesus, Catherine.* So saying, I received his head into my hands, closing my eyes in the Divine Goodness and saying, "I will."

Then I saw God-and-Man, as one sees the splendour of the sun, receiving that soul in the fire of His divine charity. Oh, how ineffably sweet it was to see the goodness of God! With what gentleness and love He waited for that soul as it left the body. . . .

But Niccolò did a gracious act that would draw a thousand hearts. And I do not wonder at it; because he already tasted the divine sweetness. He turned back like a new bride who has reached the threshold of her home, who looks round and bows to those accompanying her, showing her gratitude by that sign.

Having had the reply, my soul reposed in peace and quiet, in such fragrance of blood that I could not bear to have removed from my garments the blood that had fallen on them. Wretched and miserable, I remained on earth with the greatest envy.

Returning now to the tangle of Italian and French politics, Italy was in a ferment of growing unrest and disorder. The Communes were ruled by French Papal Legates, who misgoverned them because they did not understand the people's needs. In 1375, Florence declared war on the Church and incited the other Italian Communes to join her in throwing off French dominion in the peninsula. Ten days later, no less than eighty other towns had joined the Tuscan League. Once more the redemption of the Papacy from its Babylonian Captivity in Avignon was loudly urged as Italy's only hope of peace.

The reigning Pope Gregory XI was well known to be in favour of restoring the Papacy to Rome. Created cardinal at the age of eighteen and elected Pope at forty, his career in the Church had been brilliant. He was ordained priest only the day before he was crowned Pope. Scholarly, with poor health, in appearance he was small, slim and pallid. A good man, but not firm, he was aware of his own irresolution and he varied it with moods of obstinacy which were a trial to the Curia.

Catherine had already been in correspondence with Gregory XI before the war with Florence had broken out. She had had evidence that her words carried weight with the Head of the Church. Her letters to Gregory XI are among the most amazing documents in Christian history: she addresses him as *Dear little Babbo* and then tells him to be a man! His belief that it was his duty to return to Rome was as well known as his indecisiveness. When he wrote conciliatory messages to the Italians and told them that it was his intention to go to them so as "to live and die among the Romans," no one took him seriously. He had already said this so often that repetition had destroyed its effect. As conditions deteriorated in Italy, Catherine now tried by letter to strengthen his wavering will and persuade him to carry into action the purpose he had so often expressed.

The Dominican Order in Italy considered Catherine their responsibility because she was a tertiary who publicly wore the habit. When she was twenty-seven, they appointed as her official director, Fr. Raymond, one of the most trusted members of the province. He was a man of great learning, prudence and judgment, experienced and skilful in the direction of souls. Although he does not seem to have been fully convinced of Catherine's divine mission until after her death, nevertheless he was immeasurably generous in helping her.

The combination was providential. To Catherine it was the end of her soul's isolation. Hitherto she had been a solitary, acting without any human guidance. Despite her School of

Mystics and the fascination she exercised on her friends, she had had from them no really effective collaboration. Now, under Fr. Raymond's wise direction, she became tenfold more effective. It is impossible to imagine her succeeding without his aid in the main achievement of her life.

The Dominicans had tried to oppose the activities of the Tuscan League by preaching peace. Fr. Raymond went to Florence on this mission. The Florentine rulers suggested that he should go to the Pope in Catherine's name and prepare the way for their ambassadors who would follow with overtures for peace. Fr. Raymond readily agreed and set out at once for Avignon. Nevertheless, the subsequent Florentine embassy failed. Catherine then sent Neri to Avignon with another letter, appealing for peace. She wrote also to the Governors of Florence, offering to negotiate between them and the Pope. Their answer was to invite her to Florence for a conference. At the conclusion of this, she agreed to go to Avignon in their name and plead with the Pope on behalf of their ambassadors, who would follow her in a matter of days.

Accordingly Catherine set out for Avignon in the third week of May 1376, accompanied by the leading members of her Family, twenty-three in number, including four priests. Fr. Raymond, who had remained in Avignon, received the little company and presented Catherine to the Pope on 20 June. It was a happy interview. Gregory fully agreed that the restoration of the Holy See to Rome was the first step towards real peace in Italy. He said he would go to Rome in September and that meanwhile he would be glad to leave in her hands the negotiations for peace with Florence.

But the Florentines did not keep their word about sending ambassadors immediately. Day after day, week after week went by in an atmosphere of suspense. The enforced delay gave Catherine a useful insight into the atmosphere of the Papal Court, in which Frenchmen predominated, and of the Pope's difficulties. Avignon was at this time the centre of Christian civilisation and culture: a beautiful, gay city, its air always full of joyful ringing of church bells, but overcrowded and, like all cosmopolitan cities, corrupt. Petrarch described it as a "Shameless Babylon, bereft of all virtue, centre of grief and wrongdoing." "Stinking" was Catherine's forceful description of its social life.

Finally, in the middle of July, the long-awaited envoys from Florence reached Avignon. Catherine eagerly sent for them, but they curtly replied that they had received no mandate to treat with her, but only with the Pope. She then bitterly realised that she had just been made the dupe of politicians, who had merely used her to gain time. But the envoys' interview with the Pope was a failure and they went away again, having accomplished nothing.

Catherine held her ground. She now knew that she had been brought to this city for a purpose greater than peace with the Tuscan League, whose cause she forthwith abandoned. She began to concentrate on strengthening the Pope's wavering resolution. Since her repudiation by the Florentine ambassadors, she had become an object of derision in the public eye. The Curia were coldly hostile. The fashionable ladies, who counted for too much at court, tended to mob her out of vulgar curiosity, even crowding into the private chapel and surrounding her when she received Holy Communion. At one of those demonstrations, Lady Elys de Turenne, wife of a nephew of the Pope, feigned great devotion and stooped over Catherine's feet, which, under cover of her cloak, she stabbed viciously with a stiletto to test the veracity of the ecstasy. The feet did not even twitch and she went off in disgust. But later, when Catherine returned to consciousness, she found she could not walk and it was only then her companions discovered her wounds.

Another day three pompous prelates of the Curia came to her, armed with the Pope's permission to examine her in doctrine. Their manner was very offensive, one of their first questions being: "Couldn't the Florentines find a man to send instead of a wretched little woman like you?" Their interrogation, which lasted the whole day, bore as much on politics as on theology. When they went away, they said glumly that they had found no error. But the Pope's physician admitted to one of Catherine's friends afterwards that the visit had a sinister purpose and that if the experts had not found her solidly grounded in doctrine, her journey might have turned out most unfortunate.

Encouraged by her persuasion, the Pope sent to Italy a number of officials to prepare the way for the journey. Every detail had to be pre-arranged, including the reception that would meet him when he disembarked on Italian soil. Immediately the struggle of wills closed in around the delicate Pontiff to become the bitterest and strangest in history. It was as though the cosmic forces had issued from the camps of good and evil to engage in battle over Avignon. Catherine found herself almost alone against the opposing forces: the Pope's family to whom his human affections were closely bound; the secular might of France; the whole Sacred College.

France spoke when the King's brother, Louis, Duke of Anjou, arrived in Avignon, everyone knew to what purpose. But when this prince met Catherine, he promptly succumbed to her irresistible charm. He invited her to his castle at Villeneuve to meet his wife and Catherine became their guest for three days. She succeeded in persuading Louis that it was in the best interests of France that Gregory should return to Rome.

The Curia were a more difficult proposition. The French cardinals marshalled every argument that human ingenuity could think of in favour of remaining in Avignon. They exaggerated the dangers of the war with the Tuscan League; almost welcomed the rumours of new taxes imposed on the clergy in Florence; urged on Gregory the example of his predecessors who never acted against the advice of his brother cardinals. They had certain news of a plot to kill the Pope *en route*. An anonymous saint wrote to them from Italy revealing that poison was waiting for His Holiness on the tables in Rome and that he would be safer among the Saracens. "It was no saint wrote that," said Catherine, "but a disciple of the devil who lives not far from here."

She wrote almost daily letters to the Pope, trying to stiffen his resolution. She pointed out that the Cardinals were just playing on his fears and implored him again to be a man. Her urgent advice was to use what she called "a holy deceit" so as to escape from the anguish and travail; that is, he should pretend to postpone the day of departure and then go suddenly, without warning. She asked for a final audience and once more heartened him to take the step which his conscience told him should be taken and which he really desired with all his heart to take. When he was a Cardinal, he had so clearly seen the need for it, he had made a secret vow that if ever he were elected Pope, he would restore the Papacy to Rome. No human being knew of his vow, but Catherine told him that God had revealed it to her. It was naturally a powerful argument with the Pope. He was now Pope for seven years and still he had not fulfilled his vow. Catherine urged on him, too, that he had so often publicly announced he was going to Rome, not to keep his promise would bring ridicule on himself and on the Church.

Gregory followed her advice in the matter of secrecy. Pale and shaken, he walked down the staircase of his home in Avignon for the last time on 13 September, 1376. He was torn by conflicting emotions. The secret had been well kept; even the spies in his household did not find out until that morning. They alerted the Pope's family, who hastened to the Palace, loudly lamenting. The Pope's father, Count William de Beaufort, an old man, came running to the door, imploring his son not to go. He was firmly put aside and he then flung himself across the threshold, saying his son should not leave save over his grey hairs. Quoting the verse, "Thou shalt trample upon the asp and the basilisk," the Pope stepped across his father's prostrate body. Then the mule that was being held in readiness for him to mount, shied, backed, and finally could not be made to move. Another mule had to be brought, while murmurs arose from the mournful knot of people who had gathered to look on. But at last Gregory managed to get on board the boat which was to take him down the Rhône to Marseilles, where the Papal fleet awaited him.

Catherine and her company left Avignon the same day, travelling by land to Genoa. "Mysterious and very fruitful" was her summary of her sojourn in Avignon. The Pope made his triumphant entry into Rome on the following 16 January. He found himself the unwilling ruler of a turbulent city divided into factions. The difficulties of his life in Rome were greater than his worst fears had anticipated and at first he became unfriendly towards Catherine because she had seemed to make so light of them. After some months, however, his letters became friendly again. Peace with the Tuscan League did not immediately follow the move to Rome. Once again Catherine left Siena to negotiate this peace in Florence. While there, she heard of the Pope's illness. His health steadily declined in Rome, where the difficulties of his new life took a heavy toll of his frail physique. He did not live to see peace between the Church and the Tuscan League. Actually it was his successor who succeeded in concluding this peace.

The Conclave that followed Gregory's death was very unruly. The Roman populace made no secret of the fact that they had to have an Italian Pope, preferably a Roman one. They threatened darkly what might happen if their wishes were not respected. Eventually the Neapolitan Urban VI was elected. He began with a zeal for reform that made the Papal Court most uncomfortable. Within a matter of weeks after his election, the ten French cardinals openly expressed regret that they had elected him. It was common knowledge that there was a serious breach between the Pope and the Sacred College. In May, the French Cardinals removed to the summer residence of Anagni, where they conferred on how the Pope could be deposed. Secretly encouraged by the French King and sure of the protection of the Emperor Charles V, they issued a statement on the following 9 August that the Holy See was vacant and the Archbishop of Bari an intruder, whom they had only pretended to elect in order to save their lives from the Roman mob. Urban's reply was to nominate twenty-three new cardinals. The Frenchmen then went into Conclave and elected a rival Pope, who had previously given his promise that he would live in Avignon. Thus began the Great Western Schism which lasted for seventy years and proved the most fiery ordeal through which the Church ever had to pass. No human institution could have survived such a testing.

Catherine was overwhelmed in grief. Her sense of responsibility now turned life into a nightmare from which she was never to emerge. "Better a Pope in exile than two Popes" was the current contemporary verdict. After six hundred years, it is easy to see the justice of her action, but the people of her time could not see it. She wrote to Urban, offering her life and the lives of her friends in the cause of truth. Foreseeing that she would be called to Rome, she began to set her affairs in order. She was convinced that this was her final departure from Siena and that she would never again see her native city.

She believed that it was her duty to leave to the world some account of her mystical creed and this she now tried to incorporate in her book, *The Dialogue,* which purported to be a dialogue between God and the Christian soul. The writing of this book was an astonishing performance. Catherine dictated to three secretaries, who took turns at writing. In this way she finished it in four days, during which she herself took no rest. She made no plan of the book, but it shaped itself into sections as she went on. It has always held an honoured place among the great works of mysticism and it continues to be translated and re-edited in all the languages of the modern world.

It was only finished when the expected summons came to Rome. She set out at once with four of her fellow tertiaries, three priests and three laymen. It was agreed that the rest of the Fellowship would follow later, as soon as they could arrange to get away. The new Pope had tremendous confidence in Catherine's help because her name had now become so powerful in the counsels of Europe. He received her willingly and saw her frequently in the ensuing months.

Catherine now began what was to prove her final battle with the forces of evil. She sent out her flaming letters all over Christendom, imploring help for the Head of the Church and telling the truth about his election. She told the Italian Cardinals who had broken away from him that they could wash from head to foot in the tears and sweat that were poured out for them. Despite her heroic efforts, however, the position deteriorated month after month. Every diocese was soon divided on the issue, every parish, even every religious community. The best minds, even the holiest, in the Church could not discern the truth.

One of the worst obstacles to unity was the Pope's own character, which was harshly intolerant, gloomy and choleric. Catherine counselled him to surround himself with holy men who would advise him. She suggested names, many of which were members of her Family and to each of them the Pope sent a formal summons to Rome.

During the ensuing weeks, when the replies came filtering in, Catherine had to suffer probably the acutest disillusionment in her life because nearly all of them refused! One of them was detained in Siena by the whims of his patrician mother; another said he could not possibly pray in Rome, where he would lose all unction. Another hinted that those who had accompanied Catherine really had promotion in mind! Others made vague, long-term promises. Others got out of their difficulty by complete silence. And these were her *diletti figli,* her Family, on whose spiritual training she had generously spent herself. It has to be added that all of them achieved great things afterwards in their lives, but the Schism found them quite unprepared. They either became panic-stricken, or they totally failed to grasp the seriousness of the situation. At any rate they gave Catherine no help in her time of greatest need.

Even Fr. Raymond was disappointing. An extremely important mission had been entrusted to him twice in succession: a personal embassy to the King of France. And twice he had dilly-dallied at the frontier, enlarging on the physical danger of going further. This time Catherine had no patience with his reasoning. She wrote to him:

> If you could not have walked there, you could have crawled; if you could not have gone as a friar, you could have gone as a pilgrim; if you had no money, you could have begged your way there. . . .

The recurrent theme of her letters now is the phrase *I am living in agony*.

The New Year of 1380 was a time of great apprehension in Rome. There were daily rumours of plots to kill the Pope, or of a revolution against him both within and outside the city. Catherine felt that she was struggling physically with demons. It was in defeat that she revealed what she truly was. Daily she renewed the offering of her life for the unity of the Church and for peace. Her rapid and fiery dictation, which had been such a thrilling experience for her secretaries, now slowed into an inaudible murmur, punctuated by gasps of pain. On the third Sunday of Lent, while praying in St. Peter's, she got a stroke and had to be carried home. After prolonged and mysterious suffering, she died three weeks later at the age of thirty-three. Monna Lapa, now, too, clothed in the habit of a Dominican tertiary and her daughter's most devoted disciple, was beside Catherine at the end. The tomb selected was underneath the high altar in the Dominican church of Santa Maria sopra Minerva. Later on, Catherine's head was removed and taken to Siena, where it is enshrined in the Dominican church. She was canonised eighty-one years after her death.

St. Peter Claver

1580-1654

Katharine Chorley

WHEN I WAS A CHILD I was given a book about the saints called *In God's Garden*. The cover had a picture of St. Christopher with his staff and the tiny boy on his shoulder, and inside I read how St. Christopher, not having the gift of prayer, had dedicated himself to carrying travellers across a bridgeless stream, and how on one occasion he had carried a child whose weight in mid-stream suddenly grew intolerable. But the saint struggled across with his burden and on the far shore he learned that in his charity and courage he had given safe passage to God Himself. And I read how St. Martin of Tours divided his cloak with the beggar and later in a vision saw Christ wearing that identical half of the soldier's cloak. And I read further how St. Francis conversed with the birds and how St. Gregory the Great made a pun about certain English slave-boys which fixed them in my imagination along with those improbable children whose hands were always clean, who brushed their teeth voluntarily and who never answered back.

The result of all this was that for long enough my conception of sanctity was limited to sweetness of character and, in action, pity and kindness to those weaker than oneself. The saint in fact was a kind of holy Boy Scout, and the idea was somehow emphasised by the sentimental title of my book.

When I was asked to contribute "a saint" to this series my mind ranged through those about whom I might like to try to write, yet all the time like a swinging compass needle it came back to rest pointing at St. Peter Claver. And the reason I found was quite simple, for I realised suddenly that a couple of pages about Peter Claver, read years ago in Sir Arnold Lunn's exchange of letters with C.E.M. Joad published as *Is Christianity True?*, had exploded once and for all the boy scout or Tennysonian idea of sanctity—riding about redressing human wrongs and wearing the white flower of a blameless life. Yet oddly enough, on a surface view, this St. Peter Claver appeared as the very type of saint whose holiness is exemplified in acts of charity since thirty-eight years of his working life from 1616 onwards had been spent at Cartagena in ministering under appalling conditions to the negro victims of the African slave trade. How did it come about that in reading a few paragraphs about this particular saint I had come to perceive, dimly and yet imperatively, an altogether different, deeper and more complicated meaning in sanctity?

In her interesting and illuminating book *The Further Journey*, Mrs. Rosalind Murray has studied and contrasted the differences between the Catholic and the humanist scale of values. But there are some saints whose sanctity seems to operate in modes that are easily acceptable to the humanist. Their "heroic virtue" appears to coincide with values which he admires, values which are roughly equivalent of the boy scout-Tennysonian ideal. Thus every Englishman, whatever his creed or lack of creed, acclaims St. Thomas More; because St. Thomas More belongs to the great company of men and women of every creed and loyalty and belief who have preferred to be killed rather than betray their loyalties or give the lie to their beliefs. Moreover, St. Thomas was a statesman, a family man, and lived as the head of a highly cultivated household and circle; his private asceticisms and austerities and the intensity of his devotional life do not impinge upon the casual observer. And he did not court martyrdom; he held on so long as he could consistently with his integrity and when the decision that meant martyrdom had to be faced he made it only after a severe spiritual struggle. A psycho-analyst seeking to explain the sufferings of the saints in terms of his science could never convict him of masochism. But if we consider, say, St. Ignatius of Antioch, who also was martyred for his Faith, things become more difficult. Something is more obviously added to what we may call natural heroism—the psycho-analyst excusably catches a scent upon the breeze. For when Trajan arrested St. Ignatius in Antioch and ordered that he should be taken in chains to Rome for exposure in the Colosseum, the saint wrote to the Roman Christians imploring them to do nothing to prevent his giving his life for Christ: "Encourage the wild beasts rather so that they may become my tomb and leave nothing of my body. . ." And when we come to the mode of sanctity of such saints as St. Benedict Joseph Labre or St. Margaret Mary Alacoque things become very difficult indeed. The psycho-analyst is sure he has found his quarry and the humanist is completely baffled by a scale of values so wildly at variance with his own. Indeed, the Catholic may feel occasionally baffled too for, as Mrs. Murray has shown, humanist values are so much a part and in many cases so fine a part of our Western thinking and feeling that it is extremely difficult to stand aside and compare them detachedly.

In many ways St. Peter Claver was in this sense a difficult saint because, twisted inextricably into the pattern of his charity and love and of his private spiritual life, there are strands which seem on a humanist scale of values to be distortions or unhealthy exaggerations. And yet the sanctity belongs to the total pattern; we can alter nothing, discard nothing.

His life stands out in contrast against nineteenth and twentieth century cherished assumptions. He ministered as an individual to individuals, healing souls and bodies, giving himself utterly, and loving these slaves of his with a self-regardless love born of his consuming love of God. Yet he took the slave trade as he found it and it does not appear that he ever raised his voice against its iniquity as a system and certainly he is not to be found in the very small band of his contemporaries and immediate predecessors such as Cardinal Ximenes and Pope Leo X who believed, far ahead of the social ideas of their time, that slavery, at any rate the African slave trade, ought to be reformed or abolished altogether. His senior on the salve mission at Cartagena, Fr. de Sandoval, who wrote a book entitled *De Instauranda Ethiopicum Salute* for which he had collected from slave-traders and slaves a mass of factual and statistical information, may well have contributed far more than Claver towards educating opinion against slavery. He seems almost a modern figure, standing alongside Wilberforce and Clarkson. But the Church in her wisdom has raised Claver and not de Sandoval to her altars.

The slave ships came in to Cartagena and discharged a putrescent, half-dead swarm of black humanity—men, women and children who had been confined for two months in quarters where they scarcely had space to move, reeking with the accumulated filth of their voyage and with the stench of untended septic sores, bowel affections, all kinds of disease. De Sandoval's mission was to meet the slave ships and bring what comfort he could, physical, mental and spiritual to the newly landed slaves. It is recorded of Sandoval that "when he received notice of the arrival of a negro vessel he was covered instantly with a cold and death-like sweat at the recollection of what he had endured on the last occasion; nor did the experience and practice of years ever accustom him to it." But of Claver it is told that when news came of a slave ship sighted off Cartagena his face seemed to light up with a kind of radiant joy. This makes us uncomfortable. We can sympathise with de Sandoval's human shrinking and admire the iron will which enabled him to fulfil his duty of charity in spite of it, but Claver's "radiant joy" in face of the bitter suffering of other men disconcerts us. The bewildering challenge of sanctity to all the instincts and accepted values of humanism is involved.

Peter Claver was a Spaniard from Catalonia. He was born on a farm among the southern foothills of the Pyrenees at a small place called Verdu not far from Solsona. But though his parents were farming and relatively poor they came of ancient lineage and there was an uncle who held a rich canonry at Solsona. Peter's mother had in her own mind dedicated this son to the

Church from his early boyhood. Without in the last tainting this intention with a smear of hypocrisy, she had no doubt as time went on introduced the rich canon into her imaginative schemes for Peter. Indeed, the canon had already offered to educate the boy, but Peter's father considered that he needed the rough and tumble fellowship of school life and sent him to the Jesuit school at Barcelona. Evidently, he was shy and diffident about himself. All his life he would hate publicity though often his actions and, as a young man, his intellectual gifts inevitably drew upon him the attention of others. His school career suggested that he had the makings of a fine scholar, and the parents might legitimately have expected that their son would find not only holiness but also, sponsored by his uncle, a distinguished future as a secular priest. They would follow his career with thankfulness and pride and he would be available to watch over them in their old age. If this was the pattern of their dreams for Peter it was rudely disturbed when he asked their permission to become a Jesuit novice. They gave their consent ungrudgingly, a proof surely of both their spiritual loyalty and understanding—a climate of faith which had environed Peter since babyhood and which must have had its influence in forming his own spirituality. The parents' picture of the future was expunged for good when Peter was accepted as a missionary to the Indies and sailed for Cartagena in 1610. He was twenty-nine, and both he and they knew that he would never see them again.

The years before Peter embarked for America had been spent first in the Jesuit noviciate at Tarragona, then at Parma in Majorca where the Jesuit College of Montesione had recently been founded, finally at Barcelona where he studied and taught theology. At Montesione he had done his philosophy and in spite of his nervousness had come brilliantly through the ordeal of defending in a public debate the theses he had studied. But, more vital for his future development, he had met and come under the influence of Alphonso Rodriguez, the elderly gate-keeper at the College, a lay-brother whose *total* love for and trust in God expressed itself in ways of astonishing and naive childlikeness.

It may be [Fr. Martindale has written], that old men of this type—I will not say the complete expression of the type, like Alphonso—are not so seldom to be met with in the ranks of lay brothers of religious Orders. Perhaps anyone who has lived in a larger house of some such Order—a house of studies, for example—will remember more than one of these gentle old men, full of profound spiritual insight expressing itself often in acts of the most pathetic childlikeness or downright childishness. And such encounters come, I would dare to say, with a sweetness singularly refreshing to a mind in danger of sophistication, for the moment, by too much metaphysic or jaded at any rate by intellectual drudgeries. *Non in dialectica.* . . . .

This was the man to whom Claver turned with a spontaneous sympathy for his personal spiritual formation.

There was in Peter himself a definite streak of this same childlikeness and it may well be that he first sought Alphonso's company as a relief from the intellectual tension of his philosophical studies. Certainly he was not an "intellectual." His brain was a good instrument which he could use to cope brilliantly with philosophy or theology, but there is nothing in his life to suggest that his heart or the deeper levels of his mind were committed in these studies. He completed his theological course in America and then was told to sit for the most exacting examination of the Society. Protesting, he asked: "Is so much theology necessary in order to be able to receive ordination and baptise a few poor negroes?" This was in 1615; the following year the standard triennial report on his general progress was handed to the Jesuit Provincial. He was described as of "average intelligence, judgment below the average, little prudence and little experience." Reading of his life during his first five or six years in America it is easy to see how the hard-bitten Jesuits of the colony could have been tricked into thinking that his strange mixture of apparently incurable diffidence, childlikeness and intellectual achievement almost in spite of himself, betrayed a lack of common sense and other necessary qualities.

Old Alphonso and young Peter became intimate friends and the friendship was evidently considered good for Peter by his superiors since they even allotted a special time when he and Alphonso could meet and talk without interference. Alphonso had been a business man until he was forty when, his wife and children being all dead, he had entered the Society as a lay-brother. Despite his childlikeness he was a forceful character and also with his experience of the world behind him no doubt a shrewd judge of men. He discerned the latent quality in Peter, the steel that could be tempered, the great reservoir of his soul which was being slowly and steadily filled with spiritual strength and power. His own imagination had been fired by the Indies Mission and he determined that Peter should carry into action the zeal which he himself could only use in prayer and penance. "How many souls in America," he said, "might be sent to heaven by priests who are idle in Europe. The riches of those countries are prized, whilst the people are despised. Savage as these men may seem, they are diamonds, unpolished it is true, but whose beauty will repay the lapidary's skill. If the glory of God's house concerns you, go to the Indies...." And he urged the young man to volunteer rather than wait until he might be sent under obedience by his superiors: "Beg, urge, entreat of them to send you; reiterated entreaties are not contrary to obedience when there is reason to believe that the superior demurs only to try our constancy." He was of course not thinking then in terms of a mission to the African slaves but rather to the native Indians.

Peter's imagination took fire in its turn from Alphonso's, and as soon as he was back at Barcelona after completing his philosophy, he petitioned to go to the Indies. His Provincial temporised and told him in the meantime to stick to his theology. Two years later, Peter urgently repeated his request, and now permission was granted. Fr. Mexia, who was to lead the group of young missionaries, asked that he should be ordained before leaving Spain since bishops were rarely available in the Indies. A resurgent wave of his natural self-mistrust suddenly overmastered him and he begged—successfully—that his ordination might be put off. He landed at Cartagena with his priesthood still to come, and was sent on to the Jesuit College at Santa Fé. The College was unfinished and under-staffed—it was not until 1612 that a proper complement of professors arrived from Spain—and Claver's comrades were already priests for whom there was ample work in the town. So he was given the menial jobs of the community and for more than a year he rang the changes as porter, sacristan, sick-nurse and cook. He was so happy with these tasks that he asked his Superior to allow him to continue as a lay-brother for always. Pious biography ascribes this request to his incredible humility, but it will deepen our final estimate and admiration of Claver's character if we allow that here probably was another instance of his self-mistrust this time leading him into veritable escapism— an example of the kind of shrinking which long ago had determined his father to send him to school instead of to a private tutor. In the years to follow, for the sake of his life-work among the negroes, he would learn to distinguish humility from escapism and gloriously overcome this defect of temperament. Peter's Superior refused his request and entered him among the students of theology no doubt on the recommendation of a Father recently arrived from Barcelona who had known him in the old days as one of his ablest pupils. It was at the end of this course that he was judged worthy to be professed of the four vows though the actual profession only took place in 1622, put off perhaps by his own protestations that he could not sustain the honour. He had indeed written to the General in 1618 asking to remain without any degree of profession in the Company. Perhaps the reply gave him a final criterion by which to disentangle humility from self-mistrust: "It is good to be humble, but you should with indifference await the decision on your case by the Company; that way lies the will of God."

But already he was learning to shoulder the responsibilities for which he was destined. At Santa Fe the priesthood had again been proposed to him and he again asked for a respite, but towards the end of 1615 he left Santa Fé for the Jesuit house in Cartagena and in December of that year he was ordained subdeacon, deacon two months later and finally priest in March 1616. The humility which was so marked a trait of his spiritual character could now grow to perfection untainted by any admixture of self-mistrust. There was the occasion of a learned discussion when Fr. Claver intervened with an opinion and was rudely brushed aside by a disputant who told him to keep quiet because he was the veriest ignoramus without even a knowledge of Latin. Those who knew his past flared up in his defence, but he implored them to say nothing: "What does it matter," he said to his friends, "whether one is taken for a learned man or a fool; it is of far more importance that one should be humble and obedient." There was the occasion when an influential Spanish lady came to Mass in a costume which Fr. Claver deemed indecent. His words to her were plain and to the point. The lady lost her temper and turned on him with raised voice. At the sound of the unseemly row the sacristan came running followed by the Rector of the College who immediately blamed Claver for creating a scene by his indiscretion and imprudence. Peter fell on his knees and implored his Superior to punish him as he deserved. He made no attempt to defend himself by explaining the position.

These two stories have been chosen out of many because they instance his humility outside the context of his special work. Inside one's work occasions may arise when it is a duty to defend oneself for the sake of the work. In the interests of his mission Claver showed that he could fearlessly contest the decisions of his Superiors, clearsightedly and without confusion with his personal humbleness. He had, for example, begun after a time to acquire slaves for himself, having found by experience that this was the only way in which he could have ready at hand a team of interpreters to deal efficiently with the shiploads of slaves as they came in. At first he had done the best he could with slaves lent to him by friends or hired for a few hours. Talk of Fr. Claver's slaves reached the ears of the Jesuit Provincial who not unnaturally took alarm at this curious acquisition of property by one of the Fathers. In July 1626, Claver referred the dispute to Rome and demanded a definite ruling from the

General, Fr. Vitelleschi, the same who had reproved him for misdirected humility eight years before. Two years later the answer came:

> I am edified by the holy zeal your Reverence has displayed in this work for Our Lord and I ask you urgently to carry on your work with the same fervour and the same fine ardour; I trust that Our Lord Himself will reward you for it. I am informing the Fr. Provincial that your eight or nine black interpreters are not to be sold or bartered or otherwise taken from you since they are essential to the fulfilment of your mission.

Clearly, Claver must have put this case with confidence and ability and perhaps eight years previously the General had already recognised the intrinsic quality, not yet fully released and realised, of the man he was dealing with.

There was too the strange little incident at an execution. Part of the work he had made for himself was to visit and comfort in prison slaves who had been arrested for running away, for theft or other crimes. He would try privately to get malicious charges withdrawn and if there were the chance of successful defence in the courts he would persuade the best advocates in the town to defend his slaves without a fee. But where no defence was possible the punishment was death and Claver would then accompany the prisoner to the gibbet, having confessed him and won his trust, supporting him body and soul till the noose tightened. On one such occasion the rope broke and the condemned man dropped at Claver's feet. He comforted him once more, took him in his arms and then himself passed a new rope round the man's neck: "But this is irregular," cried a priest who was looking on at the scene. "He has taken part in an execution!" Claver was momentarily abashed. Then, collecting himself he said: "If I can save a soul at the price of an irregularity, so much the better. But no, such an action can't be irregular." The rope broke again, and once more Claver, knowing the peace that his tender hands would bring to the tortured man, fitted a third rope.

When Claver came to America he naturally supposed that his work would develop amongst the native Indians, and indeed during his first winter he went once or twice on mission into the interior. But after his ordination he was made assistant to de Sandoval, and when the latter was recalled to Lima at the end of 1616 he was left in sole charge of the mission to the slaves.

We can hardly begin to assess the spiritual quality of his work without a sustained and often painful effort of the imagination. In the first place, we have to reconstruct the conditions. Cartagena was a busy seaport and city run by rich Spaniards whose interest would be allied with the exploiters of mines and plantations in the interior for which the bulk of the slaves were destined. The stringent and amazingly enlightened laws promulgated in Spain for the protection of native Indians from slavery and forced labour—a response largely to the protests and representations made by Las Casas and his supporters—had resulted in a shortage of labour, and this was the real genesis of the large-scale African slave trade. Slaves were imported to man the mines and plantations which could not be adequately worked by the protected native labour. It is a strange irony of history that this was the indirect result of Las Casas' defence of the Indians.

The traditional theory on which the African slave trade was justified argued that it was permissible for a man to be enslaved who had been captured in a just war or who had committed certain crimes in his own land. Theoretically, the African slaves were ex-prisoners of war or criminals sold to the slavers by their own princes. But given the dimensions of the trade, it is obvious that in practice no one on either side of the Atlantic enquired into the antecedents of the slaves—no one that is except such rare men as de Sandoval who had the vision to transcend the sociology of their time. Indeed, there is extant a fascinating correspondence between de Sandoval and a Portuguese Jesuit in Angola on this very point. The Jesuit's reply to de Sandoval's honest scruples is a masterpiece of casuistry in the cant sense of the term. Churchmen like him salved their consciences by pointing out that even if free men were sometimes caught in the slave net yet their souls would benefit as they would have a chance of becoming Christians on arrival in America. Others, traders, planters and mine managers doubtless salved theirs by pointing out the practical impossibility of investigation once the slaves had been shipped. In favour of the governments of the Spanish colonies it has to be said that the laws regulating the relations of masters and slaves after the latter were settled were far more humane than those, *e.g.*, of the English plantations in Jamaica. It is as well for Englishmen to remember this. The slaves were not regarded as chattels. They had defined rights to which they could appeal, at least theoretically if not always in practice, in a court of law. The sadist had to amuse himself in private. In Jamaica he had the free public run of the island. The worst practical features of the system were the enforced exile and the appalling months' long voyage across the Atlantic.

The conditions of the voyage scarcely altered throughout the seventeenth and eighteenth centuries, and there is a particularly clear description of them in the testimony of an English captain of a slaver given at an enquiry in Liverpool in 1790, when a bill was before Parliament for a more humane regulation of the trade. According to this man, every slave whatever his size had only five feet six inches in length and sixteen inches in breadth to lie in. The floor below deck was covered with bodies stowed or packed according to this allowance. But between floor and deck there were often platforms or broad shelves in the mid-way which were covered with bodies also. The height from the floor to ceiling seldom exceeded five feet eight inches, and in some cases it did not exceed four feet. The men were chained two and two together by their hands and feet and were chained also by means of ring-bolts which were fastened to the deck. They were confined in this manner at least all the time they remained upon the coast, which was from six weeks to six months as it might happen. Their allowance consisted of one pint of water a day to each person, and they were fed twice a day with yams and horse-beans. After meals they jumped up and down in their irons for exercise. This was so necessary for their health that they were whipped if they refused to do it. They were usually fifteen or sixteen hours below deck out of the twenty-four. In rainy weather they could not be brought up for two or three days together. The mortality, taking thirty-five voyages, was approximately six per cent, exclusive of those who died after landing. But one man had lost a third of his sailors on his last voyage and also a third of his slaves.

This account scarcely varies in essentials from that given by James Barbot, a supercargo who sailed to the Congo in a slaver in 1700. About the same date a Dutch captain of a slaver made a comparison between his own (relatively) hygienic and humane methods of stowing slaves with the filthy and cruel usage of the French, English and Portuguese. There are, too, lists extant of the mortality on various voyages and the causes to which death is attributed. It is obvious from the ostensible causes listed that in almost every case misery and the terrible conditions of the slave's quarters were the real cause.

The survivors were the wrecks of humanity to whom Peter Claver ministered, winning them back to trustfulness and a semblance of human dignity by unfailing patience and an outpouring—there is no other word—of charity and love. Charity and love are abstract words; Claver made them concrete when he appeared with his baskets of provisions and fruit—delicacies which he never touched himself. There is a story that once a brother offered him a bunch of grapes which he refused but seeing the brother's chagrin he accepted two or three single grapes. He was asked whether the flavour was not finer than that of the previous year and replied that really he could not know since he had not tasted a grape since he left Spain. He made charity and love concrete too when he went among the sick tending their frightful suppurating sores, lending his cloak to one regardless of the infection when he must take it again, kissing the wounds of another in order to prove the reality of his brotherhood with these abandoned children of God. But it is not to be thought that he lacked a certain decent natural repugnance. A rich ship-owner had a slave who was so disgustingly disfigured by ulcers that he had been left to die in a squalid hole where no one could see him. Claver was called and the Spaniard watched from a distance to see what would happen. Horrified, retching with sudden nausea, Claver flinched and drew back. Then, ashamed of what he regarded as an evil cowardice in himself, he fled away and flogged himself. Returning, he fell on his knees beside the dying man, leant close to him, consoled him, lingered beside him and passed his tongue over the septic sores. After nearly three and a half centuries, we cannot even read the last part of this story without a rising nausea, a feeling that the saint was violating a natural decency. We are up once more against the terrible challenge of sanctity, the ruthless flail of an all-consuming love of God which can scatter our values to the four winds. We can call the saint's action a pathological aberration, but the explanation is too glib. It does not dispose of the searching challenge. If we try to face the challenge we begin to realise that for Claver it was a vital immediate fact that this man was made in God's image. For him to shy away was equivalent to shrinking from God Himself—and he made the most extreme reparation he could. Perhaps more than anything else we have to realise the annihilating immediacy of the impact of God on a saint like Claver.

Claver's primary duty was of course the healing of souls. The slave ships were quarantined when they docked because of the frequent epidemics on board, but Claver had special permit to visit them. After his death, the Rector of the College at Cartagena, charged with initiating the process for his canonisation, took the deposition of a Don Francis de Cavellero, an ex-captain of slavers.

> In 1628 [said this man], I was making port at Cartagena when a violent outbreak of small-pox swept my crew and the blacks I had on board. The situation was desperate and I asked for confessors to absolve the dying and if necessary baptise them. The stench which rises from below decks from a slave-ship is choking. I had perfume burnt in the hold where the slaves were crowded together. I received Fr.

Claver and, apologising for the revolting task which awaited him, I took him below. From a distance I watched him on his knees beside the sick hearing their confessions; without a thought for the risk of infection he went from one to another with a smile on his lips, comforting them, embracing them, baptising the pagans, leaving them deeply moved by so much goodness. I confess that I had not expected this marvel of charity. Every time that I met him after that, I felt as it were annihilated in his presence, convinced that sanctity could be carried no further.

It may seem strange that a captain of slavers could combine his barbarous job with this just and sincere appreciation of sanctity; his testimony gains the more weight by the contrast. It may seem strange too that Claver himself appears to have met these men without indignation or reproof though his anger flared when he found his black converts misbehaving themselves in the town in ways he specially detested, drunkenness, blasphemy and the obscene dance orgies of Africa to which occasionally they reverted. But though he never apparently questioned the system or the morality of a career made by running it, yet he protected at his own peril individual blacks from exploitation. The girl slaves, for instance, were too easily at the mercy of young Spaniards made vicious by a life of lonely luxury. Claver would rescue them whenever he could and for protection marry them off to one of their fellow negroes. More than once the balked young men ambushed him in the street and attacked him with daggers ready to stab.

When the slaves disembarked, they were herded into sheds for a few days before being sold up-country or re-shipped to ports along the coast. This short waiting period was all that Claver had for his main work of evangelisation. But there was nothing hasty or slipshod in his procedure and never a hint of forced conversions. De Sandoval, scandalised by what he had heard of the mass baptisms on the Guinea coast when shiploads of bewildered slaves were rushed wholesale into the Church without a word of instruction and without having signified their assent, had worked out a technique of instruction before he was recalled to Lima. No negro was baptised by him except willingly and after he had made it clear that he understood the rudiments of the Christian Faith—enough for his prayers and to direct his life by. Methodically, Claver developed de Sandoval's plan. Through his interpreters and using pictures and his crucifix he gave a simple forthright instruction on the *Credo* and then on the Commandments. He taught them simple prayers and invocations. He distributed rosaries made from a local berry. Only when he was satisfied that a negro understood the basic meaning of the Faith would he proceed to baptism. He concentrated on two themes; the loving fatherhood of God with the redeeming sufferings of Christ and their own sure welcome into the Christian brotherhood if they tried to live by its precepts. Pictures drove home his words. On the right side of the painting there would be groups of finely dressed smiling blacks, on the left naked pest-ridden bodies surrounded by snarling wild beasts. "Here," he would say, "you have those who have been faithful to the grace of their baptism, there you have those who have refused baptism or who have betrayed it. Thus you will be happy or miserable throughout eternity." A crude simplification of reward and punishment? Perhaps. But the talk on love and fatherhood had preceded it, and Claver knew the stops he must use in order to draw out the genuine spiritual capacity of his primitive hearers. Indeed, his own strain of simplicity, like a spontaneous child's drawing, naive but essentially true, may have enabled him to get inside their minds where another, as fervent but more sophisticated, would have failed. Yet he must have been capable of sophisticated argument too, for one of his converts was an Anglican archdeacon! This man, a chaplain, was interned at Cartagena along with a batch of English raiders. Claver met him and they talked at length in Latin. Weeks later the archdeacon lay dying in hospital and sent for Claver to receive him into the Church. It is said that after their chaplain's conversion and death, six hundred of the English prisoners eventually asked for instruction and were received.

After a few days of instruction Claver had to bid his blacks good-bye, but first those of whom he was most certain had heard Mass and received communion.

In the off-season when no slave ships could cross the Atlantic, Claver made long journeys into the hills of the interior to visit his slaves distributed now in the mines and the cotton and coffee plantations. Much had to be packed into these rapid visits; there would be marriages to solemnise, children to baptise, endless confessions to hear. And left for months to themselves, some of his converts would understandably have fallen back into the old pagan ways of their past, or they had got muddled and forgotten parts of his teaching. Patiently, he talked to them and instructed them over again and then, with the slaves crowding round him to wish him a desolated *au revoir,* he would courteously thank the master of the place for his hospitality and the time off he had allowed his slaves and move away on the next stage of his journey.

In 1650, after one of these journeys, perhaps a specially gruelling one for he was already an old man of seventy, he came back exhausted to Cartagena which was in the grip of a particularly savage outbreak of plague. At once he was off to tend the sick. But after thirty-five years during which he had passed unscathed through hotbeds of infection he caught the disease, evidence perhaps that his mission was fulfilled, so gravely that he was given the Last Sacraments. He recovered, but never again to find the full use of his limbs. A shaking in hands and legs prevented him from saying Mass. And now he was given a grimly ironic opportunity to practice that humility which already seemed perfect, to others if not to himself. Gonzalez, a lay-brother who had been with him throughout his missionary life and had watched over him with a complete devotion, on one occasion defending him with well-planted fists from a couple of thugs hired to beat him up by an amiable Spanish lady whom he had offended, was called away to help man the plague-decimated ranks of the Jesuits in the town. The saint was left to the care of a clumsy dirty and brutal negro who would not bother himself with the duties of a sick-room, forgot his meals, forgot to support him while he was dressing so that often he would fall and bruise himself. Gonzalez, indignant, wanted to report the negro. "Let it be, brother," was the reply. "I am used to Joachim now, he does not suit me too badly." "But, Fr. Claver, he is horribly lazy and so rough with you." "Oh, brother, my sins deserve worse than him."

And then, one day, Gonzalez brought him a book which had recently appeared. It was the Life of his old spiritual master, Alphonso Rodriguez. Perhaps it was the one gift for himself that Claver had ever willingly received. He clasped it to his breast beaming with joy. "Tell me," said Gonzalez, "is it true that one day when you were talking of the Trinity, you both fell into an ecstasy?" "It is true of Brother Alphonso." Physical humility, moral humility, intellectual humility, spiritual humility—he had climbed each rung in the ladder, taught and tempered in the secrecy of his private devotional life.

Yet enough is known of it for our pondering. He made a point of keeping his nights undisturbed, but only so that he might sleep for some four hours and then spend the remainder of his privacy in prayer and the practise of physical austerities. He had learned almost to do without physical nourishment and rest. Since his student days at Santa Fé and for a short time immediately after at Tunja in the mountains, where he had been sent apparently to recuperate from some unspecified illness, he had never known the relief from living at tension which is the most precious part of leisure. But he refused to cut short his one opportunity for spiritual nourishment and recuperation. One of his rectors who was also his penitent used sometimes to burst into his cell at night. "I beg of you," he said, "to choose another priest or another time to make your confession. Leave me the night."

We know relatively little about his private prayer except that it was fertilised and ripened through his devotion to Our Lady as the Mother of Divine Love, a devotion which he had first learned from St. Alphonso Rodriguez whose book of prayers and precepts he carried with him all his life and treasured as his most precious possession. Without this living sweetening warmth in his spiritual life it is possible that his harsh penances could have bound instead of suppling the sinews of his soul. Indeed, his terrible flagellations—he used a tarred rope studded with nails—seem to make him fair game for our hypothetical psycho-analyst. But we can show that he used them with the whole of his conscious mind as training for his soul and to unite himself in love with the sufferings of Christ. And we can point to the results. Muscle-bound pietists or psycho-neurotics do not spend their lives like St. Peter Claver.

Claver lingered on for four years after his partial recovery from the plague. In the town they spoke of his illness: "It is a great misfortune, but at least he is alive, he is there, he is praying for us, he loves us and thinks about us." Many others besides Don Francis Cavellero realised that they had a saint living amongst them and we have to imagine ourselves into the collective mind of that richly turbulent town to understand what such a realisation meant to those who had it. In 1654, however, Fr. de Farina arrived from Spain to take over the mission to the negroes. Claver was overjoyed. It was his soldier's discharge and he announced it quite casually to his friend and penitent Isabella d'Urbina: "Our Lord has been good enough to promise that I shall die on Our Lady's birthday."

His death-bed presented a strange scene. When the news got into the city, the locked gates of the College were stoven in by a tumultuous crowd of men, women and children who pushed their way up to his room and there knelt by his bedside praying, or shouldered and jostled for the few objects that they could take away and treasure as relics. Above his bed there was a portrait of Rodriguez. Someone, Gonzalez perhaps, defended it with his fists so that Claver might have to the last the picture of the man whom he had loved and revered more than any other human being. An unedifying scene by our reserved standards and yet a spontaneous and genuine witness of the place he had won in the heart of the scarcely tamed city, of the place he would win more than two hundred years later in the heart of the Universal Church.

It is the unconscious function of a saint like Peter Claver to force us out of our snug accustomed humanist values, in order that we may at least try, humbly and candidly, to understand his naked spiritual values.

St. Benedict Joseph Labre

1748-1783

Hugh Ross Williamson

ST. BENEDICT JOSEPH LABRE is not so popular that a general knowledge of his life can be taken for granted or so *simpatico* that the choice of him as a "favourite" saint might be assumed. At the outset, therefore, it may be permissible simply to state that the choice has been dictated by the belief that he was, in a unique way, a significant figure both for his own eighteenth century and for ours; and to quote the epitome of his life from *The Book of Saints*: "He came of a family of shopkeepers in easy circumstances and was educated by an uncle, a priest. He tried without success to join the Trappists. Then he found his vocation as a pilgrim-beggar, tramping from shrine to shrine throughout Europe, living on alms and spending long hours before the Blessed Sacrament. He died in Rome during Holy Week."

He was born in 1748, eight years before Mozart who, like him, died at the age of thirty-five. The saint and the genius were thus contemporaries whose work was done within an equal span of years and whose juxtaposition is itself revealing. In Vienna, Mozart was writing complainingly that the summer "is the worst season for anyone to make money: the most distinguished families are all in the country and all I can do is to work hard in preparation for winter"—that winter when, in the February of 1782, Pope Pius VI was to visit Vienna to try to influence the Emperor, Joseph II, who was emulating King Henry VIII of

England in his attack on the Church and his suppression and pillage of the Religious Orders.

When Pius VI left Rome on that journey to Vienna, Benedict Labre was living among the dregs of the Roman populace in the Colosseum, by choice the poorest of the beggars there, making expiation for the age, reciting his night office by the light of a candle-end in one of the ruined grottoes before standing in the empty arena, his arms outstretched in the form of a cross, in an intensity of prayer.

At the end of Lent, 1783, Mozart was able to report the success of his concert and the Emperor Joseph's patronage of him:

> The theatre could not have been more crowded and every box was full. But what pleased me most of all was that His Majesty, the Emperor, was present and goodness! how delighted he was and how he applauded me! It is his custom to send money to the box-office *before* going to the theatre; otherwise I should have been fully justified in counting on a larger sum. He sent twenty-five ducats.

In Rome, on the Wednesday of that year's Holy Week, Benedict, though quite obviously dying, insisted on going to Mass in S. Maria dei Monti near the Colosseum. He managed, by a tremendous effort, to stand through the long Gospel, but collapsed on the steps outside the church and died that evening. Almost immediately the streets were thronged by people acclaiming "il santo"; throught Maundy Thursday and Good Friday, it seemed that the whole of Rome had come to honour his body; and in the first three months after his death he worked 136 attested miracles. By 1784, news of him and the posthumous cures he had wrought were circulating in the London newspapers and the following year an English life of him was published, which gave the members of Boodle's and White's an alternative topic of conversation to the inconvenience caused to "Prinny" by his £160,000-worth of debts or Lord Barrymore's pleasant jest in dressing Tom Hooper the pugilist as a clergyman to make wild parties even wilder.

Benedict Labre thus seemed the most eccentric of exceptions in that eighteenth century "whose glory it was"—the words are Henri Gheon's—"to have lost faith, hope and charity." But today, in our age, which may be described as the end of the epilogue to the eighteenth century, the saint has acquired a new and surprising significance. The contemporary rootlessness and despair has resulted in the "tramp" becoming the symbolic, even the archetypal, figure. In the modern literature of our own country, it is still politely rather the tramp at heart than the tramp in actuality; but in America where the process has gone further and the insight is keener, the "bum" has come into his own. In Algren's latest novel, for example, his "bum" hero soliloquises:

> I feel like I been everywhere God got land . . . yet all I found was people with hard ways to go. All I found was troubles'n degradation. All I found was that those with the hardest ways of all to go were quicker to help others than those with the easiest ways. All I found was two kinds of people. Them that would rather live on the loser's side of the street with the other losers than to win off by theirselves, and them who want to be one of the winners even though the only way left for them to win was over them who have already been whipped.

Here the contracting-out which is the only protest left to the good is on the natural level only; it is not, like Labre's, on the supernatural and for the love of God. Yet there is in it an echo of Labre's voice speaking across the continents and the centuries.

But, to me, the story of Labre has an even deeper historical meaning. In 1770, on his way to Rome, he called by chance at a house in Dardilly where he was given a bowl of soup and shelter for the night. It was the house of Pierre Vianney and among his host's children whom he blessed on leaving was Mathieu who, sixteen years later, was to become the father of the future Curé d'Ars. Benedict is said to have written a letter of thanks to the Vianneys, which the Curé kept in his possession. Whether or not there was this tangible link between them, Benedict Labre and the Curé are indeed "two spiritual brothers, separated in time by the fall of the old régime, two humiliated figures standing as a frame to the Revolution."

They are more than that. History, it has been truly said, is not a record of things that have happened but an evaluation of significant events. But still this leaves undefined the criterion of "significance" and the standard of "value." Without at this point advancing a lengthy argument, a Catholic may be permitted to hold that "history" is essentially the story of the dealings of God with men. The Old Testament is significant, and therefore *history,* in a sense in which Herodotus is not. In such history, the term of value is definite enough. The Chosen People in the Old Testament are not only under judgment: they also judge. Foreign nations and people are "good" in so far as they aid the work of God by safeguarding the Covenant or recalling the Covenant-nation to a sense of its purpose and responsibilities. To take one obvious example, the battle of Salamis merely occurs "offstage" in the second chapter of the book of Esther and for the importance of Xerxes (Assuerus) in the scheme of things, the hanging of Aman is more relevant than the whipping of the Hellespont.

When, after the Incarnation, the Catholic Church replaced the Chosen Race as the heir to the Promises, it became, too, the touchstone of history and the old Chroniclers who made their value-judgments depend on men's attitude to it are nearer the truth than their modern, "impartial" successors. But the contracting-party of the New Covenant no less than that of the Old is under judgment. The Church, too, at times has compromised with and become corrupted by the world; and to see the conflict as a simple antithesis between right and wrong is neither good history nor good theology. Yet the Church, merely because it belongs to the New Covenant, possesses within itself an absolute standard which the Old lacked—the saints. It is by reference to the saints that we come to certainty and a history of Europe written in terms of the saints would be a true—perhaps the only true—history of Europe. They imply judgment and dictate perspective.

So it is that the whole of French history from the middle of the eighteenth to the middle of the nineteenth century can be comprehended in and evaluated by the lives of two men—St. Benedict Joseph Labre and the Curé d'Ars. Between the visit of Benedict to Dardilly and the death of the Curé, France experienced everything from the reign of Madame Dubarry, the ferment of the Revolution, the "Enlightenment" of the Encyclopaedists and the flurry of Napoleon to the novels of George Sand, the Communist uprising in Paris, the Crimean War and the beginning of the Suez Canal. And, among it all, Labre made himself a beggar, poorer than the poorest *sansculotte,* and the Curé (dying in the year that Darwin published the *Origin of the Species*) stayed for fifty years in the smallest parish in France and brought the world to it on its knees.

In conventional, secular history, the French Revolution, with its causes and its results, dominates the age and we still live under its shadow. But before it happened Benedict Labre judged it. In simple fact, he foresaw what he was not to live to see. The dream which persistently troubled him to the extent of making him think it was some mirage sent by the devil was of a "huge fire driving across my country." In the blaze, abbeys were burnt; the Blessed Sacrament was profaned on the altars; priests were persecuted. That he realised with exactitude what it was is improbable (though the spirit which informed it, when it came, recognised him for what he was, and two women were sent to the guillotine for possessing relics of him); but by his life he corrected its false assumptions.

"Expiation," Voltair was explaining in the *Dictionnaire Philosophique,* is "a wild and absurd notion." Labre spent a life of expiation; and to those who wondered at the intensity of it, he would say: "With God's help you can do anything, anything at all; you can even stand in the fire and not get burnt, like the three young men in the Babylonian furnace." To the false notion of "liberty," he opposed the true concept of obedience.

There was a moment in his own life when obedience seemed to deny his most profound perceptions and he was ordered to receive the Sacrament to show that he was not a secret Jansenist. No act of obedience could have been more difficult for him. "I am a sinful man," he said, "I am not worthy to receive the Bread of Angels." But he did as his confessor told him, explaining: "It is better to go to Communion out of obedience than to stay away out of humility."

In what is called "the Age of Reason" but which was rather the age of that rationalism which is the antithesis of reason (in that, while asserting the rights of reason over nature it denied the rights of super-nature over reason), Benedict almost made a cult of what was deemed the superstitious. His pilgrimages were to what the age considered the more suspect of relics—to the Holy Shroud, to the incorrupt body of St. Claude, above all to the Holy House which had been carried by angels from Nazareth to Loreto. Kneeling there, he never doubted that this was the very room where, by the power of the Holy Ghost, Our Lady had conceived the Son. And his faith and devotions so clarified his intellectual perceptions that he understood, as few have, that greatest of mysteries, the Holy Trinity. When he spoke of the Godhead, his confessors thought they were listening to a prophet. One, hearing him speak of the Trinity in the most profound and at the same time theologically exact terms, asked him if he read St. Teresa, Benedict managed to stammer out: "I'm not an educated man, Father."

In dealing with the poverty of the age, he answered its evil and drew the sting of its envy, by immersing himself in its very depths and, for nothing but the love of God, drawing upon himself all its suffering and humiliation and distortion. Lazarus, whose sores the dogs licked, was bright with the promise of redemption. As one of Benedict's biographers has put it: "When Benedict spoke of poverty it no longer meant the absence of something good: it became a possession itself to be defended." But Benedict himself did more than teach: "We must trust ourselves utterly to God's goodness and wait with hope and resignation for whatever life may bring"; he acted on it, refusing a few pence offered to him as he set off for one of the shrines with "the poor don't carry money on their journeys" and rejecting a gift of food with "the poor have scraps of bread, not whole loaves . . . they must mortify themselves and overcome their flesh just like everyone else." Alone, this might have seemed a fanaticism which would justify the suspicion of Jansenism or even more heretical asceticism. Even set against the background of his age, Benedict's stringency might seem excessive were it not for the balancing part of the picture, of which the strange happening of Maundy Thursday, 1773, may be taken as an example.

Benedict was at Moulins, living temporarily in an attic which the Franciscans had found for him. On that Maundy Thursday, when the Church, imitating the humility of Christ, was giving officially to the poor, Benedict, too, felt that he must give something. He went to the town and collected twelve other beggars who might be pardoned for their ribald jests at the suggestion that the most ragged of them all could give them anything. For a joke more than anything else, they followed him to his attic where he had for them a few pennyworth of peas and some crusts. "They held out their bowls derisively; and he held up his as if his few scraps were to be consecrated. And suddenly they fell silent, for he became absolutely transfigured; under his glowing fingers, the tiny pittance grew—the bowls they held were filled to the brim." Somebody whispered the word "miracle," but Benedict merely smiled and "murmured something about a generous patron who gave him everything he wanted."

Thus Benedict spoke to his age, opposing his expiation to its materialism, his obedience to its drive towards anarchy, his simplicity of faith to its sterile rationalism. But he spoke for the most part in silence. Even in this, he stood apart. In all that eighteenth-century welter of epigram and argument, he remained a Trappist who had, against his own will, been forced into the world and who lived by the Rule of the Order he had chosen in his youth, but which had not been able to receive him.

Benedict was born at Amettes, near Boulogne, the eldest of

fifteen children. Even in childhood, though of a happy disposition, he showed an inclination to austerity. He preferred giving things away to getting them and practising how much he could do without. In the coldest weather, his mother noticed, he would sit far from the fire. He liked talking to tramps and beggars, giving them food which he himself should have eaten. Though his masters at school said he was a most intelligent pupil, his real interest was only in religious instruction. When he was twelve he went to live with his uncle, the parish priest of Erin, not far from his home, who completed his education and fostered the vocation which Benedict seemed undoubtedly to have, training him as his successor. At sixteen the boy wished to enter La Trappe. His uncle, thinking him neither strong nor old enough for such austerity, tried to dissuade him, pointing out that his duty seemed to lie there in the parish which would one day be in his spiritual charge. He even reproached Benedict for ingratitude to receive the reply: "I did not want to hurt you: I fought it as long as I could." The Abbé Labre then insisted that Benedict returned to his parents to gain their approval, but they told him he was to wait till he was older and sent him back to his uncle.

In the summer of 1766, the town was struck by the plague and the Abbé was one of the victims. The way to La Trappe at last seemed open. Benedict's parents withdrew their opposition to his becoming a religious, fearing they might be opposing the will of God; but his maternal uncle, who also was a priest, suggested that he should ask admission to a Carthusian rather than a Trappist house. He set off for the Chartreuse du Val de Sainte-Aldegonde and was refused. With another uncle— Benedict had six priest uncles—he then went to another house of the Order at Neuville-sous-Montreuil. Here he was told that as he was not yet twenty there was no hurry and that he was not sufficiently versed in dialectic and plainsong. He put himself under a new tutor to study them and, armed with a certificate stating that he was "a good-living boy of well-ordered and edifying behaviour, with a meek and docile character, who goes often to the sacraments, loves study and finds pleasure only in being apart from the world," returned to Neuville, this time to be admitted. But, in a few weeks he was back in Amettes, informing his parents in his matter-of-fact way; "God does not want me to be a Carthusian but a Trappist." He set out for La Trappe at last, at the end of 1767, with his parents' blessing, but the Abbot, considering him too delicate for so rigorous a life, told him to wait a few years, entertained him "as the most transient of visitors" and sent him home again. For a year he seemed to settle down on the farm which he one day, as the eldest, would inherit; but the call of his curious vocation was too strong. In spite of his parents' entreaties, of his village's anger, of his parish priest's reproaches, this delicate young man whose determination to enter a monastery was equalled only by the monasteries' determination to keep him out, announced once more his intention to go back to La Trappe; but since the opposition was so general he went first to make a retreat and ask the advice of the Bishop.

The Bishop, who knew his family, asked whether they approved of his becoming a Trappist. Benedict said that they would rather he became a Carthusian. "In that case, my son," said the Bishop, unaware of the previous experiences at Neuville, obey your parents. Become a Carthusian." Obediently, Benedict set off for Neuville the third time on 16 August, 1769. In October, he wrote a letter home saying:

My dearest Father and Mother, This is to tell you that the Carthusians find me unsuited to their life and that I left them on the second of October. I look on this as a command from God calling me to something more perfect still—they said themselves that it was the hand of God taking me from them. I am therefore setting out for La Trappe, where I have always longed to go. I ask your forgiveness for all my disobedience and for all the sorrow I have caused you. I ask both of you to give me your blessing so that Our Lord will be with me. I shall pray for you every day of my life; please do not worry about me. I wanted to stay here, but they would not have me. So I am glad to be able to feel quite sure that God Almighty is leading me. . . . I will have the fear of Him always before me and the love of Him in my heart. I have every hope of being received at La Trappe; if not, I am told that Sept-Fonts is not quite so harsh and they take people younger; but I shall certainly be received at La Trappe. . . .

But once again La Trappe refused him. It was pointed out to him that he had, on his first visit, been told to wait several years. He had come back much too soon. So he went to the Cistercian abbey of Sept-Fonts where at last he had his wish and on 11 November put on the habit of a novice as Brother Urban. But, five months later, he fell seriously ill; the Abbot told him when he was out of danger, "My son, God is not calling you to our Order," and when he was strong enough at the beginning of July 1770, Benedict left to journey to Rome. But it is worth recording that the infirmarian at Sept-Fonts, who, perhaps, knew him best, gave it as his opinion: "This young man is a saint." From Piedmont, that August, he wrote again to his parents—the second of the only two letters of his that are known:

You know that I left the Abbey of Sept-Fonts and you must be worried about what I have done since then and what sort of life I want to take up. I am writing this to do my duty and relieve you of your worries. I must then tell you that I left Sept-Fonts on 2 July; I still had a fever when I came away, but it had gone by the fourth day; and I set out towards Rome. I am now half-way there; I have not got very far since leaving Sept-Fonts because all through August it has been terribly hot in Piedmont, where I am; and also I was kept for three weeks, just lately, by a slight illness I had, in a hospital where I was very well looked after. Apart from that I have been very well since I left Sept-Fonts. There are several monasteries in Italy where the life is very regular and very austere. I intend to enter one of these and hope God will allow me to. I have even heard of one Trappist monastery whose Abbot wrote to a French Abbot saying he would receive any Frenchman who came, because he is so short of subjects. At Sept-Fonts they gave me good references. Do not worry about me. . . . Please give me your blessings so that God will bless my plans. It was His Providence that directed me to undertake this journey. . . .

Benedict was twenty-two-and-a-half years old when, on the final rejection, he set out on the unceasing pilgrimage over Europe from shrine to shrine which was to be so mysteriously his true vocation.

The importance of these early events is that they show without any possibility of doubt that the last thing that he himself wished was to be an eccentric tramp. No one could have tried more fiercely, against all odds, to withdraw into a hidden anonymity of silence and suffering. Even his own purpose, as he saw it, was not quite that for which God used him. The last person to have known what he in fact was to his age was himself. He did not even become a pilgrim because he could not become a monk; it was because he wanted to retain the integrity of a monk in surroundings which were not designed to help it that he went from shrine to shrine and made Europe his La Trappe. "Labre is the great patron for all who are trying to find out what they are meant to do," Agnes de la Gorce has so perceptively said in her life of him: "for he spent his life trying to find that out for himself. It may be that only in the peace of the very end did he realise that he really had found it."

He set out on his long pilgrimage clad in an old coat, with a large rosary round his neck and a small one in his hand and on his back a sack which had in it a New Testament, a breviary—he said the Divine Office daily—and his favourite book, *The Imitation of Christ*. He took nothing else. He never begged though he accepted any alms that were given him and dispensed to other tramps what was left after his small needs were satisfied. In summer he slept in the open, though in winter he would accept a bed if anyone offered it to him.

We have a description of him at the beginning of his twelve-and-a-half years of journeyings, from some who met him in

Fabriano where he had gone to venerate the shrine of St. Romuald. He had a small, fair beard and rather long hair falling over his shoulders "like a Nazarene." He spoke with great courtesy, had scrupulously good manners, ate with careful cleanliness—"not like a common beggar at all"—and gave no appearance of exhaustion. The sisters who preserved this memory of him preserved also his saying: "To love God, you need three hearts in one—a heart of fire for Him, a heart of flesh for your neighbour, and a heart of bronze for yourself."

We have, too, a description of him near the end of his journey, from Fr. Marconi who became his confessor:

> In the month of June, 1782, just after I had celebrated Mass . . . I noticed a man close beside me whose appearance at first sight was decidedly unpleasant and forbidding. His legs were only partially covered, his clothes were tied round his waist with an old cord. His hair was uncombed, he was ill-clad and wrapped about in an old and ragged coat. In outward appearance he seemed the most miserable beggar I had ever seen.

Between the two there exists a picture of Labre painted under strange circumstances by André Bley. As this somewhat obscure artist from Lyons was making a sketch, in 1777 in Rome, for a picture of the call of St. Peter, he noticed, among a crowd of mendicants "a young man in beggar's garb with a short red beard" who, though not handsome, had a peculiar beauty which made the artist approach him to ask him to come to his studio and pose as the model for Christ. Benedict shuddered, shook his head and went on saying his rosary. Bley asked again. Benedict, this time, gave his decided negative in French. Then Bley tried the third time, representing it as a kindness to a fellow-countryman, and Benedict, who taught that charity to one's neighbour should outweigh everything else, followed the painter to his studio. "He came," wrote Bley to his brother in Paris, "posed like a statue and refused any kind of sitter's fee." From this sketch, after Benedict's death, a portrait was made—a strong, peasant face with emaciated cheeks and downcast eyes. Two years later, another and better painter, Cavalucci, came upon Benedict praying and "with the eye of a genius made him the incarnation of mysticism."

In Rome at the time of Benedict's death was a twenty-eight-year-old American Congregational minister, John Thayer, trying to understand Catholicism "just as I should have wished," as he wrote, "to understand the religion of Mohammed if I had been in Constantinople." He spoke of the strange, by now verminous, beggar in terms which even his friends considered unnecessarily tasteless. His detestation of Catholicism reached its peak when the Roman crowds insisted on making a popular canonisation of this unpleasant eccentric— when the guard of police on duty outside the church where Benedict's body lay had to be doubled and Corsican soldiers had to be brought in to beat back the superstitious crowds. But, fascinated as well as repelled, John Thayer watched events and when the report of miracles started to shake the city, he could not resist investigating the phenomena by calling on some who claimed to have been cured by Benedict's intercession. Six weeks after Benedict's death, John Thayer became a Catholic, and in due course a priest—the first native of New England to be ordained to the priesthood. Even in the nature of his first convert, St. Benedict Joseph Labre revealed his "significance."

St. Bernadette

1844-1879

James Brodrick

BERNADETTE SOUBIROUS, canonised on 8 December, 1933, is one of the most surprising saints in the Church's calendar. Of her the late Fr. Herbert Thurston wrote:

> In all the annals of sanctity it would be hard to find the counterpart [of her history]. She did nothing out of the common, she said nothing memorable, she gathered no followers around her, she had in the ordinary sense no revelations, she did not prophesy or read men's secret thoughts, she was remarkable for no great austerities or striking renunciations, or marvellous observance of rule, or, conspicuous zeal for souls. And yet . . . for all future time, as long as this earth shall last, the Holy Sacrifice will be offered in her honour, and petitions will be addressed to her to intercede with God, the common Father of us all.[1]

These are the carefully pondered words of a very great scholar whose chief field of study was the lives of the saints. What he says is completely endorsed by a more recent authority on Bernadette and Lourdes, Dr. René Laurentin, who maintains that her holiness was not a particular form of sanctity, but sanctity free of accessories and reduced to its essence, the sanctity without human grandeur or accidental charisms, which was that of the Holy Family at Nazareth. From this point of

211

view, Dr. Laurentin continues, the sanctity of Bernadette could be said to mark a turning-point in the annals of hagiography. She herself had no patience with lives of saints which dehumanised them and spoke only of their revelations and miracles. She held that the faults of the saints should be pointed out as well as the means they took to overcome them, for that would be a real help to us.[2]

Bernadette was in fact a new type of saint, whose very ordinariness is her great attraction. Her story, at once simple and sublime, is so familiar that the merest bald sketch of her life will be enough for the refreshment of memory. She was born at Lourdes on 7 January, 1844, the eldest child of two easygoing, illiterate millers, François and Louise Soubirous, kindly, Christian people whose reputation was not of the highest among their neighbours. As a result of their shiftlessness and mild addiction to the bottle, they lost their mill and were reduced eventually to almost complete destitution. At the age of six, Marie-Bernarde, known to everybody in the Soubirous's small circle as Bernadette, became subject to attacks of asthma and four years later fell victim to the cholera raging then in Lourdes. So was the poor child's health permanently undermined and her growth retarded. At the time of the Apparitions in 1858, when she had passed her fourteenth birthday, she looked no more than twelve or less and was only four and a half feet tall. In November 1859, her mother told a priest inquirer that "she was hardly ever free from ill-health and suffering of one kind or another down to the day when she was favoured with the vision of Our Lady." After that great day, Louise Soubirous continued, her health had become progressively worse: "From time to time her body becomes so distended that she can no longer fasten her dress. Her cough is incessant and harassing while she is suffering from these distensions, and the attack lasts for three weeks or a month together, quitting her only to recur with renewed violence."[3]

In 1857, the family, mother, father and four children, were evicted from their last poor lodging in Lourdes through inability to pay the rent, and had to fall back on the charity of a relative, André Sajoux, tenant of a former town gaol, who allowed them the use of one ground-floor room, the notorious *cachot,* where drunks and other undesirables had been locked-up in the past. In the small walled yard outside were a dunghill and cesspool, Bernadette's only prospect from the single window for seven months of her young life. It is touching to find that Louise Soubirous tried hard to keep this insanitary hole as clean as might be, though for all her battles with them the vermin would return. Bernadette when not crippled with her asthma was her mother's great ally in this unending campaign. Sajoux who lived upstairs over their heads testified that the Soubirous, though half starving and never properly warm, always ended their hard days with evening prayers before retiring to their miserable beds. The parents undoubtedly had their faults but must have been fine people down deep to have retained their human dignity and integrity in those appalling circumstances. It was said of them that they would rather die than beg, and the children, though poorly clad in old patched garments, were kept clean and, as far as possible, neat. The scarf which Bernadette wore tightly over her dark hair was originally striped, but the colours in it had run through incessant washing. Her big billowing skirt, which once in innocent vanity she tried to arrange like the crinolines worn by the fashionable young ladies of Lourdes, was kept by her own diligent fingers in good repair and thoroughly brushed. She was always gifted with her needle, and in later years worked really beautiful lace for the albs of priests, examples of which are still to be seen.

In September 1857, the farmer's wife at the village of Bartrès, less than three miles from Lourdes, who had suckled Bernadette as a baby on a strictly commercial basis, because her own young mother (Louise was only seventeen at the time) had been unable to do so on account of an accident, asked for the services of her former foster-child on board and lodging terms. Bernadette's parents were only too glad to get her out of the fetid atmosphere of the *cachot,* even though it meant a severe pang to part with her who was the one comfort of their dreadful existence. So off she went with her few pitiable belongings to slave from morning to night at kitchen chores, or looking after the farmer's small children, or tending from time to time his sheep and lambs. Her only reference to the third very temporary occupation was that she loved the smallest lambs best. In spite of their subsequent loud protestations of love for Bernadette, after she had become celebrated, there is every indication that the farmer and his wife overworked her, and they certainly neglected her religious instruction, in spite of their express promise to her parents. Another, older servant of the family testified that when she brought Bernadette to Bartrès, she had assured her parents on behalf of her employers that she would be sent to the village school to learn her catechism, of which till then she had been taught nothing.

But work prevented her from being sent [continued this witness], and I do not think that she was even given time to attend Sunday school. The mistress of the house tried to teach her a little in the evenings, before bed, but poor Bernadette was very slow to learn, and even though the same word was repeated to her three or four times she still could not retain it. It was so bad that her foster-mother said to her, "You will never learn anything," and threw the catechism book aside in exasperation. All the same, Bernadette knew the Our Father, the Hail Mary and the I believe in God, though she missed out a few words in the I believe. We were good friends and never had a disagreement. *Elle était si brave.*[4]

Owing to the child's persistent ill-health and the need of her at home to look after her younger brothers and sisters while her parents were out, doing any casual jobs they could find, she was not sent to school at all and could neither read nor write. The farmer's wife at Bartrès, described by the village schoolmaster as a "cold and rather parsimonious woman," was herself barely literate, so we may fairly guess that her catechetical methods lacked something of enlightenment. It is little wonder that Bernadette could not memorise the abstract words dinned into her poor head, without explanation, at the end of a tiring day. It made the weary little drudge very unhappy because, until she knew the catechism, she would not be able to make her first Communion. This child of predilection really pined for Holy Communion, and to the frustration of being kept from it was added another sorrow in the persistent unkindness shown to her by some member of the rural household. She bore it all, the distress of her asthma, the hard work, the deprivation of school and the ill-treatment, with a "gay and laughing" front, because, as she told a friend, she thought it to be God's will for her. But she grieved in secret and ate out her affectionate heart, longing for God in His Sacrament. One day, seeing a woman from Lourdes pass by, she called to her and said: "Would you tell my parents that I am weary of this place and want to return to join the class of those preparing for first Communion. Tell them to come for me." Things must have reached a sad pass in the Pyreneean Arcady to make Bernadette yearn for the dreadful *cachot* in the Petits-Fossés. At any rate she would have affection there, even if never enough to eat, and, being herself a most loving and lovable little person, she needed affection as a flower, however humble, needs water and light. But Francois and Louise Soubirous were in no hurry to bring their first-born back to the misery in which they themselves lived, for they had not the slightest suspicion of the distress which she felt. When a second urgent message to her parents brought no result, Bernadette packed her few things in a bundle, gave her employers notice, and on Thursday, 28 January, 1858, took the road to Lourdes. She never again visited Bartrès, a fact surely significant in the conduct of a person always so grateful for kindness and so naturally friendly. It might almost serve to banish from the books in future the charming but fanciful eclogue of Bernadette the happy shepherdess, to which even Mgr. Trochu, that excellent biographer, shows himself somewhat addicted.[5]

Exactly a fortnight after Bernadette's return to Lourdes, on 11 February, 1858, the tremendous thing happened, Heaven's most signal visitation on earth since the Incarnation. As she knelt in ecstasy that bitter winter day before her strangely youthful Vision, "no taller than myself," her friend Jeanne Abadie who saw her from some distance on her knees remarked impatiently to her sister Toinette: *Ellè ne sait que prier Dieu*—all she's good at is praying!"[6] It was a revealing exclamation at the very outstart of Bernadette's mission and "martyrdom" of fame. Her prayer, always of the simplest, consisted at first in the devout use of her cheap little rosary, and then, as she grew in grace, in loving adoration of the will of God which had chosen her for suffering, a vicarious victim for the sins of the world, especially those of bad Catholics, the only people capable of making her really afraid. That she saw, not as an interior, intellectual vision such as St. Teresa experienced of Jesus, but with her eyes of flesh the holy Mother of God, on eighteen distinct occasions, is as certain as any event in history, though it rests entirely in the long run on her uncorroborated witness, as nobody else beheld the Apparitions. But what majesty and power there was in the witness of this young, ailing, illiterate, defenceless girl from the slums! Nearly all those who saw her in ecstasy at Massabielle, including such a lifelong free-thinker as Dr. Dozous, believed in the reality of her visions without further proof. Heaven shone on her transfigured face and convinced them, even while officialdom remained obdurately opposed.

How familiar the names of those excellent functionaries, immortalised by their encounters with Bernadette, have become to us, Jacomet, the Commissioner of Police, Dutour, the Procureur Impérial, Rives, the Examining Magistrate, D'Angla, Captain of the Lourdes gendarmerie, Peyramale, the Parish Priest. All of them came round to belief eventually, in the long or short run. It took Captain D'Angla twenty years to shed his doubts about the Apparitions. When questioned by Père Cros why he held out so long, he made an interesting answer, which might have been given by Jacomet and Dutour also: "I used to ask myself, Is it possible that the Blessed Virgin can have revealed herself to such a little *drôlesse*? I use the word in the sense of vagabond, good for nothing, the daughter of a disreputable family."[7] D'Angla was not himself acquainted with Bernadette, but he found her father's name in the police records as having spent a week in gaol for appropriating an unclaimed joist of timber. That and the fact that François was a palpable failure in business sufficed to blind the good Captain to all other aspects of the situation and to condemn poor Bernadette unseen and unheard. Jacomet and Dutour allowed themselves to be guided by the same prejudices. Nothing good could come out of the Rue des Petits-Fossés. But to the ill-repute of the parents, so largely unjustified, was added the grave fact that Bernadette was associated with a certain Mme. Millet, indeed had stayed for a few days in her house, and this woman, a mere servant, had committed the unpardonable crime in small town society of marrying her employer and becoming modestly rich. If she showed off a bit, that surely did not necessarily prove her disreputable.

M. Dutour, an admirable Catholic and very fair-minded official, reported to his immediate chief, the Procureur Général at Pau, on 1 March 1858, that in his opinion, after examination of the child,

> Bernadette Soubirous has never seemed, and does not now seem, to look for any temporal advantage likely to result from the supernatural favour of which she considers herself to be the object. Her family are less exempt from suspicion. . . . A certain Madame Millet, once a domestic servant, but now the possessor of a snug little fortune derived from marriage with her former master, . . . being ignorant and idle, is the easy prey of any form of excitement which gratifies her caprice. This woman, having heard people speak of the grotto of Massabielle, . . . set her heart on visiting it in company with Bernadette. For three days she carried the poor child off and lodged her in her own house, during which time they went each morning to the grotto where they lit candles and said the rosary . . .

Though darkly suspicious of the *nouveau-riche* widow and her presence at the Grotto, the Procureur was honest enough to admit that the Blessed Virgin, if it *was* the Blessed Virgin and not Bernadette's imagination, seemed to have nothing against her. Indeed, it was while she was there that the Vision first spoke to the child and requested her with such delicate courtesy to return every day for a fortnight.

But Dutour felt in his bones that Bernadette's parents, though not Bernadette herself who impressed him against his will, must be getting something out of the opulent Mme. Millet. "Is it possible," he asked his chief at Pau, "that She who is the purest of creatures can have chosen such abject emissaries through whom to communicate her wishes?" It was perfectly possible, and it is now absolutely certain that Francois and Louise had taken on something of their daughter's almost miraculous integrity, and steadfastly refused the many offers made by kind people to relieve their dreadful circumstances. André Sajoux, their host at the *cachot,* underwent the same influence, and said that he might have become a rich man if he had accepted all the money gifts pressed upon him by visitors to Bernadette at his address. He laid no claims to special nobility, but he never accepted a sou. Well known is the story of how the gentle Bernadette boxed her small brother's ears and made him immediately return the two francs, a fortune in that household, which some ladies had given him for acting as their guide to the Grotto. Such disinterestedness was out of this world altogether and marked Bernadette while still only a child as on the high road to canonisation. It was one of the things that astounded the Curé, M. Peyramale, and helped to break down his initial hostility to Bernadette and her message for, as he told his Bishop, he could only regard it as a miracle of divine grace.

But there was much more in the story than that sublime detachment. As a witness for Heaven, Bernadette holds a place apart among all those, saints included, who, through the Christian centuries, have received private revelations from God. Our Lady, if not M. Jacomet, M. Dutour, Captain D'Angla, Mother Vauzou and the rest of the good honest folk, knew exactly what she was about when she chose Bernadette as her herald, for grace builds on nature and there was in this lowly child a strange native aristocracy of disposition which made a lie, an exaggeration, an embroidery of a message, abhorrent. Standing, a poor little waif with none to plead for her, before the hostile authorities of state and church, she became a very rock on which broke unavailingly every effort of theirs to frighten, cajole or trick her into denying her Vision or confusing her message. A good authority on these matters has written as follows:

> Heroism is most nobly exhibited in constancy, and the constancy of this poor little half-starved, ailing, defenceless child, standing up to the alternate threats and cajolery, the menaces and flattery, of civil and ecclesiastical authorities, and to the stupid if well-meaning efforts of pious sensationalists to get her to elaborate her simple narrative of what she had seen into something more consonant with their conception of what she *ought* to have seen, profoundly stirs one's imagination. She would not concede a point to such insinuations, nor on the other hand would she go back on any of her original statements, and she clearly preferred to say nothing at all about her experiences and in fact never did so except under question.... One is bewildered by the spectacle on the one hand of the commotion occasioned by the recent events, and on the other by the perfect balance and calmness of her who was the centre of it all.[8]

In the constancy and purity of her witness, Bernadette resembled in her humble fashion Him who said: "My teaching is not my own but His who sent Me." She would sooner have died than change one jot or tittle of the commands given to her in the Lourdes patois by her Heavenly Visitant. Jacomet in his impressive regalia thought it his duty to bully her unmercifully and, when he threatened her with prison, she had no reason to think that he was bluffing. Her answer is famous: "So much the better. I shall be less expense to my father, and while I am in prison you will come and teach me the catechism." Similarly, she outfaced the thundering Abbé Peyramale who had made her tremble, and returned to the lion's den with a racing heart to give him the second part of her Lady's command, which his fulminations had driven out of her head on the first occasion. It made no difference whether she understood the Lady's commands or not, as when she was bidden to wash and drink at a tiny puddle and to eat a bitter herb, actions which made the crowd gathered there shake their heads and consider her demented. She bore the sneers and jeers with the same gentle serenity that she did the tiresome veneration.

The veneration indeed turned into a form of martyrdom which the profoundly humble, self-effacing child had to endure almost daily for eight years on end. As Fr. Thurston wrote in an article which he called *The "Martyrdom" of Bernadette*:

> The visitors to Lourdes considered that, being a poor peasant girl, she might be sought out and interrogated with impunity. Her simplicity, gentleness and evident lack of education made her the prey of every self-opinionated bore, of every chattering, curious or impertinent busybody who considered that he paid her and her visions a compliment by condescending to inquire about them.[9]

The article is well worth study as showing to what lengths crass, insensitive, misguided people were prepared to go in order to establish a connection with the celebrated Bernadette. One man brought her from her bed with a racking cough, right across Lourdes to his hotel, on a January day of howling, icy winds and torrential rain, that he might interrogate her for two solid hours. This we know because he wrote and published an account of his exploit, saying how much he was edified by Bernadette's firm refusal to accept three louis d'or which he pressed upon her as reward for her trouble in coming out in such vile weather. He tried to inveigle her, as did many others, into telling him what were the three secrets committed to her by the Blessed Virgin, but there he came up against a rock as solid as Massabielle. The secrets went intact with their little guardian to the grave. Another shocking example of crude publicity-mongering is given in the article cited, and such things went on without intermission for eight weary years. This is another example of Bernadette's heroism, for she hardly ever refused a visitor, or many visitors at the same time, even when she was ill in bed. The many, sceptics or ecclesiastics who endeavoured, like Jacomet, to catch her out in her words or to make her contradict herself were dumbfounded by her quiet tenacity. And how she hated those interminable interviews! Big tears would gather in her eyes when she was summoned to the parlour of the nuns' Hospice in Lourdes, perhaps for the tenth time in one day, to repeat her story to some inquiring bishop or priest or journalist or *grande dame,* but she would brush them away and give a smiling greeting to her visitors. Then, when the interview was over, she would clap her hands and laugh out loud in relief, just like a small child let loose from school.

Bernadette remained to her dying day the most charmingly unstarched and spontaneous of holy souls, one who loved to mimic the portentous mien of her doctor or the thundering of her parish priest, at first her foe and then her doughtiest champion and her friend. She wept bitterly when she heard that the grand old man, massive like his native mountains, was dead. When she left Lourdes and the Grotto with all its heavenly associations for ever in 1866, to become a nun at Nevers, three hundred miles and more away, she was in her twenty-third year, but still looked the ageless fourteen she had been at the time of the Apparitions. She seemed to have acquired something of the timelessness of the Immaculate Conception, as a priest who spoke with her and gave her Holy Communion in 1865 testified. "I do not believe," he wrote, "that it would be possible to find a child of thirteen with a younger face than Bernadette's at twenty-one, and her youthfulness has a supernatural charm impossible to miss."[10] And she was still as young of heart, as unspoilt and unspoilable, as on the gloomy, glorious February morning when she went off with Toinette and Jeanne to collect sticks and bones along the banks of the Gave. A rather pompous abbé who visited Bernadette at Lourdes in 1859 delivered to her a homily on the danger of having her head turned by the tributes of respect paid to her on all sides, even by princes of the Church. When people showed her marks of veneration, he continued, she must clasp her rosary tightly and give the glory to the Mother of God. Humbly and in utter sincerity the child replied, as the homiletic abbe recorded: "Monsieur, I thank you for your good advice and I will try to put it in practice from this day forth." Now, if there was one person in Lourdes, in France, in the wide world, who had no need of such advice, that person was Bernadette. It was part of her charm, of her heavenly childlikeness, to be either completely unaware of the veneration shown her, or to treat it as a silly thing, a bore or a joke. Yet good, well-meaning people at Lourdes and Nevers went out of their way to humiliate and snub her publicly, for fear she might become conceited.

Her disconcerting naturalness, concealing such unfathomable depths of suffering and union with God, greatly disturbed a number of people with preconceived notions of what sanctity involved. The Mother Superior of the Hospice in Lourdes and the formidable Mother Vauzou, Mistress of Novices at Nevers, were two who could never fit the homely, merry *paysanne* into their stuffy Second Empire notions of the conduct to be expected from a girl singularly favoured by God. Poor, able, complicated Mother Vauzou could never have even begun to understand or appreciate the beauty of the wild flower which had timidly shown its humble head in her well-regulated garden. Whether or not one of Bernadette's three secrets was, as Fr. Thurston ventured to surmise, a pact with the Blessed Virgin never under any circumstances to try to draw to herself the attention of the world, that was exactly how she acted for the rest of her crucified existence. She shunned notice as others might shun the plague, but she was a loving soul, and a little affection from those in charge of her would have done her no spiritual harm. She suffered greatly from the lack of it, a "martyrdom of the heart," one observant nun called the snubs and the coldness. Before thirty-six she was dead, after years of atrocious physical suffering, borne with superhuman cheerfulness and fortitude.

In our time of stars and personalities and pathological craving for the limelight, it is a benediction to think of Bernadette and her unselfconscious holiness, which involved no miracle nor prophecy nor memorable word. On her and on her alone Lourdes and its world-wide consequences depended, like some mighty inverted pyramid balanced on a very small stone. She was the mustard seed from which grew the great tree for the sheltering and healing of the nations. People would have swarmed after her to do her bidding, had she given them a lead. But she never dreamt of any such thing, nor of offering a modest opinion about arrangements at Massabielle. The basilica went up entirely unknown to her, though she was its real foundations. Magnificent processions and international pilgrimages were organised, which she, the *fons et origo* of them all, never witnessed. She was given permission and even encouraged to attend the solemn consecration of the basilica at Lourdes in July 1876. It was the crown of all that she had lived and suffered for, her supreme interest on earth, but she could not be present, as she knew from hard experience, without riveting all men's attention, and that was something her profound conviction of her worthlessness was unable to bear. "Oh, if I could only see without being seen!" she was heard to exclaim, and so she stayed away, the broom of Our Lady that had worn out its every bristle in her sweet service, and now lay contentedly discarded behind the door. Others might fight for the headlines and welcome, but this little nun, trailing her clouds of glory, hungered only to be forgotten, and to serve God as best she knew how in the tiny lost world behind convent walls, peeling potatoes or polishing candlesticks. Many years after her death, Bernadette did work some miracles to please the Congregation of Rites, but she was herself Our Lady's most beautiful miracle.

St. Thérèse of Lisieux

1873-1897

J.B. Morton

ON JANUARY 2ND, in the year 1873, a daughter was born to the wife of a retired jeweller in the Norman town of Alençon. At the age of fifteen, by a Papal dispensation, she entered the Carmelite Convent in Lisieux. There, nine years later, after a long and painful illness, she died. In 1925, only twenty-eight years after her death, she was canonized by Pope Pius XI. "Our Mother Prioress," a Sister had once said, "will not find much to write about her in the obituary notice. Though she is very good, she has never done anything worth talking about."

I made my first visit to Lisieux more than a quarter of a century ago, three or four years after I had become a Catholic. I knew nothing of the story of Thérèse Martin; and there is little enough of that story to be learned from the smiling statue which is to be found in Catholic churches all over the world, or from the shrine at Lisieux, with its theatrical decorations. I was beginning to get the impression of a nun who would be bound to make a strong appeal to sentimental women. That gentle smile on the face of the statue suggests serene happiness, and I found it not difficult to imagine her untroubled existence in the Carmel, out of reach of temptation, shielded from conflict; an uneventful life of prayer and meditation and contemplation, without problems or difficulties. She would be a nun like so many others, conscientiously following the rule of her Order. But, at that point, there was a question to be answered. The

225

Church does not canonize such nuns. What was the secret behind that smile? My companion at Lisieux, a man of robust character, a lover of song and laughter and jest, began to talk of her while we sat in a café after our lunch. He said: "It always amuses me that people who know nothing about her, think that they know what is going on in the world of our time. Her canonization was almost forced on the Pope by popular clamour." He told me enough of the story to arouse my interest, and to make me realize that my picture of her must be completely false. I began to read about her, in a haphazard fashion, and at once I was amazed. What I was reading was a chronicle of heroic virtue. The smile on the face of the statue hides the secret which even the nuns of her community did not suspect, the secret which she disclosed, under obedience in the *Histoire d'une Ame.*

One of the first things that strikes the reader of the story of St. Thérèse is that it is an unusual story. We are accustomed in hagiography to reading of one who lived amid ecstasies and visions and mystical experiences of every kind. We expect marvels. But such things were rare in her life. There were, in her childhood, the prophetic vision of her father's death, the last-minute reconciliation to the Church of the condemned criminal Pranzoni, and the vision of Our Lady which ended her mysterious sickness. In the Carmel she experienced a moment of ecstasy while making the Stations of the Cross. For the rest, she seemed to the community to be an exemplary nun and no more. Another striking thing about the story is that she knew, towards the end of her life, the effect her teaching would have. In her humility, she disliked calling attention to herself, and asked only to fulfil her duties to the best of her ability; to be ignored or even despised. She said that answering promptly when you are summoned is more important than the writing of books about the saints. And when, in 1894, the Prioress asked her, in what little spare time she had, to write about her early years, she feared that such a task would distract her from the rule of life which she had made for herself. But she obeyed. She wrote out her memories of her childhood at home and of her first years in the Carmel for the second of her sisters, who was then Prioress. In 1896, Mother Marie de Gonzague, who had been Prioress when St. Thérèse entered the convent, was re-elected. She asked that the autobiography should be completed, and the second part was written during the last illness. The third part was written for her eldest sister, Marie, Sister Marie of the Sacred Heart. The book was neither planned nor divided into chapters, and some of it was written when she was almost too weak to form the letters. When she had delivered the manuscript she showed no further interest in it. It was unread for some time, but she made no reference to it. It was an act of obedience performed. The task was finished. Neither she nor her sisters had any thought of publication. But later on she knew that what she had written was of importance to the world outside the Carmel, and, a few weeks before her death, she was urging publication "after my death, without the least delay." Asked if she thought the book would benefit souls, she said, "Yes. It is a means which God will employ." She realized that the *Histoire d'une Ame* would play an important part in her mission, that mission of which she spoke to her sister at the end of her life: "To make the good God loved as I love Him, to give to souls my little way."

The book, which tells the story of her first years, of her life in the Carmel, and of her "little way" of love and self-denial, will be a disappointment to those who look for a work of great literary merit. It is the spontaneous and ingenuous outpouring of a soul. There is no literary artifice, no attempt to captivate by tricks of style. Its merit is in its content, and considering the conditions in which it was written, without time for shaping or revision, it is surprising that it can be read with such ease. The character it reveals is one of utter simplicity and indomitable courage and strength of mind. Those sayings of hers which are most treasured today are the simplest. He who finds something tedious in her insistence on her littleness and weakness is finding true humility tedious. All through the book she is giving herself as an example of man's powerlessness when relying solely on himself, and explaining that to rely on God as a child relies on its parents, is the only way to live as we are intended to live. The childishness of her language has frequently been criticized with impatience, but she always chose the simplest way of saying what she had to say, and it is what she said that is important. Some have been discouraged from enquiring into her life by this very simplicity of heart, and have found her style of writing difficult to digest without embarrassment. Let them be embarrassed, but let them read on. I myself suffer from this embarrassment, but it is a fault in me, not in her. I also, like many, have deplored the tawdriness of the decorations of her shrine at Lisieux, the sentimentality of the harp, the roses, the angels. But I remember Villon's mother, who is one of the earliest examples of a woman who "knew what she liked." The ballade her son made for her still today challenges intellectual pride. St. Thérèse is the people's saint, and her shrine is surrounded by examples of the popular taste of her day. It is not the humble and the childlike who are repelled by the mawkish in art.

We must remember that, though she did not know it, while she was writing the story of her soul she was speaking to an audience of all races and all kinds of people. The directness of her style has the great advantage of making it impossible for her to be misunderstood. Some of her sayings could be put into a more literary form, but they would lose thereby. Nobody can read her book or her recorded sayings without realizing that she was highly intelligent, and had a sense of humour. But the last thing she wanted was to be "clever." Her dislike of drawing attention to herself was part of her humility. She once said this remarkable thing: "It would not disturb me if (to suppose what is impossible) God Himself did not see my good actions. I love Him so much that I would like to give Him joy without His knowing who gave it. When He does know, He is, as it were, obliged to make some return. I should not like to give Him the trouble."

The family in the midst of which Thérèse Martin was brought up differed from other middle-class French families of the time only in the exemplary lives led by her parents, both of whom were extremely devout. Thérèse was the spoilt child. She was by nature affectionate, and her love of home and of her sisters was unusually strong. She was impulsive, not easily amenable to discipline, precociously intelligent, and extremely sensitive. A casual observer would have seen a pretty, vivacious child, happy by temperament, with a deep appreciation of the beauties of nature, and with a tendency to day-dreaming. These dreams, at a very early date, were not the usual reveries of a child. Beneath the surface of her life there was an undercurrent. Her vocation had come to her at an age when children are content to play their games. She had set her heart on becoming a Carmelite nun, and was confident that she could become a saint. The stubbornness with which she fought all opposition to her one overriding desire was the first indication of that iron will which was to become unbreakable during her nine years of perpetual warfare. Two of her elder sisters entered the Carmel at Lisieux. The eldest, Marie, discouraged her, reminding her that she was far too young to enter the convent. The Mother Prioress was of the same opinion. So was the Canon who represented the Bishop as ecclesiastical superior of the Community. An interview with the Bishop himself produced only a promise that he would consider the matter. Both he and the Vicar-General had decided that she must have patience, and take time to prove that she had a true vocation. But patience, which she was to possess to an outstanding degree later in life, was impossible to her now. She was utterly convinced that she must begin her work without delay. There remained one more resource: an appeal to the Pope himself. And to the Pope himself, during a pilgrimage to Rome with her father, she appealed.

An audience with Leo XIII was arranged for the pilgrims from her diocese. The Vicar-General of Bayeux, who led the pilgrimage, seems to have had an idea that the audacity of this little girl of fourteen might lead to an unusual scene. He therefore announced to the waiting group of pilgrims that on no account whatever must anyone address the Holy Father. But Thérèse, kneeling before the Pontiff, begged to be allowed to enter the Carmel next year, at the age of fifteen. The Vicar-General, standing by, explained to the Pope that her case was under consideration, which was a hint that her request was opposed by those who had examined the matter. Leo XIII could only advise her to await their decision. But she was not yet defeated. "If you, Holy Father," she said, "would give permission, the others would agree." "You shall enter if it is God's will," replied the Pope. Even then, she was about to speak further. She clung to the Pope's knees, and was finally led away in tears. On January 1st of the next year, 1888, she learned that the Bishop had given his permission for her to enter the Carmel that year.

So, at the age of fifteen, she left home and family, and abandoned the world. From the moment she crossed the threshold of the Carmel her physical and spiritual torment began. This was no surprise to her, since she already understood that there is no way to perfection but through suffering. Of a delicate constitution she had to accustom herself to unappetizing food, to intense suffering from cold, to lack of sleep. She was harshly treated and often rebuked by the Mother Prioress, and had to bear the small irritations inseparable from life in a community. She was under constant temptations against faith, was repeatedly attacked by dryness of spirit, and, asking nothing but to give herself completely to God, received no encouragement, no response from Him. But, even in the worst trials, in the depths of her soul she was serene and confident, for she knew that God had called her, and she told herself that every tribulation was a proof that He was testing her trust in Him, and making trial of her love for Him. The more grievous the trial became, the more certain she was that she had a task to perform and that it must be performed at whatever cost to herself. From Holy Communion she received no consolation. "Is not this to be expected, since I do not desire to receive Our Lord for my own satisfaction, but to please Him?" She was ready to forgo spiritual consolation, because she had united her will to the will of God, and not only bore her sufferings patiently, but learned to rejoice in them. The more she was tried, the more that love of God increased, that fervour of self-sacrifice which refused to be discouraged.

But Thérèse had made up her mind to be something more than an exemplary nun. She had long wanted to be a saint, and had said so with that complete candour of hers. She had once longed to emulate the spectacular saints, to be a St. Joan or a St. Francis Xavier. But when she compared herself with them, she realized that their feats were beyond her power. Yet, she told herself, God does not inspire a desire such as this if it is impossible of fulfilment. Searching the Scriptures she was struck by the words, "Whoever is a little one, let him come unto me." On these words, and on similar texts, she based her doctrine of spiritual childhood, which, as Pope Pius XI said, "consists in thinking and acting under the influence of virtue, as a child feels and acts in the natural order." This was her Little Way, the method by which, in her own humble and unobtrusive fashion, she set about the task of attaining perfection, so far as it can be attained on this earth, and of so loving God that after death it should be her reward to bring souls to Him to the end of time. In a word, it is a system by which the teachings of the Church may be applied to the minutest details of the most uneventful existence. It is possible at a first reading of her own description of how she made this discovery to see nothing remarkable in what she set out to do. The obtuse may even ask, "What new teaching, what revolutionary idea had she discovered?" But the point of the story is that she discovered a very old teaching, something in danger of being forgotten. And the idea of becoming as little children may certainly be called revolutionary in the present state of the world. Her Little Way was important enough to be examined and discussed by professional theologians, and Pope Pius XI believed that, if it were generally acted upon, it might bring Europe back to the Faith. He saw in the system which the Saint made for herself not merely an example to be followed by religious communities, but a cure for a sophisticated age. The full force of her teaching was timed to coincide with the despair of our day, and to confront the preposterous dogmas of the godless. She made old words fresh and living.

Dissatisfaction with herself and disappointment at her slow progress towards sanctification made her suspect that she had been relying too much upon herself. This led to her determination to become, spiritually, a little child, and to use the grace that God gave her to attain complete forgetfulness of self, by accepting, with love and confidence and humility, whatever came to her. This was no doctrine of quietism. Her love was a militant love, her confidence was vigilant against her own weakness, and her humility was a joyous, not a sad humility. So thoroughly did she understand and accept the necessity for suffering as a means of showing her love of God that, on the day of her profession, she had prayed to be granted martyrdom of soul and body. When this prayer was answered, so profound was the peace of mind which nothing could disturb that, in admitting to the Mother Prioress in the *Histoire d'une Ame*, that she had suffered much, she wrote, "You would have to know me thoroughly not to smile when you read these words, for has ever a soul been apparently less tried than mine?" It was a part of her charity and her humility to hide from the Sisters both her physical pain and her mental anguish. She was always cheerful, as though nothing was troubling her. Even when she had become seriously ill, she succeeded in hiding the fact from the Mother Prioress and from the nuns. Her only concern in this matter was that nobody should be distressed or even inconvenienced by what she was enduring.

As an illustration of the extent of her physical suffering we may take her confession that she was never adequately warm, and in winter had often thought that she would die of cold. When she fell ill, she naturally became still more sensitive to cold. In the very worst weather a fire occasionally burned in the community room, and there was no other warmth anywhere in the convent. But if she came here to warm herself, she had to face fifty yards of open cloister to return to her cell. At the end of a day in which she had carried out all her duties cheerfully, she would come, exhausted, sick and numbed with cold, back to the freezing cell for a few hours' rest. This torture of cold, which went on day and night, day and night, gives us, I think, some idea of her courage and singleness of purpose; especially when we remember that, shortly after she became ill she was assailed by those temptations against faith which were to continue for more than a year. But, far from being discouraged, she still accepted every new trial as evidence that she was being tested. From the test she emerged triumphant, and it is literally true that she loved God more and more the harder the struggle became, until, at the end of her life, she asked nothing but to suffer, in order that the profound joy in her soul might be evidence of her love, and that she might offer her tribulations to Him for souls in need. Only by making an effort of the imagination can the ordinary man or woman understand this paradox of agony welcomed with rejoicing which is the explanation of what a saint is. "It is for us," she said, "to console Our Lord, not for Him to be always consoling us."

In mortal sickness and in dryness of spirit the saint continued to carry out her duties, and, at the same time, to practise her system. Daily she sought opportunities for humiliating herself— for instance, by allowing herself to be unjustly rebuked. She forced herself to appear serene, and always courteous, and to let no word of complaint escape her, to exercise charity in secret, and to make self-denial the rule of her life. St. Teresa of Avila (whose teaching, with that of the Gospels and St. John of the Cross and the *Imitation of Christ,* she studied closely) warned her Carmelites against false humility. Not to believe that God is bestowing certain gifts is to lessen our love for Him. True humility consists in knowing that we, of ourselves, have no merit; but that humility should be accompanied by confidence and by a realization that God is using us as an instrument to do His work. True humility in one who leads a devout life, is not diffidence. St. Thérèse was in no danger of falling into this error. She knew very well what God would accomplish in her, as we see from the most famous of all her words: *"Ma mission va commencer, ma mission de faire aimer le bon Dieu. . . . Je veux passer mon ciel a faire du bien sur la terre. . . ."* "He has done great things in me," she wrote once in a letter.

What Thérèse herself wrote of her "little way," and the examples she gave of it in practice, make quite clear that it is no mere counsel of perfection for nuns or for the excessively devout. It is a system simple enough to be easily understood by anybody. Yet it is obvious that even the most ardent soul could set itself no more difficult task than to imitate the saint with any degree of success. But any Catholic, without the saint's virtues of utter abandonment of self to the will of God, and her ever-active charity, could set his feet tomorrow on the path she followed to the end. He could not do what she did, but he could try to keep her counsel in mind. There never was any teaching, when once its meaning has been grasped, so free from obscurities and complications, or from the things that often alarm us and keep us away from the lives of the saints. With that common sense which is one of her most striking qualities, St. Thérèse devised a method of conduct which encourages us to be as simple and natural with God as is a child with its parents. Nothing is too small or insignificant to find its place in her system, and, for that reason, every hour of every day brings opportunities for applying it. What may look like a ridiculous triviality becomes a battle in a campaign, part of a pattern of planned strategy. A man going about his affairs in the world today can plead the impossibility of setting aside regular periods for recollection. He says his morning and evening prayers. He goes to Mass; perhaps, if he can fit it in, to Benediction. What else can he do? He has little chance, with his manifold cares and responsibilities, to get himself into a mental state in which he can think of more important things. For this man and millions like him, little acts of mortification and self-sacrifice are the answer. For it will be noticed that, in the many examples she gave of her "little way," there are many that can be transferred to the context of life in the world. Take her advice to the novices: "If, during any period of recreation, you are telling a sister something you think entertaining, and she interrupts to tell you something else, show yourself interested, even though her story may not interest you at all. Be careful also, not to resume what you were saying. . . . You have not sought to please yourself but others." There is a short sermon, crammed with common sense, and made to fit the club bore and his unwilling victim as closely as any two religious. Take, again, her words about suffering unjust rebukes in silence: "Having nothing to reproach myself with, I offer gladly to God this small injustice. Then, humbling myself, I think how easily I might have deserved the reproach." In many a good Catholic home children are brought up to practise self-denial and patience and charity, but how many remember the lessons and act on them when they grow up? The merit of her system is not that it is original, a new doctrine, but that it is a statement in elementary terms, of an old doctrine; a very lucid re-statement of the Church's teaching in the matter of humility. And her own life was an example of what can be achieved if God is loved enough. She showed that an accumulation of the smallest and most unspectacular actions is as good a use of God's grace as those more startling triumphs which are reserved for saints of another kind.

The common sense which I have spoken of as being one of the saint's characteristics may be studied in her attitude to mortification and to prayer.

She began her life in the Carmel without questioning the tradition of mortification and penance which was at that time the rule. In fact, she admitted later that she had felt drawn to exaggerated asceticism. But as she observed the daily life in the Convent she began to doubt the wisdom of making certain forms of physical mortification the rule for a community, without taking into account the health, the temperament, the character of the individual. She herself fell ill after wearing an iron cross with points. The points wounded her. From that moment she began to clarify her ideas on mortification, and she came to the conclusion that it is absurd to expect that the torture of the body will have the same effect (in the development of holiness) on one person as on another. She realized that if the health is destroyed by violent penance, and one's daily duties thereby interfered with, then the penance is excessive, and defeats its own end. She continued to take the discipline, like all the other nuns, but she was careful not to attribute too much importance to this method of subduing the body. She said that for impetuous and ardent natures excessive mortification might be regarded as a temptation to be resisted, since it broke their health, and so prevented them from doing the work they were called to do. But she saw a graver danger. She held that an insistence on the more violent forms of mortification might easily lead to self-satisfaction and complacency. A religious might come to believe that such practices were not only essential in themselves, but were inseparable from any system of self-perfection. As for herself, her mortification were the acts of charity and self-sacrifice, most of them unnoticed, and even unsuspected by the Sisters, which she performed every day. But she never attempted to avoid the scourging, and the other forms of penance enjoined.

Her method of prayer, which, strictly speaking, was no method at all, is another illustration of her common sense. She said, of course, the great, universal prayers of the Church. When God seemed to have turned away from her, and she could find no consolation, she said the Our Father and the Hail Mary very slowly, as nourishment for her soul. But from her earliest years she had found it difficult and unsatisfactory to read prayers in a book. They all seemed beautiful to her, as she wrote later, but there were so many that she could not say them all, and did not know which to choose. "So I act like a child who cannot read. I tell God quite simply all that I want to say." St. Thomas Aquinas says that in praying you can concentrate on the words you are saying, or better, on the sense of the words, or best of all, on Him to Whom you are praying. St. Thérèse had learned to talk to God in the most natural fashion at a very early age, and the habit remained with her. She prayed better when she composed her own prayers, or meditated. When she was a small child her elders noticed that she seldom followed the Mass in her missal. Someone would direct her attention to the right place on the page, but after a moment she would look up again, and lose the place. It was assumed that she was giving way to distractions, but what distracted her was the book. Without any training, without any understanding of such things, she was making a prayer of contemplation. Later, when distractions came to her as she prayed, she invented an ingenious method of making them serve her purpose. She prayed for the people the thought of whom was distracting her. "In this way they benefit by my distractions."

There are many people who find it difficult to concentrate their attention on set prayers, and they would probably say that this idea of an unpremeditated prayer is all very well for one whose whole life is a prayer. But a moment's consideration of the matter will reveal something so obvious that it is difficult not to overlook it. The undeniable truth is that anyone, anywhere, at any time can accustom himself to praying in this spontaneous fashion. Once more, it seems to me, this common sense of St. Thérèse teaches a very simple lesson which is worth learning by ordinary men and women going about their business in the world. No special holiness is needed, no preparation, since it soon becomes a habit. It is invaluable advice to all who are too busy or too lazy to make a daily visit to a church, to all whose wills are too weak to combat the distractions which so often accompany the reading of long prayers. "Prayer," she said, "is, for me, an expression of love and gratitude in the midst of trial as in times of joy."

This having been said, it is important to point out that praise of St. Thérèse's way of praying is not intended to suggest that it is a better way than any other. Her distaste for set prayers was a personal matter, as was her distaste for extraordinary mortification. She condemned neither. She merely said that it is unreasonable to suppose that there is one road to perfection which must be trodden by everyone; she said that in religion, as in everything else, one is dealing with individuals, even in a community; that, outside the observance of the rule of an Order, one must allow for temperament and character. Far from even suggesting that her way was the best, she repeatedly said that it was intended as a kind of lift to Heaven for those who were too feeble to walk up the stairs.

It was in 1896, on the night between Holy Thursday and
Good Friday, that the presentiment of her childhood that she
would die young became a certainty. A bloodstained hand-
kerchief warned her that she was gravely ill. Her first thought
was one of joy, her second, a determination that she must
conceal her illness as much as possible. On Good Friday, and on
the days that followed, she carried out all her duties with her
customary cheerfulness. It was noticed that she was paler than
usual, but even the Prioress, whom she had told of her
haemorrhage, was deceived into underestimating the seriousness of her malady. But Thérèse, though she could smile and
disguise her fatigue and weakness, could not conceal her
coughing. A doctor was summoned, and for a few weeks she was
better. In the damp and cold of the winter of 1896-1897 she
grew weaker, and the doctor gave up hope of curing her. And
then began that slow death which can be read in all its edifying
details in Monseigneur Laveille's biography of the saint. She
asked to remain in her cell, rather than move to the less
uncomfortable infirmary, so that her coughing might not
disturb anyone, and so that her suffering might not be lessened.
A Sister who found her walking slowly and painfully in the
convent garden instead of resting, was told that she was walking
for some weary missionary priest in a far land, and offering her
pain and weakness to God, in order that the priest might be
strengthened. On another occasion, when the community was
singing a hymn, she was too exhausted to rise to her feet. A
Sister, not knowing how ill she was, signed to her to stand up.
She stood up at once, and remained on her feet until the hymn
was over. Never did she miss a chance of following her little
way; not even though, at this time, she was battling with her
worst temptations against faith. We are reminded of her prayer
that she might suffer martyrdom of soul and body as we read of
the increasing physical and mental torment to which she was
submitted. One is tempted, and the temptation must be
resisted, to say, "Surely she had earned an easier death," and it
sounds paradoxical to say that on the contrary, she had earned
this kind of death. Day by day her pain increased. The doctor

said, "Never have I seen anybody suffer so intensely with such an expression of supernatural joy. She was not made for this world." Day by day, not only was consolation withheld, but her soul was assaulted, and she had to fight all the time. After the middle of August, with her death six weeks distant, she could not even receive Holy Communion. As she lay gasping for breath and drenched in sweat, she thought of "All the good I wish to do after my death." On August 28th she said to the Prioress, "My soul is in darkness. Yet I am at peace." The time came when she could hardly make the least movement in her bed, so great was her weakness. Yet it was not until September 29th that the end seemed to have come. The prayers for the dying were read. But the agony continued through the day and the night and the next day. She died shortly after seven o'clock on the evening of September 30th. Her last words were "My God, I love Thee."

Her body was taken to the cemetery, with but a small procession following after. All that the townspeople knew was that a Carmelite nun had died and was being buried. A few days afterwards visitors to the cemetery were surprised to see, carved on the cross of wood which bore her name, the words: *Je veux passer mon ciel à faire du bien sur la terre.* In October 1898 her secret was given to the world, her autobiography was published, and what followed is well known. People everywhere had discovered a saint for today, one whose teaching contained nothing difficult to understand, whose precepts might be followed, however clumsily and imperfectly, by anyone who believed in God. The fame of her miracles and of her interventions on earth spread far and wide. She had said: "Would God give me this ever-growing desire to do good on earth after my death unless He wished me to fulfil it? No. He would give me rather the longing to take my repose in Himself." Her mission, as she had foretold, began immediately after death, and her words, and the amazing story of her brief life travelled across the world. More and more people discovered that she had spoken not only to Carmelite nuns, not only to the devout, but to the unhappy everywhere, to those burdened with sin, to those tempted to despair. She brought—she brings to all hope and confidence. She is the answer to the man who thinks that the enclosed life is a life wasted and misdirected in the world of today; to him who doubts or denies the power of prayer. She herself once expressed astonishment that there could be atheists, and her own life, as one studies it, helps one to share that astonishment.

Notes

St. Basil

1. Orationes XLIII, 19; I,785, ed. Boulenger, 98-100.

2. St. Basil the Great, p. 23.

3. From St. Basil, Letters (Vol. II), translated by Sister Agnes Clare Way, D.P., Fathers of the Church Inc., 1955, p. 128.

4. Letter, 14, 2; III, 94C.

5. *Op. cit.*, Vol. I, Letters 2, I; III, 70 D.

St. Bernadette

1. *The Month,* December 1933.

2. Laurentin, *Sens de Lourdes,* 1955, pp. 86-87. It is worth noting that Fr. R.H. Steuart anticipated this interpretation in his study of Bernadette, *Diversities in Holiness,* 1936, pp. 168-70.

3. Quoted by Fr. Thurston from a rare little book, *La Grotte des Pyrénées,* published at Lourdes in 1862 by a certain Abbé Azun de Bernétas. *The Month,* July 1924.

4. Cros, *Histoire de Notre-Dame de Lourdes d'après les Documents et les Temoins.* Vol. I, 3rd ed., Paris, 1925, p. 58. Bernadette's reference to her love for the smallest lambs mentioned above was made in reply to a question from Père Cros.

5. *St. Bernadette,* English trans., p. 30.

6. Cros, *Histoire,* I, p. 73.

7. Cros, *Histoire,* I., p. 214.

8. Steuart, *Diversities in Holiness,* pp. 174-75.

9. *The Month,* July 1924, p. 28.

10. Cros, *Histoire,* III, p. 181.